A PRIMER
ON
THE FINITE ELEMENT METHOD

B. L. Manocha, Ph.D. (Engineering)

ISBN
Paperback 979-8-89929-087-9
Hardcase 979-8-89929-088-6

CONTENTS

PREFACE

The Finite Element Method (FEM) has revolutionized the way engineers and scientists solve complex problems in various domains, including structural mechanics, heat transfer, fluid flow, and electromagnetics. Over the decades, FEM has evolved into a powerful and versatile computational tool that enables practitioners to find approximate solutions to problems that are otherwise analytically intractable. This book is designed to introduce readers to the fundamental principles and practical applications of the finite element method, providing a bridge between theoretical concepts and real-world problem-solving.

The primary purpose of this manuscript is to provide an accessible yet comprehensive introduction to FEM for students, researchers, and professionals. By balancing theory with practical examples, this book enables learners to develop a deep understanding of the methodology, its applications, and its limitations. While commercial FEM software like ANSYS, ABAQUS, and COMSOL are widely used, a solid foundation in the underlying principles is essential for effectively utilizing these tools. To this end, the text emphasizes manual calculations in early chapters, fostering an intuitive grasp of FEM concepts before transitioning to automated computations.

The book is structured to guide readers through the entire process of FEM—from the basics of differential equations and numerical approximations to advanced topics like three-dimensional problems and unsteady-state analysis. Chapters are supplemented with numerous examples, illustrations, and practice problems that showcase the application of FEM in diverse fields such as heat transfer, structural mechanics, and fluid flow. Special attention has been given to concepts such as shape functions, global stiffness matrices, and time-stepping techniques, which are foundational to the method.

Key features of this book include:

- Step-by-step explanations of fundamental concepts like Galerkin's method, residual equations, and interpolation using shape functions.
- Practical applications of FEM in solving heat transfer, structural, and fluid flow problems.
- A review of essential matrix algebra and numerical techniques for solving algebraic systems.
- Worked examples and practice problems to reinforce theoretical concepts.
- Coverage of both steady-state and transient phenomena, providing a holistic understanding of FEM applications.

This manuscript is intended to serve as a self-contained resource for readers with a basic understanding of calculus and linear algebra. While it is particularly suited for undergraduate and graduate students in engineering disciplines, it is also a valuable reference for professionals seeking to refresh or deepen their knowledge of FEM.

I am grateful to the countless researchers and educators whose contributions to the field of finite element analysis have shaped the content and approach of this book. Special thanks are also due to the students and colleagues whose questions and feedback have enriched my teaching and writing.

It is my hope that this book will empower readers to approach engineering and scientific challenges with confidence and creativity, leveraging the finite element method to uncover innovative solutions.

B. L. Manocha, Ph.D. (Engineering)

January 2025

CHAPTER 1

THE PRELIMINARIES

The **purpose of the finite element method** is to find approximate numerical solutions of intractable differential equations. This method is also used to solve many other difficult problems in engineering and science. A computer is required to solve even simple problems by the finite element method. However, in this book, we have solved many examples manually to enable learners to master this method to enable them to use commercial software such as ANSYS and others. First, we demonstrate the earlier techniques which were employed for this purpose.

Galerkin's Method

A technique, called Galerkin' method, is used to find approximate solutions of differential equations. This method is explained below with two examples.

Example 1.1 Consider the differential equation,

$$E\,I\,\frac{d^2y}{dx^2} \ - \ M(x) \ = 0 \ \textit{which applies to a simply supported beam}$$

Or

$$\frac{d^2y}{dx^2} \ - \ \frac{M(x)}{EI} \ = 0$$

We will solve the above equation if $M(x) = M_0 =$ Constant bending moment on the beam of length L.

E = Young's modulus of the material of the beam.

I = Second moment of area of the beam's area of cross-section.

It is given that y (0) = 0 and y(L) = 0.

Residual of a Given Differential Equation

The given differential equation is written down with its right-hand side as zero.

The left-hand side is then called the residual R of the given equation. For example,

$$\frac{d^2y}{dx^2} - \frac{M_0}{EI} = R \ (\textit{residual}) \ \textit{of the given equation}$$

Trial function

We assume a **trial function** that obeys the given boundary conditions. The trial function may have one or more constants in it. For example, we assume that for the differential equation given here, the trial function is, $A \sin \dfrac{\pi x}{L}$ because it satisfies the given boundary conditions, y (0) = 0 and y(L) = 0.

Weighting Function

There is only one constant A in the trial function assumed here. Multiplier of constant A is $\sin \dfrac{\pi x}{L}$. It is called a weighting function, W. The number of weighting functions is equal to the number of constants in the assumed solution.

Weighted Residual Integral

The product of the weighting function and the trial function integrated over the interval over which the solution is desired is called the weighted residual integral.

For example, in the problem given here, the the weighted residual integral is,

$$\int_0^L W_i \ R \ dx \tag{1.1}$$

where i is the number of weighting functions = number of constants in the trial solution).

i = 1 in the given problem.

According to Galerkin's method, each integral of the weighted residual is equated to zero to determine the constants in the assumed solution. This means that,

$$\int_0^L W_i \ R \ dx = 0, \text{ where i = 1, 2…etc.} \tag{1.2}$$

or in the present example,

$$\int_0^L \left(\frac{d^2y}{dx^2} - \frac{M_0}{EI} \right) \left(\sin \frac{\pi x}{L} \right) dx = 0 \tag{1.3}$$

Since $y = A \sin \dfrac{\pi x}{L}$, $\dfrac{dy}{dx} = \dfrac{A L}{\pi} \cos \dfrac{\pi x}{L}$ *and* $\dfrac{d^2y}{dx^2} = -\left(\dfrac{A L}{\pi} \right)^2 \sin \dfrac{\pi x}{L}$.

the given *equation becomes,*

$$\int_0^L \left[-\frac{A\pi^2}{L^2}\sin\frac{\pi x}{L} - \frac{M_0}{E\,I}\right]\left(\sin\frac{\pi x}{L}\right)dx = 0 \tag{1.4}$$

Equation (1.4), gives $A = -\dfrac{4\,M_0\,L^2}{\pi^2 E\,I}$

Thus, the solution of the given differential equation is,

$$y(x) = \frac{-4M_0 L^2}{\pi^3 E\,I}\sin\frac{\pi x}{L} \tag{1.5}$$

Example 1.2

Let us consider another differential equation, $\dfrac{d^2T}{dx^2} - 9\,T = x^3$ given that T (0) = 0 and T (1) = 2.

Solution: Assume a trial function, $T = c_0 + c_1 x + c_2 x^2 + c_3 x^3.$

Applying T (0) = 0 gives $c_0 = 0.$

Applying T (1) = 2 gives, $c_1 + c_2 + c_3 = 2$

Therefore, $c_1 = 2 - c_2 - c_3$

$T = \left(2 - c_2 - c_3\right)x + c_2 x^2 + c_3 x^3$

or $T = 2x + c_2\left(x^2 - x\right) + c_3\left(x^3 - x\right)$

Thus, the two weighting functions are,

$W_1 = \left(x^2 - x\right)$ *and* $W_2 = \left(x^3 - x.\right).$

The derivatives of T are,

$$\frac{dT}{dx} = \left(2 - c_2 - c_3\right) + 2\,c_2 x + 3\,c_3 x^2$$

$$= 2 + c_2(2x - 1) + c_3\left(3x^2 - 1\right)$$

$$\frac{d^2T}{dx^2} = 2\,c_2 + 6\,c_3 x$$

The residual is,

$$R = \left[2c_2 + 6\,c_3 x - 9\left\{c_2\left(x^2 - x\right) + c_3\left(x^3 - x\right)\right\} - x^3 - 18\,x\right]$$

According to Galerkin's method, *integral of each weighted residual* must be equated to zero. Using this approach, we will be able to evaluate the remaining constants c_2 *and* c_3. This means that,

$$\int_0^L W_1 R \, dx = 0 \tag{1.6}$$

$$= \int_0^1 (x^2 - x)\left[2c_2 + 6c_3 x - 9\left\{c_2(x^2 - x) + c_3(x^3 - x)\right\} - x^3 - 18x\right] dx = 0$$

After carrying out the above integration, we get

$$0.63\, c_2 + 0.95\, c_3 = 1:533 \tag{a}$$

$$\int_0^L W_2 R \, dx = 0$$

$$= \int_0^1 (x^3 - x)\left[2c_2 + 6c_3 x - 9\left\{c_2(x^2 - x) + c_3(x^3 - x)\right\} - x^3 - 18x\right] dx = 0$$

After carrying out the above integration, we get,

$$0.95\, c_2 + 1.485\, c_2 = 2.457 \tag{b}$$

Simultaneous solution of equations (a) and (b) gives

$$c_2 = -1.74 \text{ and } c_3 = 2.77.$$

The constants can then be substituted in the assumed solution to obtain the final solution.

Thus, the solution is,

$$T = \left(2 - c_2 - c_3\right)x + c_2 x^2 + c_3 x^3 = (2 - (-1.74) - 2.77)x + (-1.74)x^2 + 2.77\, x^3$$

$$or \quad T = -0.97\, x - 1.74\, x^2 + 2.77\, x^3$$

A Brief Review of Matrix Algebra

It is important to refresh your knowledge of Matrices and Determinants before starting your study of the Finite Element Method. It is also necessary to understand Gauss's method of elimination to solve a set of algebraic equations.

Let us consider two algebraic equations:

$$a_{11} x_1 + a_{12} x_2 = b_1$$

$$a_{21} x_1 + a_{22} x_2 = b_2$$

We can rewrite these two equations as one matrix equation,

$$\begin{bmatrix} a_{11} & a_{12} \\ a_{21} & a_{22} \end{bmatrix} \begin{Bmatrix} x_1 \\ x_2 \end{Bmatrix} = \begin{Bmatrix} b_1 \\ b_2 \end{Bmatrix}.$$

$\begin{bmatrix} a_{11} & a_{12} \\ a_{21} & a_{22} \end{bmatrix}$ is called a 2 x 2 matrix. A larger matrix may consist of more rows and columns.

$\begin{Bmatrix} x_1 \\ x_2 \end{Bmatrix}$ is called a column vector of two rows.

A matrix of size n x 1 size called a column vector of size n.

$\begin{Bmatrix} b_1 \\ b_2 \end{Bmatrix}$ is a column vector of two rows.

$\begin{Bmatrix} c & d \end{Bmatrix}$ is a row vector of two columns.

Note the use of symbol [] for matrix and the symbol { } for a vector.

Transpose of a Matrix

If each row of a matrix is interchanged with its column, then the new matrix is called the transpose of the old matrix. Transpose is denoted by superscript T.

For example, transpose of $\begin{bmatrix} a_{11} & a_{12} \\ a_{21} & a_{22} \end{bmatrix} = \begin{bmatrix} a_{11} & a_{12} \\ a_{21} & a_{22} \end{bmatrix}^T = \begin{bmatrix} a_{11} & a_{21} \\ a_{12} & a_{22} \end{bmatrix}$

A matrix of size 1 x n is called a row vector.

Transpose of a row vector becomes a column vector. Transpose of a column vector becomes a row vector.

A formula used in transpose of matrices is, $[A][B][C] = [C]^T[B]^T[A]^T$

Addition of Matrices

Matrix A of size m x n may be added to another matrix of size m x n. A new matrix C of size.

m x n results from this addition. The elements of these matrices are related as $c_{ij} = a_{ij} + b_{ij}$.

Multiplication of a Matrix by a Scalar

If we multiply a matrix by a scalar, then every element of the resulting matrix gets multiplied by that scalar.

As an example, $5 \begin{bmatrix} 2 & 6 \\ 3 & 4 \end{bmatrix} = \begin{bmatrix} 10 & 30 \\ 15 & 20 \end{bmatrix}$.

Multiplication of a Matrix by Another Matrix

Two matrices, A of size m x n and B of size n x m can be multiplied and the result is a matrix C of size m x m. For example,

$$\begin{bmatrix} 2 & 6 & 1 \\ 3 & 4 & 5 \end{bmatrix} \begin{bmatrix} 1 & 3 \\ 2 & 5 \\ 6 & 7 \end{bmatrix} = \begin{bmatrix} (2\times1+6\times2+1\times6) & (2\times3+6\times5+1\times7) \\ (3\times1+4\times2+5\times6) & (3\times3+4\times5+5\times7) \end{bmatrix} = \begin{bmatrix} 20 & 43 \\ 41 & 64 \end{bmatrix}$$

Here, [A] is 2 x 3 matrix and [B] is 3 x 2 matrix. Such two matrices are called consistent matrices.

The result of their product is a 2 x 2 matrix.

We may write [A] [B] = [C], where [C] is m x p matrix such that

$$c_{ij} = \sum_{i}^{m} \sum_{j}^{p} a_{ij} b_{ji} .$$

(1.7)

Differentiation and Integration of Matrices

Suppose we have a matrix [B] whose elements are functions of x and y.

For example,

$$[B] = \begin{bmatrix} x+y & y^2 - xy \\ 6+x & y \end{bmatrix},$$

then,

$$\frac{\partial[B]}{\partial x} = \begin{bmatrix} \dfrac{\partial(x+y)}{\partial x} & \dfrac{\partial(y^2 - xy)}{\partial x} \\ \dfrac{\partial(6+y)}{\partial x} & \dfrac{\partial y}{\partial x} \end{bmatrix} = \begin{bmatrix} 1 & -y \\ 0 & 0 \end{bmatrix}$$

A formula for differentiation is, $\dfrac{d\,\{U\}^T [A]\,\{U\}}{d\{U\}} = 2\,[A]\,\{U\}$

(1.8)

Diagonal Matrix

A diagonal matrix has elements on its diagonal only. At other places of the diagonal matrix, elements are all zeros.

For example, $\begin{bmatrix} 2 & 0 & 0 \\ 0 & 5 & 0 \\ 0 & 0 & -4 \end{bmatrix}$ is a diagonal matrix.

Identity Matrix

An identity matrix has unity on its diagonal and zeros everywhere else.

For example,
$\begin{bmatrix} 1 & 0 & 0 \\ 0 & 1 & 0 \\ 0 & 0 & 1 \end{bmatrix}$ is an identity matrix. An identity matrix is written down as [I].

Symmetric Matrix

If a matrix is equal to its transpose, then this matrix is a symmetric matrix.

$[A] = [A]^T$ means that $[A]$ is a symmetric matrix.

Determinant of a Matrix

Determinant of a matrix is a scalar. This relationship is written as

$det\,[A] = |A|$

For example,

$$det \begin{bmatrix} a_{11} & a_{12} \\ a_{21} & a_{22} \end{bmatrix} = \begin{vmatrix} a_{11} & a_{12} \\ a_{21} & a_{22} \end{vmatrix} = \left(a_{11} a_{22} - a_{21} a_{12} \right)$$

and

$$det \begin{bmatrix} a_{11} & a_{12} & a_{13} \\ a_{21} & a_{22} & a_{23} \\ a_{31} & a_{32} & a_{33} \end{bmatrix} = \begin{vmatrix} a_{11} & a_{12} & a_{13} \\ a_{21} & a_{22} & a_{23} \\ a_{31} & a_{32} & a_{33} \end{vmatrix}$$

$$= a_{11} \left(a_{22} a_{33} - a_{32} a_{23} \right) - a_{12} \left(a_{21} a_{33} - a_{31} a_{23} \right) + a_{13} \left(a_{21} a_{32} - a_{31} a_{22} \right)$$

Inverse of a Matrix

Inverse of a matrix, [A] is another matrix, $[A]^{-1}$ such their product,

$[A][A]^{-1} = identity\ matrix\ [I]$.

Minor of a Matrix

Minor of a matrix [A] is denoted by $[M_{ij}]$. It is the determinant of matrix obtained by omitting row i and column j of [A].

For example, $[M_{23}]$ of $\begin{bmatrix} a_{11} & a_{12} & a_{13} \\ a_{21} & a_{22} & a_{23} \\ a_{31} & a_{32} & a_{33} \end{bmatrix} = det \begin{bmatrix} a_{11} & a_{12} \\ \\ a_{31} & a_{32} \end{bmatrix}$

$$det \begin{bmatrix} a_{11} & a_{12} \\ a_{31} & a_{32} \end{bmatrix} = a_{11} a_{32} - a_{31} a_{12}$$

Cofactor of a Matrix

The product of a Minor $[M_{ij}]$ of [A] with $(-1)^{i+j}$ gives us the cofactor [C] of the matrix [A].

This means that,

$[C_{ij}] = (-1)^{i+j} [M_{ij}]$.

Adjoint of a Matrix

The adjoint of a matrix [A] is defined as the transpose of the cofactor of matrix [A].

Thus,

$adj\ [A] = [C]^T$

Inverse of a Matrix

$Inverse\ of\ [A] = [A]^{-1} = \dfrac{adj\ [A]}{det\ [A]}.$

Inverse of a 2 x 2 Matrix

If $[A] = \begin{bmatrix} a_{11} & a_{12} \\ a_{21} & a_{22} \end{bmatrix}$ is a given 2×2 matrix, then

$$inv\ [A] = inv \begin{bmatrix} a_{11} & a_{12} \\ a_{21} & a_{22} \end{bmatrix} = \frac{1}{det\ [A]} \begin{bmatrix} a_{22} & -a_{12} \\ -a_{21} & a_{11} \end{bmatrix} = \frac{1}{a_{11}a_{22} - a_{21}a_{12}} \begin{bmatrix} a_{22} & -a_{12} \\ -a_{21} & a_{11} \end{bmatrix}$$

Quadratic Form of a matrix

Suppose we have a (n x n) matrix [A]. Suppose a (n x 1) vector is also given.

Then, the product $\{X\}^T[A]\{X\}$ is called the quadratic form of $[A]$.

For example, an expression,

$$u = 3x_1^2 - 4x_1x_2 + 6x_1x_3 - x_2^2 + 5x_3^2$$

may be written in quadratic form as

$$u = \{x_1\ x_2\ x_3\} \begin{bmatrix} 3 & -2 & 3 \\ -2 & -1 & 0 \\ 3 & 0 & 5 \end{bmatrix} \begin{Bmatrix} x_1 \\ x_2 \\ x_3 \end{Bmatrix}$$

$$= \{X\}^T[A]\{X\}.$$

Eigenvalues and Eigenvectors

Consider the eigenvalue problem,

$$[A]\{y\} = \lambda\{y\}. \tag{a}$$

Here we want to find the eigenvector $\{y\}$ and the corresponding eigenvalues of

λ that satisfy the above equation.

$$([A] - \lambda[I])\{y\} = \{0\} \tag{b}$$

Equation (b) has the solution,

$$det([A] - \lambda[I]) = 0. \tag{c}$$

Equation © will give us several values of λ. We can then use each value of λ in equation (b) to get a different value of eigenvector corresponding to it.

Positive Definite Matrix

A symmetric matrix is said to be positive definite matrix if all its eigenvalues are positive. Another way of defining a positive definite matrix is that

$\{X\}^T [A] \{X\} > 0$ *for any value of* $\{X\}$.

Gaussian Elimination Method

Gaussian elimination method is **a technique for solving a system of linear algebraic equations**.

The Gaussian elimination technique is also called row reduction method.

Example 1.3 Consider a given set of linear equations. Find tie solution of this set.

$3x + 2y = 12$

$9x + 3y - 2z = 17$

$4y - 3z = -3$

Solution: Let us write coefficients and constants of the above set of equations as an augmented matrix:

$$\begin{bmatrix} 3 & 2 & 0 & 12 \\ 9 & 3 & -2 & 17 \\ 0 & 4 & -3 & -3 \end{bmatrix}$$

Here the first goal is to make the coefficients of X in the first column of all rows below row 1 as zero.

For this purpose, we multiply the first row by the coefficient factor,

$$F_{21} = -\frac{coefficient\ of\ x\ in\ row\ 2}{coefficient\ of\ x\ in\ row\ 1} = -\left(\frac{9}{3}\right) = -3 \text{ and add it to the second row, that is,}$$

$$R_2 = R_2 + F_{21}R_1$$

$$\begin{bmatrix} 9 & 3 & -2 & 17 \end{bmatrix} + (-3)\begin{bmatrix} 3 & 2 & 0 & 12 \end{bmatrix} = \begin{bmatrix} 0 & -3 & -2 & -19 \end{bmatrix}$$

Thus, we get a new second row in which the first column of the second row will become zero

The augmented matrix now is

$$\begin{bmatrix} 3 & 2 & 0 & 12 \\ 0 & -3 & -2 & -19 \\ 0 & 4 & -3 & -3 \end{bmatrix}$$

The coefficient of x in the first column of the third row is already zero.

Next goal is to make the coefficient of y as zero in all rows below second row. For this purpose, we multiply the second row by the coefficient factor, and add it to the third row, that is,

$$R_3 = R_3 + F_{32}R_2$$

$$\begin{bmatrix} 0 & 4 & -3 & -3 \end{bmatrix} + \frac{4}{3}\begin{bmatrix} 0 & -3 & -2 & -19 \end{bmatrix} = \begin{bmatrix} 0 & 0 & -5.667 & -28.333 \end{bmatrix}$$

Thus, we get a new third row in which the second column of the third row will become zero

The augmented matrix now is

$$\begin{bmatrix} 3 & 2 & 0 & 12 \\ 0 & -3 & -2 & -19 \\ 0 & 0 & -5.667 & -28.333 \end{bmatrix}$$

From the third row of the augmented matrix, we get

$$5.667\, z = 28.333$$

$$or\ z = \frac{28.333}{5.667} = 5$$

From the second row we get, -3 y - 2 z = -19

or -3 y = -19 + 2(5) = -9

or y = 3

From the first row we get, 3 x + 2 y = 12

or 3 x = 12 - 2(3) = 6

or x = 2

Example 1.3 Consider the following set of linear equations. Solve this set.

$$1.0536\, x_1 - 0.3501\, x_2 = 29.1862$$

$$-0.3501\, x_1 + 1.0536\, x_2 - 0.3501\, x_3 = 1.1782$$

$$-0.3501\, x_2 + 0.6\, x_3 = 0.9572$$

Solution: Let us write coefficients and constants of the above set of equations as an augmented matrix:

$$\begin{bmatrix} 1.0536 & -0.3501 & 0 & 29.1862 \\ -0.3501 & 1.0536 & -0.3501 & 1.1782 \\ 0 & -0.3501 & 0.6 & 0.9572 \end{bmatrix}$$

Here the first goal is to make the coefficients of x_1 in the first column of all rows below row 1 as zero. For this purpose, we multiply the first row by the coefficient factor

$$F_{21} = -\frac{coefficient\ of\ x\ in\ row\ 2}{coefficient\ of\ x\ in\ row\ 1} = -\frac{-0.3501}{1.0536} = 0.3323$$

and add it to the second row, that is, $R_2 = R_2 + F_{21} R_1$

Thus, we get a new second row in which the first column of the second row will become zero

$$\begin{bmatrix} -0.3501 & 1.0536 & -0.3501 & 1.1782 \end{bmatrix} + (0.3323)\begin{bmatrix} 1.0536 & -0.3501 & 0 & 29.1862 \end{bmatrix} = \begin{bmatrix} 0 & 0.9373 & -0.3501 & 10.8765 \end{bmatrix}$$

The augmented matrix now is

$$\begin{bmatrix} 1.0536 & -0.3501 & 0 & 29.1862 \\ 0 & 0.9373 & -0.3501 & 10.8765 \\ 0 & -0.3501 & 0.6000 & 0.9572 \end{bmatrix}$$

Now the next goal is to make the coefficients of x_2 in the second column of of all rows below row 2 as zero.

For this purpose, we multiply the second row by the coefficient factor,

$$F_{32} = -\frac{coefficient\ of\ y\ in\ row\ 3}{coefficient\ of\ y\ in\ row\ 2} = -\left(\frac{-0.3501}{0.9373}\right) = 0.3735$$ and add it to the third row, that is,

$$R_3 = R_3 + F_{32}R_2$$

Thus, we get a new third row in which the second column of the third row will become zero.

$$\begin{bmatrix} 0 & -0.3501 & 0.6 & 0.9572 \end{bmatrix} + (0.3735)\begin{bmatrix} 0 & 0.9373 & -0.3501 & 10.8765 \end{bmatrix} = \begin{bmatrix} 0 & 0 & 0.4693 & 5.0197 \end{bmatrix}$$

The augmented matrix now is

$$\begin{bmatrix} 1.0536 & -0.3501 & 0 & | & 29.1862 \\ 0 & 0.9373 & -0.3501 & | & 10.8765 \\ 0 & 0 & 0.4692 & | & 5.0197 \end{bmatrix}$$

From the third row, we get,

$$0.4692\,x_3 = 5.0197$$

$$or\ x_3 = \frac{5.0197}{0.4692} = 10.7$$

From the second row we get,

$$0.9373\,x_2 - 0.3501\,x_3 = 10.8765$$

or

$$0.9373\,x_2 - 0.3501\,(10.7) = 10.8765$$

or

$$x_2 = \frac{0.3501(10.7) + 10.8765}{0.9373} = 15.6$$

By substituting the values of

$x_2\ and\ x_3\ in\ the\ first\ row\ we\ get,$

$$1.0536\,x_1 - 0.3501\,x_2 + 0 = 29.1862$$

$$Therefore,\ x_1 = \frac{29.1862 + 0.3501(15.6) + 0}{1.0536} = 32.9$$

CHAPTER 2

THE FINITE ELEMENT METHOD

What is the Central Idea of 'The Finite Element Method'?

We are given a region in which a differential equation applies with its boundary conditions.

However, a closed form solution of the given differential equation is sometimes too difficult to find.

In order to find an approximate solution of such a differential equation, we divide the given region into smaller regions, called elements. These elements would have nodes. The Finite Element Method is a technique for finding an approximate numerical solution at the nodes. Corresponding to the given differential equation, we can write down a residual equation for each node where the approximate solution is desired. The residual equation is an algebraic equation corresponding to the given differential equation. For example, if we have two continuous elements (e) and (e+1) with nodes i, j, k, as shown below, then corresponding to the given differential equation,

$$D\frac{d^2T}{dx^2} + Q = 0,$$

(2.1)

the nodal (algebraic) equation at node j is

$$R_j = \left(D\frac{dT}{dX}\right)_j^{(e+1)} - \left(D\frac{dT}{dx}\right)_j^{(e)}$$

$$-\left(\frac{D}{L}\right)_i^{(e)} T_i + \left[\left(\frac{D}{L}\right)^{(e)} + \left(\frac{D}{L}\right)^{(e+1)}\right] T_j - \left(\frac{D}{L}\right)^{(e+1)} T_k - \left(\frac{Q\,L}{2}\right)^{(e)} - \left(\frac{Q\,L}{2}\right)^{(e+1)} = 0$$

(2.2)

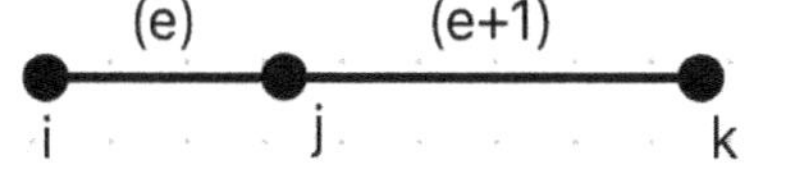

Fig. 2.1

This equation is called residual equation at node j. (2.3)

The derivative boundary conditions, which may apply at one end node or the other end node or both nodes, are ignored here since, at any interior node such as j, the difference of dbcs as represented by the first two terms of equation (2.2) must become zero. Thus, for any interior node such as j, the nodal residual equation becomes,

$$R_j = -\left(\frac{D}{L}\right)_i^{(e)} T_i + \left[\left(\frac{D}{L}\right)^{(e)} + \left(\frac{D}{L}\right)^{(e+1)}\right] T_j - \left(\frac{D}{L}\right)^{(e+1)} T_k - \left(\frac{QL}{2}\right)^{(e)} - \left(\frac{QL}{2}\right)^{(e+1)} = 0 \qquad (2.4)$$

Here, we have written down an expression for the nodal residual directly. It is not easy to use this expression in the computer programming of the finite element method. The following alternative approach is used instead.

We may determine an element's residual contribution to its nodes. A node may have many elements to its residual. These residual contributions at each node from all elements joining there are summed up. This summed up value at each node is equated to zero, thus forming an algebraic equation at each node. When all such algebraic equations are solved, we get the approximate values of the dependent variable of the given differential equation at the nodes.

We will now give an example of application of equation (2.4)

Example 2.1 We consider a composite wall with two layers. The first layer has a thickness of 0.02 m and thermal conductivity, $k = 10\ \frac{W}{m \cdot {}^\circ C}$. The second layer is of thickness 0.05 m and has a thermal conductivity, $k = 4\ \frac{W}{m\ {}^\circ C}$. The composite wall is represented by two elements (e) and (e+1) as shown in Fig. 2.2. The temperature at node i is 100 deg C and that at node k is 20°C. Find the temperature at node j.

Solution: we need to write down one equation, that is at node j only, to find

T_j because T_i and T_k are already known.

Fig. 2.2

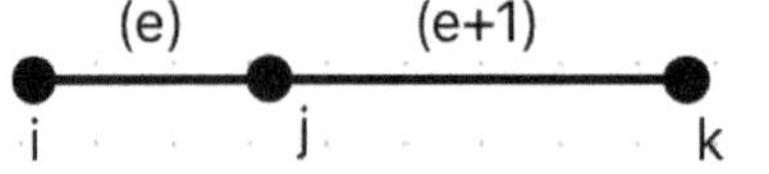

Fig. 2.3

Using equation (2.4), we get,

$$R_j = -\left(\frac{D}{L}\right)^{(e)}_i T_i + \left[\left(\frac{D}{L}\right)^{(e)} + \left(\frac{D}{L}\right)^{(e+1)}\right] T_j - \left(\frac{D}{L}\right)^{(e+1)} T_k - \left(\frac{QL}{2}\right)^{(e)} - \left(\frac{QL}{2}\right)^{(e+1)} = 0$$

Or

$$R_j = -\left(\frac{10}{0.02}\right)(100) + \left[\left(\frac{10}{0.02}\right) + \left(\frac{4}{0.05}\right)\right] T_j - \left(\frac{4}{0.05}\right)(20) - 0 - 0 = 0 \tag{2.5}$$

Or

$$580 \, T_j = 51600$$

$$T_j = \frac{51600}{580} = 88.965\,°C$$

Another way of writing a residual nodal equation is to write it as an element (e)'s residual contribution to its nodes i and j. (Please skip this method on the first reading)

$$R_j^{(e)} = -\left(D\frac{dT}{dx}\right)_{x=X_j} + \left(\frac{D}{L}\right)(-T_i + T_j) - \left(\frac{QL}{2}\right)$$

$$R_i^{(e)} = \left(D\frac{dT}{dx}\right)_{x=X_i} + \left(\frac{D}{L}\right)(T_i - T_j) - \left(\frac{QL}{2}\right) \tag{2.6}$$

This way of writing residual contribution is more useful when writing a computer program for FEM application. We may write the set of two equations as

$$\begin{bmatrix} 500 & -500 & 0 \\ -500 & 500+80 & -80 \\ 0 & -80 & 80 \end{bmatrix} \begin{Bmatrix} T_1 \\ T_2 \\ T_3 \end{Bmatrix} = \begin{Bmatrix} 0 \\ 0 \\ 0 \end{Bmatrix}$$

$$R_i^{(e)} = \left(D\frac{dT}{dx}\right)_{x=X_i} + \left(\frac{D}{L}\right)(T_i - T_j) - \left(\frac{QL}{2}\right) \tag{2.7}$$

$$R_j^{(e)} = -\left(D\frac{dT}{dx}\right)_{x=X_j} + \left(\frac{D}{L}\right)(-T_i + T_j) - \left(\frac{QL}{2}\right) \tag{2.8}$$

For any interior element, we ignore the derivative terms. Thus, for an interior element,

$$R_i^{(e)} = \left(\frac{D}{L}\right)(T_i - T_j) - \left(\frac{QL}{2}\right) \tag{2.9}$$

$$R_j^{(e)} = \left(\frac{D}{L}\right)(-T_i + T_j) - \left(\frac{QL}{2}\right) \tag{2.10}$$

Finally, we may rewrite the above two equations in matrix form as shown below:

$$\{R^{(e)}\} = \frac{D}{L}\begin{bmatrix} 1 & -1 \\ -1 & 1 \end{bmatrix}\begin{Bmatrix} T_i \\ T_j \end{Bmatrix} - \begin{Bmatrix} \dfrac{QL}{2} \\ \dfrac{QL}{2} \end{Bmatrix} \tag{2.11}$$

$$\{R^{(e)}\} = [k^{(e)}]\{T\} - \{f^{(e)}\}, \tag{2.12}$$

where $[k^{(e)}] = \dfrac{D}{L}\begin{Bmatrix} 1 & -1 \\ -1 & 1 \end{Bmatrix}$ is called the element stiffness matrix.

and

$$\{f^{(e)}\} = \begin{Bmatrix} \dfrac{QL}{2} \\ \dfrac{QL}{2} \end{Bmatrix} \text{ is called the element force vector.} \tag{2.13}$$

The global equation to use is, $[K]\{T\} = \{Q\}$

Or

$$\frac{10}{0.02}\begin{bmatrix} 1 & -1 \\ -1 & 1 \end{bmatrix} + \frac{4}{0.05}\begin{bmatrix} 1 & -1 \\ -1 & 1 \end{bmatrix} = \begin{Bmatrix} 0 \\ 0 \end{Bmatrix}$$

Or

$$\begin{bmatrix} 500 & -500 & 0 \\ -500 & 580 & -80 \\ 0 & -80 & 80 \end{bmatrix}\begin{Bmatrix} 100 \\ T_2 \\ 20 \end{Bmatrix} = \begin{Bmatrix} 0 \\ 0 \\ 0 \end{Bmatrix}$$

Since temperature at node 1 is known, we delete row one in the above matrix equation and **modify the remaining ones. Similarly, since the temperature at node 3 is known, we delete row 3** and modify the remaining ones. The result is,

$$580\,T_2 - 80\times 20 = 50000$$

Or

$$T_2 = \frac{51600}{580} = 88.965$$

which is the same result that we obtained by using equation (2.5).

By now we may have realized that the finite element method is a numerical technique which is used to find approximate solutions of differential equations. Many ordinary and partial differential equations occur in structural mechanics, heat transfer, fluid mechanics and electrical engineering.

It is difficult to find exact solution to many such equations.

The finite element method is eminently suitable for solving such problems. In all problems solved by the finite element, we solve one matrix equation, $[K]\{T\} = \{F\}$, where $[K]$ is called the global stiffness matrix,

{T} is a vector of field variable to be approximated, and {F} is the global force vector. The global matrix [K] is assembled from element stiffness matrices $[k^{(e)}]$, and the global force vector{F} is assembled from the element force vectors, $\{f^{(e)}\}$. The expressions for $[k^{(e)}]$ and $\{f^{(e)}\}$ are available in literature for heat transfer problems, structural problems, and others. Please see the Appendix of this book.

Methods are also available to derive these expressions. The procedure used for assembling [K] and {F} from the element matrices is called 'Direct Stiffness Procedure.' We will explain this method at the appropriate time.

Summary of Steps in the Finite Element Method (FEM) Application

1. **Discretization (Mesh Generation)**

   o **Divide the region into a finite number of elements of appropriate shape (e.g., line, triangular, rectangular).**

   o **Define nodes at element junctions and number them sequentially.**

   o **Assign notation to elements and nodes (e.g., for a line element:** nodes i and j; for a triangular element: nodes i, j, k).

2. **Formulation of Element Matrices**

   o **Derive or use pre-defined expressions for the element stiffness matrix and element force vector for each element. These expressions are typically obtained from theoretical derivations or standard references.**

3. **Application of Boundary Conditions**

   o **Incorporate derivative boundary conditions where necessary.**

   o **This step modifies the element matrices and force vectors accordingly.**

4. **Assembly of Global Matrices**

   o **Construct the global stiffness matrix [K] and global force vector {F} by assembling individual element contributions.**

   o **The Direct Stiffness Procedure is commonly used for assembly.**

5. **Formation of Global System of Equations**

   o **Represent the assembled system using the matrix equation:**

   Here, [K] is the global stiffness matrix, {T} is the unknown vector (e.g., displacement, temperature), and {F} is the global force vector.

6. **Modification for Boundary Conditions**

   o **Adjust the global equation to account for any fixed nodal values (essential boundary conditions).**

7. **Solution of the System**

   o **Solve the modified global matrix equation using numerical methods (e.g., Gaussian elimination, iterative solvers) to obtain the unknown nodal values.**

This stepwise approach ensures that the problem is systematically transformed from a complex domain into a solvable algebraic system using the Finite Element Method (FEM).

CHAPTER 3

SHAPE FUNCTIONS

Meaning of a Shape Function: Interpolation Inside a Linear Line Element

The Finite Element Method makes extensive use of shape functions for interpolation between nodes. A shape function is an interpolation function used to define the variation of a physical quantity <u>inside an element</u> in terms of its values at its nodes. *<u>The nodal values are usually written in capital letters.</u>*

We will now consider a line element (e) with its nodes i and j. We assume that values of a variable y at nodes i and j are Y_i and Y_j respectively. Then the value of y, at a point P located inside the element as shown in Fig. (3.1), can be written as

$$y = a + b\,x \tag{3.1}$$

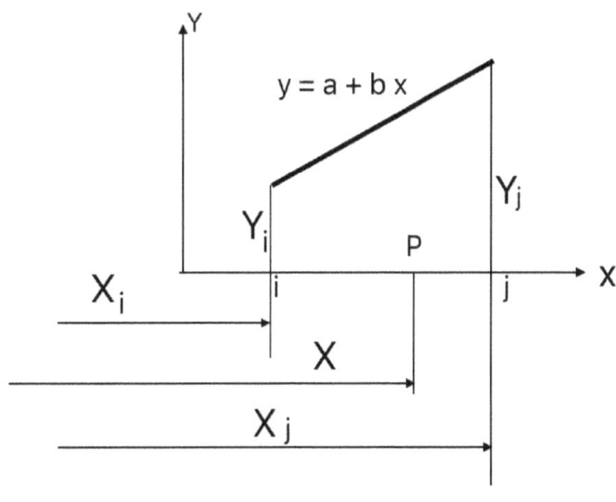

Fig. 3.1

Substituting the condition that $y = Y_i$ *at* $x = X_i$ at node i we get, $Y_i = a + b\,X_i$. $\tag{3.2}$

– 25 –

Substituting the condition that $y = Y_j$ at $x = X_j$, we get, $Y_i = a + b X_j$ (3.3)

Solving equations (2.3) and (2.4) simultaneously, we get

$$a = \frac{Y_i X_j - Y_j X_i}{X_j - X_i}$$

$$b = \frac{Y_j - Y_i}{X_j - X_1}$$

Substituting these values in eqn. (2.1), we get,

$$y = \frac{Y_i X_j - Y_j X_i}{X_j - X_i} + \frac{Y_j - Y_i}{X_j - X_i} \; x = \frac{X_j - x}{L} Y_i + \frac{x - X_i}{L} Y_j \tag{3.4}$$

We may write equation (3.1) in terms of shape functions as

$$y = N_i Y_i + N_j Y_j \tag{3.5}$$

Comparing equations (3.1) and (3.5), we get,

$$N_i = \frac{X_2 - x}{L} \quad and \quad N_j = \frac{x - X_i}{L} \tag{3.6}$$

$N_i = \dfrac{X_j - x}{X_j - X_i}$ is called the shape function of element (e) corresponding to node i

$N_j = \dfrac{x - X_i}{X_j - X_i}$ is called the shape function of element (e) corresponding to node j

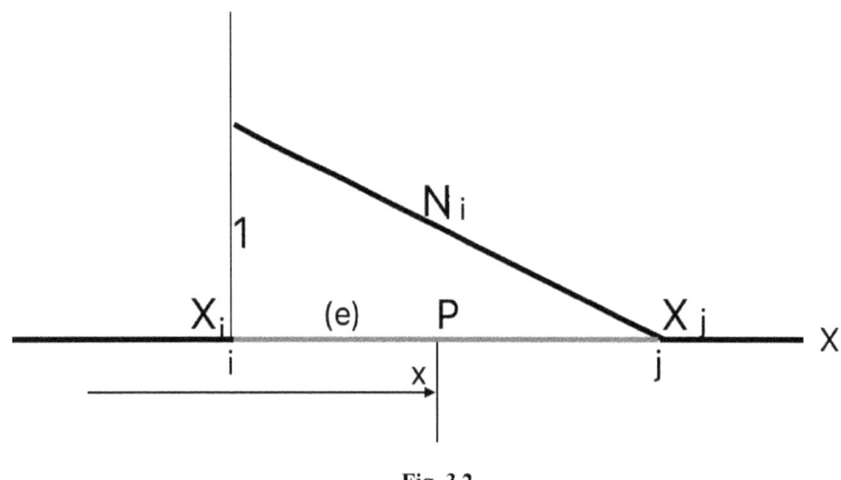

Fig. 3.2

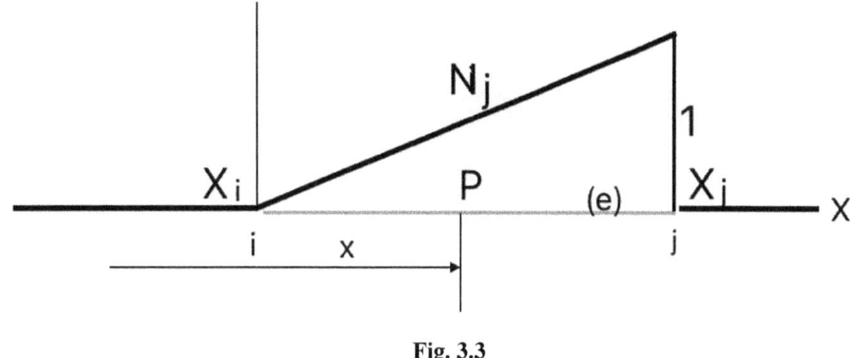

Fig. 3.3

Writing an interpolated value in terms of shape functions and nodal values as in equation (3.5) is important and should be well understood.

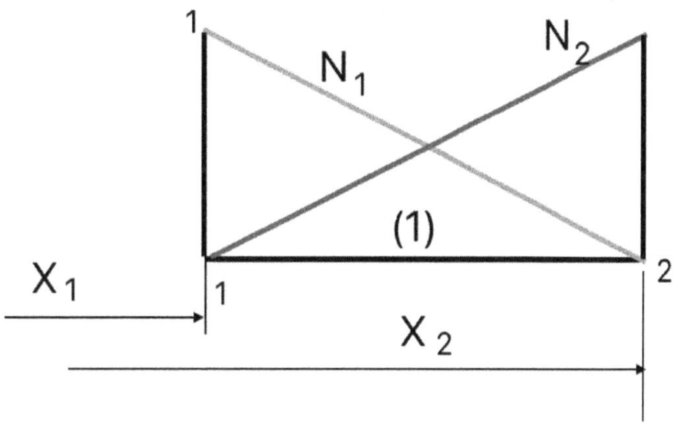

Fig. 3.4

Note that in Fig. 3.4,

N_1 *is a sloping straight line over element* (1) *which has a value 1 at* X_1 *and zero at* X_2

N_2 *is a sloping straight line over element* (1) *which has a value 1 at* X_2 *and zero at* X_1

So far, we have used x-coordinate system to express linear shape functions. The x-coordinate system (or later x-y and x-y-z systems) is called global coordinate system.

$$N_i = \frac{X_j - x}{X_j - X_i}$$

$$N_j = \frac{x - X_i}{X_j - X_i}$$

Shape Functions in Local Coordinate Systems

Line Element: Origin of the s - coordinate system at node i

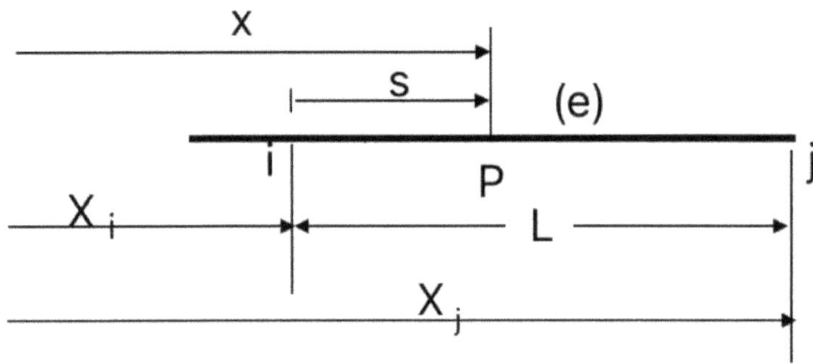

Fig. 3.5

$$N_i = \frac{X_j - x}{X_j - X_i} = 1 - \frac{s}{L} \qquad N_j = \frac{x - X_i}{X_j - X_i} = \frac{s}{L}$$

Line Element: Origin of the q-coordinate system at the mid point of the element

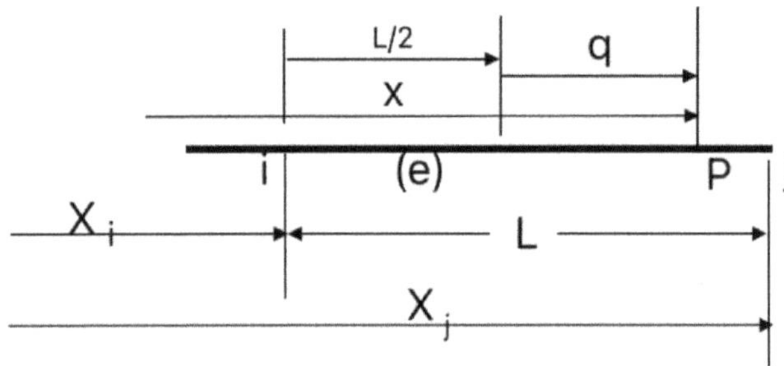

Fig. 3.6

$$N_i = \frac{X_j - x}{X_j - X_i} = \frac{X_j - \left(X_i + \frac{L}{2} + q \right)}{L}$$

$$= \frac{X_j - X_i - \frac{L}{2} - q}{L} = \frac{\frac{L}{2} - q}{L}$$

$$= \frac{1}{2} - \frac{q}{L}$$

Similarly, $N_j = \dfrac{1}{2} + \dfrac{q}{L}$

Line Element: Origin of the natural or ξ - coordinate system at the mid point of the element

If we write $\dfrac{q}{L/2} = \xi$, then we get, $N_i = \dfrac{1}{2} - \dfrac{\xi}{2} = \dfrac{1}{2}(1 - \xi)$ and $N_j = \dfrac{1}{2}(1 + \xi)$

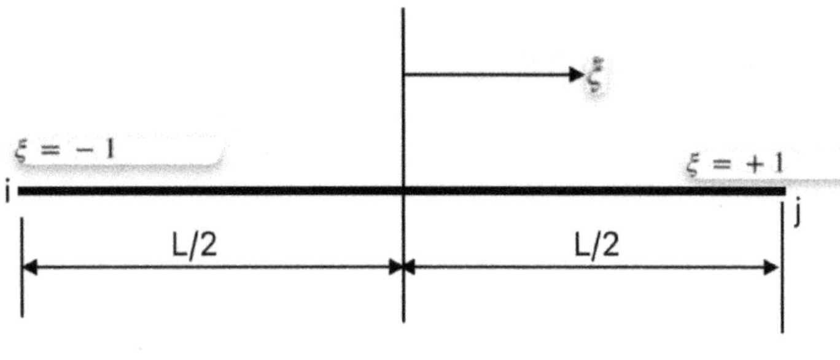

Fig. 3.7

Consider a triangular element, 123. Let us take a point P inside thus triangle and join P with nodes 2 and 3. Then the area ratio of the the triangle P23 and triangle 123 is written as L_1, that is,

$$L_1 = \frac{area\ of\ triangle\ P23}{area\ of\ triangle\ 123}$$

$$L_2 = \frac{area\ of\ triangle\ P31}{area\ of\ triangle\ 123}$$

$$L_3 = \frac{area\ of\ triangle\ P12}{area\ of\ triangle\ 123}$$

If the local coordinates corresponding to the nodes 1, 2, 3 are I, j, k, then it can be shown that the area coordinates are the same as the shape functions of the triangular element 123. This means that

$$L_1 = N_i$$

$$L_2 = N_j$$

$$L_3 = N_k$$

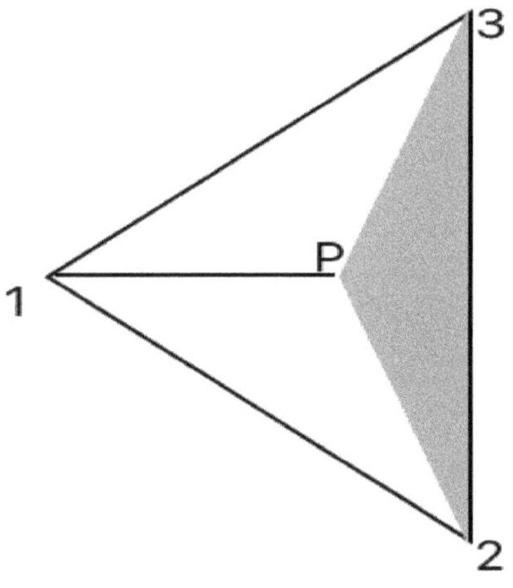

Fig. 3.8: Triangular Area

If we draw any line parallel to side 2-3 of the triangle, any point on this line will have the same area coordinates as the point P, and therefore the same value of shape function N_i.

Interpolation Inside a Triangular Element

Following a procedure of the linear line element for shape functions, we get the shape functions of the triangular linear element as,

$$N_i = \frac{1}{2A}\left(a_i + b_i x + c_i y\right)$$

$$N_j = \frac{1}{2A}\left(a_j + b_j x + c_j y\right)$$

$$N_k = \frac{1}{2A}\left(a_k + b_k x + c_k y\right)$$

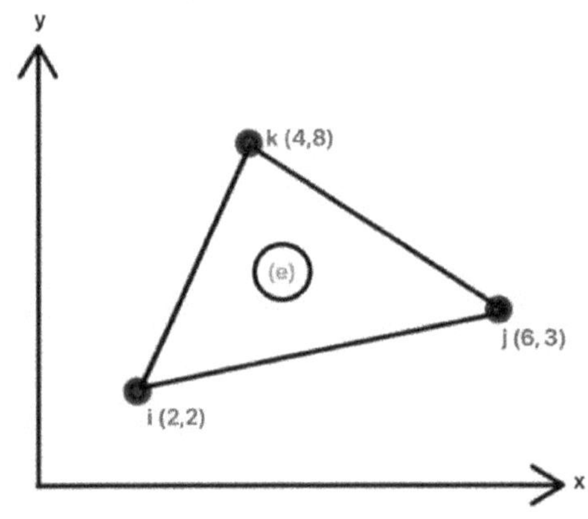

Fig. 3.9

where,

$$2A = det\begin{bmatrix} 1 & X_i & Y_i \\ 1 & X_j & Y_j \\ 1 & X_k & Y_k \end{bmatrix} \tag{3.7}$$

$$a_i = X_j Y_k - X_k Y_j,\ b_i = Y_j - Y_k,\ c_i = X_k - X_j$$

$$a_j = X_k Y_i - X_i Y_k,\ b_j = Y_k - Y_i,\ c_j = X_i - X_k$$

$$a_k = X_i Y_j - X_j Y_i,\ b_k = Y_i - Y_j,\ c_k = X_j - X_i \tag{3.8}$$

Thus, for the given triangular element,

$$a_i = 6\times 8 - 4\times 3 = 36, \; b_i = 3 - 8 = -5, \; c_i = 4 - 6 = -2$$

$$a_j = 4\times 2 - 2\times 8 = -8, \; b_j = 8 - 2 = -6, \; c_j = 2 - 4 = -2$$

$$a_k = 2\times 3 - 6\times 2 = -6, \; b_k = 2 - 3 = -1, \; c_k = 6 - 2 = 4$$

$$T = \frac{1}{2A}\left[N_i T_i + N_j T_j + N_k T_k\right]$$

$$\text{where, } 2A = det\begin{bmatrix} 1 & X_i & Y_i \\ 1 & X_j & Y_j \\ 1 & X_k & Y_k \end{bmatrix}$$

$N_i = (36 - 5x - 2y)/2A = 8/2$

$N_j = (-8 + 6x - 2y)/2A = 8/22$

$N_k = (-6 - x + 4y)/2A = 6/22$

$$2A = det\begin{bmatrix} 1 & 2 & 2 \\ 1 & 6 & 3 \\ 1 & 4 & 8 \end{bmatrix} = 1(6\times 8 - 4\times 3) - 2(1\times 8 - 1\times 3) + 2(1\times 4 - 1\times 6) = 22$$

Notice that the sum of all shape functions is equal to 1. Interpolation can be used to find the value of a quantity, say T at a location X inside the triangular element if we know T at node (i) (say 54 units), T at node j (say 45 units) and T at node k (say 60 units). For example, we can find T at a point (4, 4). At this point,

$$T = T_i N_i + T_j N_j + T_k N_k$$

Thus, T at the desired location X is,

T = (1/22) [(8)(54) + (8) (45) + 6 (60)] = 52.36 units.

Interpolation Inside a Rectangular Element with Sides oof Length 2b and 2a.

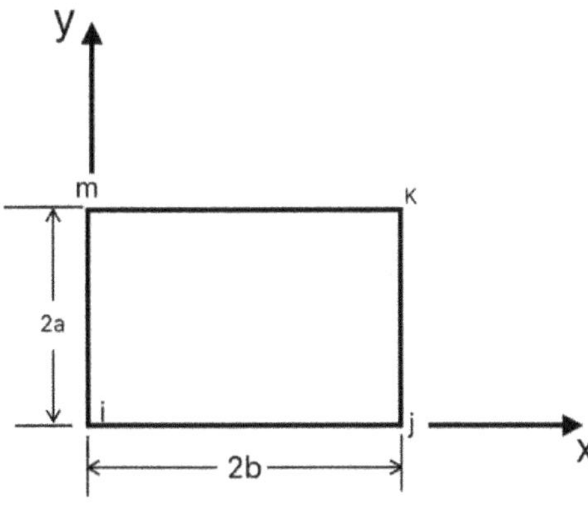

Fig. 3.10

Shape functions for a rectangular element are known as

$$N_i = \frac{1}{4ab}\left(X_j - x\right)\left(Y_m - y\right)$$

(3.9 a)

$$N_j = \frac{1}{4ab}\left(X_i - x\right)\left(Y_m - y\right)$$

(3.9 b)

$$N_k = \frac{1}{4ab}\left(x - X_i\right)\left(y - Y_i\right)$$

(3.9 c)

$$N_m = \frac{1}{4ab}\left(X_j - x\right)\left(y - Y_i\right)$$

(3.9 d)

Shape Functions of a Rectangular Element in Local Coordinate Systems

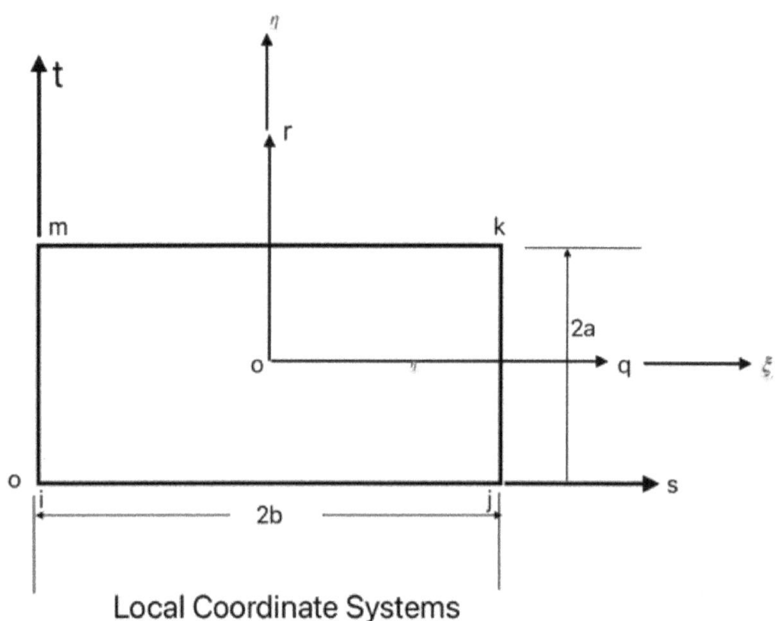

Fig. 3.11

Rectangular Element: Origin of the s-t coordinate system at the bottom left corner

$$N_i = \left(1 - \frac{s}{2b}\right)\left(1 - \frac{t}{2a}\right)$$

$$N_j = \left(\frac{s}{2b}\right)\left(1 - \frac{t}{2a}\right)$$

$$N_k = \frac{s\,t}{4\,a\,b}$$

$$N_m = \frac{t}{2\,a}\left(1 - \frac{s}{2\,b}\right)$$

Rectangular Element: Origin of the q-r coordinate system is at the mid point of the element

$$N_i = \left(1 - \frac{q}{b}\right)\left(1 - \frac{r}{a}\right)$$

$$N_j = \left(1 + \frac{q}{b}\right)\left(1 - \frac{r}{a}\right)$$

$$N_k = \left(1 + \frac{q}{b}\right)\left(1 + \frac{r}{a}\right)$$

$$N_m = \left(1 - \frac{q}{b}\right)\left(1 + \frac{r}{a}\right)$$

Rectangular Element: Origin of the natural coordinate $\xi - \eta$ system system is at the the mid point of the element

$$N_i = \frac{1}{4}\,(1 - \xi)\,(1 - \eta)$$

$$N_j = \frac{1}{4}\,(1 + \xi)\,(1 - \eta)$$

$$N_k = \frac{1}{4}\,(1 + \xi)\,(1 + \eta)$$

$$N_m = \frac{1}{4}\,(1 - \xi)\,(1 + \eta)$$

Element Stiffness Matrix, Element Force Vector

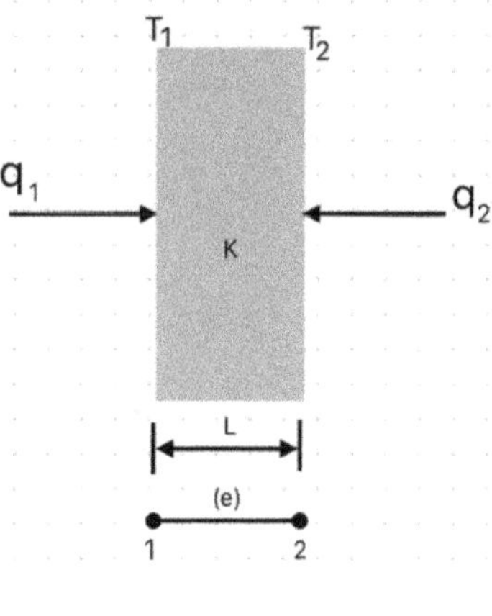

Fig. 3.12

Let us consider a plane wall of thickness L as shown in Fig. 2.3. The thermal conductivity of this wall is k. The temperature of its left surface is T_1 and that of its right surface is T_2 heat is entering the wall from its left surface and from its right surface.

In steady flow, net heat entering = 0. This means that $q_1 + q_2 = 0$

All the information stated above can be represented by one line element called (e) with two nodes 1 and 2.

By **Fourier's Law of heat conduction,** $q_1 = \dfrac{kA}{L}\left(T_1 - T_2\right)$

Since $q_1 + q_2 = 0$,

$$q_2 = -q_1 = -kA\frac{T_1 - T_2}{L} = \frac{kA}{L}\left(-T_1 + T_2\right)$$

Both the above equations can be combined and written as one matrix equation,

$$\left\{\begin{array}{c} q_1 \\ q_2 \end{array}\right\} = \frac{kA}{L}\left[\begin{array}{cc} 1 & -1 \\ -1 & 1 \end{array}\right]\left\{\begin{array}{c} T_1 \\ T_2 \end{array}\right\}$$

In the language of the Finite Element Method, the vector $\left\{\begin{array}{c} q_1 \\ q_2 \end{array}\right\}$ is called the element force vector and is written as $\{f^{(e)}\}$.

The matrix, $\dfrac{kA}{L}\left[\begin{array}{cc} 1 & -1 \\ -1 & 1 \end{array}\right]$ is called the element stiffness matrix and is written as $[k^{(e)}]$.

The vector $\left\{\begin{array}{c} T_1 \\ T_2 \end{array}\right\}$ is called the vector of unknown temperatures and is written as $\{T\}$.

When there are many elements in a problem, these element matrices are written as an assembled matrix equation $[K]\{T\} = \{F\}$. The assembly is done using the 'Direct Stiffness Procedure.'

This matrix equation is solved to obtain the solution of a given problem.

Applying Derivative Boundary Conditions

Heat conducted through a surface in the direction of the positive normal to that surface = heat convected from that surface to the fluid in contact with that surface.

$$-kA\frac{dT}{dx} = hA\left(T - T_{fluid}\right) = hAT - hAT_{fluid}$$

or

$$-kA\frac{dT}{dx} = MT - S \tag{3.11}$$

where $M = hA$ and $S = hAT_f$. For example, matrix $\left[\begin{array}{cc} 0 & 0 \\ 0 & M \end{array}\right]$ is added to the element stiffness matrix $[k^{(e)}]$ if the convection boundary condition occurs at the end node. Similarly, force vector $\left\{\begin{array}{c} 0 \\ S \end{array}\right\}$ is added to the force vector $\{f_Q\}$ if the convection boundary condition occurs at the end node.

For example, it is known that on side 2 of the rectangular element shown below,

$$kA\frac{\partial T}{\partial x} = 4T_b - 5,$$

Thus,

$$-kA\frac{\partial T}{\partial x} = -4T_b + 5 = MT_b - S$$

Therefore, M = -4 and S = -5

If heat flux q is entering a surface along its normal, then M = 0 and S = q.

Hat Function

A hat function is shown shown in Fig. 3.13. Its role is explained below:

Meanings of Symbols

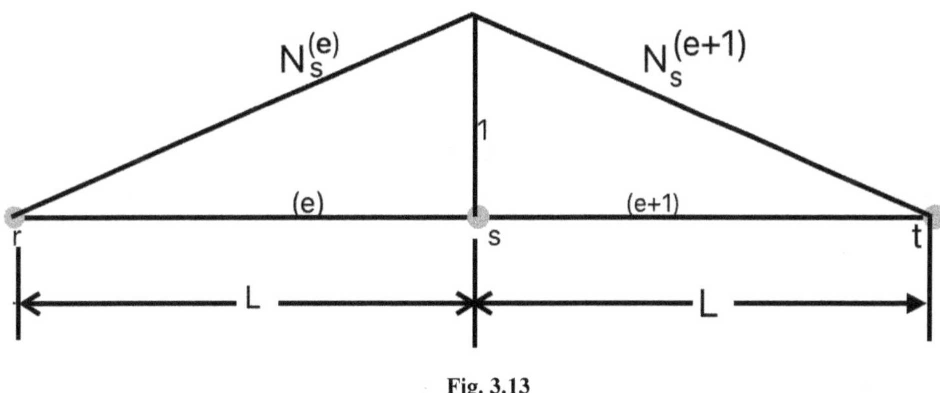

Fig. 3.13

Consider two elements (e) and (e+1) of a grid joined at fore node s as shown above.

$N_s^{(e)}$ *means shape function of element* (e) *at its fore node s*

which is located at X_s.

$N_s^{(e+1)}$ *means shape function of element* ($e + 1$) *at its hind node s*

which is located at X_s

Fig. 313 looks like a hat. The hat function is used as a weighting function to determine the weighted residual at node s. This figure can be used to find the residual contribution to the node s. Using this approach, the residual contribution of an element (e) to its nodes i and j has been derived as,

$$\{R^{(e)}\} = \{I^{(e)}\} + [k^{(e)}]\{T^{(e)}\} - \{f^{(e)}\} \text{ or}$$

$$\begin{Bmatrix} R_i^{(e)} \\ R_j^{(e)} \end{Bmatrix} = \begin{Bmatrix} I_i^{(e)} \\ I_j^{(e)} \end{Bmatrix} + \frac{D}{L}\begin{bmatrix} 1 & -1 \\ -1 & 1 \end{bmatrix}\begin{Bmatrix} T_i \\ T_j \end{Bmatrix} - \frac{QL}{2}\begin{Bmatrix} 1 \\ 1 \end{Bmatrix} \text{ } corresponding\ to\ the\ equation, \text{ } D\frac{d^2T}{dx^2} + Q = 0$$

where,

$$I_i^{(e)} = D\frac{dT}{dx}\bigg|_{x = X_i}$$

$$I_j^{(e)} = -D\frac{dT}{dx}\bigg|_{x = X_j}$$

Review Questions of Shape Functions and other Basic Terms

Please correct mistakes, if any, in the following statements

For an element (e) with nodes i and j, $\dfrac{dN_i}{dx} = \dfrac{d}{dx}\dfrac{L-x}{L} = \dfrac{d}{dx}\left(1-\dfrac{x}{L}\right) = -\dfrac{1}{L}$

For an element (e) with nodes i and j, $\dfrac{dN_j}{dx} = \dfrac{d}{dx}\dfrac{x}{L} = \dfrac{1}{L}$

A line element in s − t coordinates has $N_s = \dfrac{L-s}{L} = 1 - \dfrac{s}{L}$ *and* $N_t = \dfrac{s}{L}$

If $[N] = \begin{bmatrix} N_i & N_j \end{bmatrix}$, *then* $[N]^T[N] = \begin{bmatrix} N_i \\ N_j \end{bmatrix}\begin{bmatrix} N_i & N_j \end{bmatrix} = \begin{bmatrix} N_i^2 & N_iN_j \\ N_iN_j & N_j^2 \end{bmatrix}$

If $[B] = \dfrac{1}{L}\begin{bmatrix} N_i & N_j \end{bmatrix}$, *then* $[B]^T = \dfrac{1}{L}\begin{bmatrix} N_i \\ N_j \end{bmatrix}$

then, $[B]^T[B] = \dfrac{1}{L^2}\begin{bmatrix} N_i \\ N_j \end{bmatrix}\begin{bmatrix} N_i & N_j \end{bmatrix} = \dfrac{1}{L^2}\begin{bmatrix} N_i^2 & N_iN_j \\ N_iN_j & N_i^2 \end{bmatrix}$

CHAPTER 4

HEAT TRANSFER

Fourier's Law of Heat Conduction

If we a assume that a positive outward normal to a surface is directed away from a surface, the heat conducted to that surface from within the body per unit surface area per unit time is given by

$$- k \frac{dT}{dn} = q''_n$$

(4.1)

Equation (4.1) is known as the Fourier's Law of Heat Conduction.

A more general form of the Fourier' Law is,

$$\frac{\partial}{\partial x}\left(k\frac{\partial T}{\partial x}\right) + \frac{\partial}{\partial y}\left(k\frac{\partial T}{\partial y}\right) + \frac{\partial}{\partial z}\left(k\frac{\partial T}{\partial z}\right) + Q = \rho\, c\, \frac{\partial T}{\partial t}$$

where,

Q = rate of heat generation per unit volume of the body

t = time

k = *thermal conductivity of material of the body*

c = *constant pressure specific heat of the material of the body*

ρ = *density of the material of the body*.

α = *thermal diffusivity of the body*

The following boundary conditions may exist on the surfaces of heat conducting bodies:

I. **surface may have a given, constant temperature. In this case, we apply,**

$$T = T\big|_{x=0}$$

We delete the corresponding algebraic equation in the global equation and modify the remaining algebraic equations in the global equation.

II. **The surface may be insulated. In this case, we use,**

$$\frac{\partial T}{\partial x}\bigg|_{x=0} = 0$$

There is no need to alter anything in the global equation because of this boundary condition.

III. **Convective boundary condition or derivative boundary condition or dbc**

$$-k\frac{\partial T}{\partial x}\bigg|_{x=0} = h\left(T\big|_{x=0} - T_f\right) = M\,T_b - S, \; \textit{if dbc is at } x = 0$$

Note that we write the temperature at the boundary as T_b

The left hand of this equation stands for the heat conducted in the direction of the outward normal directed away from the surface x = 0. This means that heat is leaving body at surface at x = 0. *In this case we can see that $M = h$ and $S = h\,T_f$.*

$$-k\frac{\partial T}{\partial x}\bigg|_{x=0} = h\left(T_f - T\big|_{x=0}\right) = MT_b - S, \; \textit{if the dbc is at } x = 0$$

The left hand of this equation stands for the heat conducted in the direction of the inward normal directed into the surface x = 0

In this case also we can see that $M = h$ and $S = h\,T_f$.

Thus, in both case, whethe heat is entering the body or leaving the body,

$$M = h \text{ and } S = h\,T_f.$$

IV. **A heat flux q''_x may be entering through a surface. In this case, we use,**

$$M = 0 . \text{ and } S = q''_x$$

A heat flux q''_x may be leaving through surface. In this case,

$$M = 0 . \text{ and } S = -q''_x$$

V. **Why do we need M and S?**

Note that M multiplies surface temperature T_b.

S is a costant. These help us in applying the boundary conditions

to complete the element matrices to which these apply.

These boundary conditions will be explained further when we solve problems involving these.

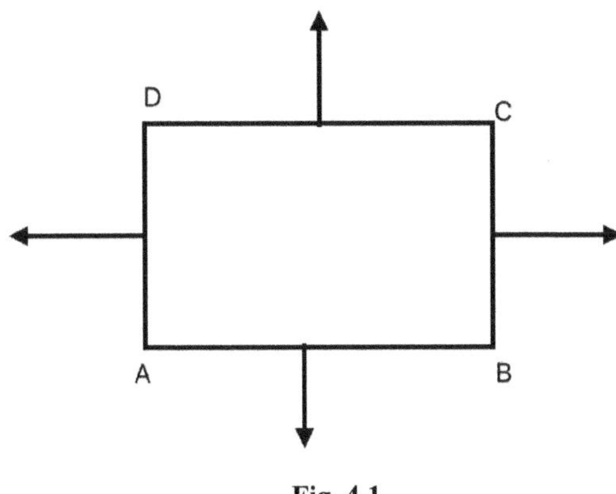

Fig. 4.1

Surface BC: By Fourier's Law, heat conducted in the direction of the

positive normal to BC extending away from BC, $- k\dfrac{dT}{dx} = h\left(T_b - T_f \right)$

Standard method of writing the Fourier's law gives, $- k\dfrac{dT}{dx} = MT_b - S$

Thus, by comparison, on surface BC, M = h and S = h T_f
Similarly, we can use comparison as above on the remaining sides to find M and S on these sides.

Example 4.1 A composite wall consists of three materials as shown in Fig. 3.1. The outermost surface is at 20 deg. C.

$$k_1 = 25 \; \frac{W}{m.K} \quad ; k_2 = 30 \; \frac{W}{m.K} \; and \; k_3 = 70 \; \frac{W}{m.K}$$

Convection heat transfer takes place on the inner surface of the wall with

$$T_f = 800 \, deg. \, C.$$

$$h = 30 \frac{W}{m^2 \cdot K}$$

a) The temperature distribution in the composite wall without any heat generation in the wall.
b) The temperature distribution in the wall if heat generation occurs in the composite wall at the rates in the first, second and third composite respectively:

$$Q_1 = 2000 \; \frac{W}{m^3}, \; Q_2 = 1500 \; \frac{W}{m^3} \; and \; Q_3 = 2500 \; \frac{W}{m^3} \; occur \; in \; the \; first, \; second \; and \; third \; wall, \; respectively.$$

Solution (4.1 a) The differential equation that applies in this case is,

$$D\frac{d^2T}{dx^2} = 0 \tag{4.2}$$

Applicable heat trander equation in this case i.e., no internal heat generation case is,

Fig. 4.2

Or

$$k\frac{d^2T}{dx^2} = 0 \tag{4.3}$$

Since there is no constant term such as Q in the applicable equation, there is no element force vector such as $\{f\,_Q^{(e)}\}$. Convection at surface 1, however, adds one matrix $\left[k_M^{(e)}\right] = h\,A\begin{bmatrix} 1 & 0 \\ 0 & 0 \end{bmatrix}$ and one force vector Here we choose 3 elements with 4 nodes.

Element stiffness matrix

$$\left[k^{(1)}\right] = \frac{k_1 A}{L_1}\begin{bmatrix} 1 & -1 \\ -1 & 1 \end{bmatrix} = \frac{25 \times 1}{0.3}\begin{bmatrix} 1 & -1 \\ -1 & 1 \end{bmatrix} = \begin{bmatrix} 83.33 & -83.33 \\ -83.33 & 83.33 \end{bmatrix}\begin{matrix} 1 \\ 2 \end{matrix}$$

$$\left[k^{(2)}\right] = \frac{k_2 A}{L_2}\begin{bmatrix} 1 & -1 \\ -1 & 1 \end{bmatrix} = \frac{30 \times 1}{0.2}\begin{bmatrix} 1 & -1 \\ -1 & 1 \end{bmatrix} = \begin{bmatrix} 150 & -150 \\ -150 & 150 \end{bmatrix}\begin{matrix} 2 \\ 3 \end{matrix}$$

$$\left[k^{(3)}\right] = \frac{k_3 A}{L3}\begin{bmatrix} 1 & -1 \\ -1 & 1 \end{bmatrix} = \frac{70 \times 1}{0.15}\begin{bmatrix} 1 & -1 \\ -1 & 1 \end{bmatrix} = \begin{bmatrix} 466.67 & -466.67 \\ -466.67 & 466.67 \end{bmatrix}\begin{matrix} 3 \\ 4 \end{matrix}$$

$$\left[k_M^{(1)}\right] = h\,A\begin{bmatrix} 1 & 0 \\ 0 & 0 \end{bmatrix} = (30) \times (1)\begin{bmatrix} 1 & 0 \\ 0 & 0 \end{bmatrix} = \begin{bmatrix} 30 & 0 \\ 0 & 0 \end{bmatrix}\begin{matrix} 1 \\ 2 \end{matrix} \qquad \{f\,_S^{(e)}\} = h\,A\,T_f\begin{Bmatrix} 1 \\ 0 \end{Bmatrix} \text{ to the element force vector.}$$

$$or\ \{f\,_S^{(e)}\} = h\,A\,T_f\begin{Bmatrix} 1 \\ 0 \end{Bmatrix}\begin{matrix} 1 \\ 2 \end{matrix} = 30 \times 1 \times 800\begin{Bmatrix} 1 \\ 0 \end{Bmatrix}\begin{matrix} 1 \\ 2 \end{matrix} = \begin{Bmatrix} 24000 \\ 0 \end{Bmatrix}\begin{matrix} 1 \\ 0 \end{matrix}$$

Thus, complete $\left[k^{(1)}\right] = \begin{bmatrix} 83.33 & -83.33 \\ -83.33 & 83.33 \end{bmatrix}\begin{matrix} 1 \\ 2 \end{matrix} + \begin{bmatrix} 30 & 0 \\ 0 & 0 \end{bmatrix}\begin{matrix} 1 \\ 2 \end{matrix} = \begin{bmatrix} 113.33 & -83.33 \\ -83.33 & 83.33 \end{bmatrix}\begin{matrix} 1 \\ 2 \end{matrix}$

Global stiffness matrix is,

$$[K] = \begin{bmatrix} & 1 & 2 & 3 & 4 & \\ 113.33 & -83.33 & 0 & 0 & 1 \\ -83.33 & 83.33+150 & -150 & 0 & 2 \\ 0 & -150 & 150+466.67 & -466.67 & 3 \\ 0 & 0 & -466.67 & 466.67 & 4 \end{bmatrix}$$

$$= \begin{bmatrix} & 1 & 2 & 3 & 4 & \\ 113.33 & -83.33 & 0 & 0 & 1 \\ -83.33 & 233.33 & -150 & 0 & 2 \\ 0 & -150 & 616.67 & -466.67 & 3 \\ 0 & 0 & -466.67 & 466.67 & 4 \end{bmatrix}$$

$$\left\{ f_Q^{(1)} \right\} = \left\{ f_Q^{(2)} \right\} = \left\{ f_Q^{(3)} \right\} = \begin{Bmatrix} 0 \\ 0 \\ 0 \\ 0 \end{Bmatrix} \begin{matrix} 1 \\ 2 \\ 3 \\ 4 \end{matrix}$$

$$\left\{ f_S^{(1)} \right\} = h\,A\,T_f \begin{Bmatrix} 1 \\ 0 \\ 0 \\ 0 \end{Bmatrix} = (30)\,(1)\,(800) \begin{Bmatrix} 1 \\ 0 \\ 0 \\ 0 \end{Bmatrix} = \begin{Bmatrix} 24000 \\ 0 \\ 0 \\ 0 \end{Bmatrix} \begin{matrix} 1 \\ 2 \\ 3 \\ 4 \end{matrix}$$

Thus,

Global force vector,

$$\{F\} = \begin{Bmatrix} 24000 \\ 0 \\ 0 \\ 0 \end{Bmatrix} \begin{matrix} 1 \\ 2 \\ 3 \\ 4 \end{matrix}$$

Using the **global matrix equation**, $[K]\{T\} = \{F\}$, *we get*

$$\begin{bmatrix} 113.33 & -83.33 & 0 & 0 \\ -83.33 & 233.33 & -150 & 0 \\ 0 & -150 & 616.67 & -466.67 \\ 0 & 0 & -466.67 & 466.67 \end{bmatrix} \begin{Bmatrix} T_1 \\ T_2 \\ T_3 \\ T_4 \end{Bmatrix} = \begin{Bmatrix} 24000 \\ 0 \\ 0 \\ 0 \end{Bmatrix}$$

Since $T_4 = 20\,deg.C$ is given, we delete row 4 and column 4

After shifting $(-466.67)\,(20) = -9333.34$ to the right-hand side. This means that 9333.34 will be added to the last column where there is zero existing there.

$$\begin{bmatrix} 113.33 & -83.33 & 0 \\ -83.33 & 233.33 & -150 \\ 0 & -150 & 616.67 \end{bmatrix} \begin{Bmatrix} T_1 \\ T_2 \\ T_3 \end{Bmatrix} = \begin{Bmatrix} 24000 \\ 0 \\ 9333.34 \end{Bmatrix}$$

Resulting 3 algebraic equations are:

$113.33\,T_1 - 83.33\,T_2 = 24000$

$-83.33\,T_1 + 233.33\,T_2 - 150\,T_3 = 0$

$-150\,T_2 + 616.67\,T_3 = 9333.34$

The solution (without any heat generation) is: $T_1 = 319.79$; $T_2 = 146.91$; $T_3 = 50.87$

Solution (4.1 b)

Applicable heat transfer equation in this case i.e., with internal heat generation case, is,

$$D\frac{d^2T}{dx^2} + Q = 0 \tag{4.4}$$

or

$$k\frac{d^2T}{dx^2} + Q = 0. \tag{4.5}$$

Adding the term Q does not change element stiffness matrices.

Only element force vectors change and now these are:

$$\{f_Q^{(1)}\} = \frac{Q\,L_1}{2}\begin{Bmatrix}1\\1\\0\\0\end{Bmatrix} = \frac{2000\times0.3}{2}\begin{Bmatrix}1\\1\\0\\0\end{Bmatrix} = \begin{Bmatrix}300\\300\\0\\0\end{Bmatrix}$$

$$\{f_Q^{(2)}\} = \frac{Q\,L_2}{2}\begin{Bmatrix}0\\1\\1\\0\end{Bmatrix} = \frac{1500\times0.2}{2}\begin{Bmatrix}0\\1\\1\\0\end{Bmatrix} = \begin{Bmatrix}0\\150\\150\\0\end{Bmatrix}$$

$$\{f_Q^{(3)}\} = \frac{Q\,L_3}{2}\begin{Bmatrix}0\\0\\1\\1\end{Bmatrix} = \frac{2500\times0.15}{2}\begin{Bmatrix}0\\0\\1\\1\end{Bmatrix} = \begin{Bmatrix}0\\0\\187.5\\187.5\end{Bmatrix}$$

$$\{f_S^{(1)}\} = h\,A\,T_f\begin{Bmatrix}1\\0\\0\\0\end{Bmatrix} = 30\times1\times800\begin{Bmatrix}1\\0\\0\\0\end{Bmatrix} = \begin{Bmatrix}24000\\0\\0\\0\end{Bmatrix}$$

Thus,

$$\{F\} = \begin{Bmatrix}300\\300+150\\150+187.5\\187.5\end{Bmatrix} = \begin{Bmatrix}24300\\450\\337.5\\187.5\end{Bmatrix}$$

The global matrix equation $[K]\{T\} = \{F\}$ now becomes,

$$
\begin{bmatrix}
113.33 & -83.33 & 0 & 0 \\
-83.33 & 233.33 & -150 & 0 \\
0 & -150 & 616.67 & -466.67 \\
0 & 0 & -466.67 & 466.67
\end{bmatrix}
\begin{Bmatrix}
T_1 \\ T_2 \\ T_3 \\ T_4
\end{Bmatrix}
=
\begin{Bmatrix}
24300 \\ 450 \\ 337.5 \\ 187.5
\end{Bmatrix}
$$

Since $T_4 = 20\, deg.C$ is given, we delete row 4 and column 4

After shifting $(-466.67)(20) = -9333.34$ to the right-hand side. This means that 9333.34 will be added to the last column where there is 187.5 existing there.

Thus,

$$
\begin{bmatrix}
113.33 & -83.33 & 0 \\
-83.33 & 233.33 & -150 \\
0 & -150 & 616.67
\end{bmatrix}
\begin{Bmatrix}
T_1 \\ T_2 \\ T_3
\end{Bmatrix}
=
\begin{Bmatrix}
24300 \\ 450 \\ 9520.84
\end{Bmatrix}
$$

Thus, the 3 algebraic equations are:

$113.33\, T_1 - 83.33\, T_2 = 24300$

$-83.33\, T_1 + 233.33\, T_2 - 150\, T_3 = 450$

$-150\, T_2 + 616.67\, T_3 = 9520.84$

Solution using Gauss elimination method is:

$T_1 = 326.33;\ T_2 = 152.20:\ T_3 = 52.46$

Heat Conduction in One-dimensional Fins

A one-dimensional, steady state heat transfer equation is,

$$\frac{d}{dx}\left(kA\frac{dT}{dx}\right) - hPT + hPT_f = 0$$

For a fin shown in Fig. 4.2, the above equation becomes,

$$kA\frac{d^2T}{dx^2} - hPT + hPT_f = 0$$

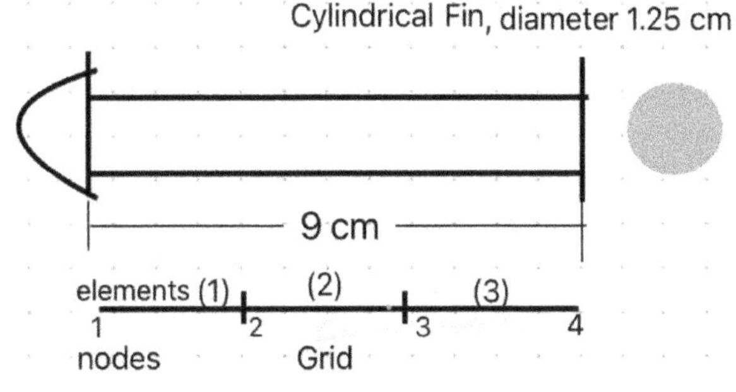

Fig. 4.3

Here we take an example to illustrate the method of solving equation (1.3) by using the Finite Element Method or F.E.M for short.

Example 4.2 A cylindrical fin has a base temperature of 80 deg C. Its other end is, in contact with water at 5 deg C with a transfer coefficient of $0.06 \ \dfrac{W}{cm^2.\,^\circ C}$.

The exterior surface of the fin is in contact with air at 5 deg C with a heat transfer coefficient of $0.03 \ \dfrac{W}{cm^2.\,^\circ C}$. The fin diameter = 1.25 cm and fin length = 9 cm. The thermal conductivity of the fin material is 1.0. Use three equal-length finite elements to obtain solution for the temperature distribution in the fin.

Solution: For steady state heat conduction from a one-dimensional fin which is exposed to a *fluid of temperature* T_f,

$$kA\frac{d^2T}{dx^2} - h\,P\,T + h\,P\,T_f = 0$$

(4.6)

where A is the area of cross-section and $P = fin\ perimeter$

Those terms in the above equation which have the dependent variable T in them will each contribute to the element conductance matrix (also called stiffness matrix) $[k^{(e)}]$.

$$[k^{(e)}] = [k_D^{(e)}] + [k_G^{(e)}] = \frac{kA}{L}\begin{bmatrix} 1 & -1 \\ -1 & 1 \end{bmatrix} + \frac{GL}{6}\begin{bmatrix} 2 & 1 \\ 1 & 2 \end{bmatrix}$$

Let us assume that the fin base has a constant temperature on it and the fin end is exposed to convection. The fin end is said to be subjected to a derivative (or convective) boundary condition or dbc. Conduction into the fin end from inside the fin = convection away from the fin end into the fluid.

Or

$$-k\,A_e\frac{dT}{dx} = h_e A_e\left(T - T_f\right) = h_e A_e T - h_e A_e T_f$$

$$\begin{bmatrix} 0 & 0 \\ 0 & h_e A_e \end{bmatrix} \text{ to the element matrix } [k^{(e)}] \text{ which has convection at its end.}$$

The constant term Q or $\left(h\,A\,T_f\right)$ *in the applicable differential equation contributes to the*

element force vector, $\{f^{(e)}\} = \{f_Q^{(e)}\} = \dfrac{h\,A\,T_f\,L}{2}\begin{Bmatrix} 1 \\ 1 \end{Bmatrix}$

The term $h_e A_e$ *multiplies* T. *Thus, it adds a matrix*

$$[k_M^{(e)}] = h_e A_e \begin{bmatrix} 0 & 0 \\ 0 & 1 \end{bmatrix}$$

(4.7)

and a force vector,

$$\{f_S^{(e)}\} = S\begin{Bmatrix} 0 \\ 1 \end{Bmatrix} = h_e A_e T_{fe}\begin{Bmatrix} 0 \\ 1 \end{Bmatrix}$$

(4.8)

Thus, complete element force vector is,

$$[k^{(e)}] = \left(\frac{kA}{L}\right)^{(e)}\begin{bmatrix} 1 & -1 \\ -1 & 1 \end{bmatrix} + \left(\frac{hpL}{6}\right)^e\begin{bmatrix} 2 & 1 \\ 1 & 2 \end{bmatrix} + M\begin{bmatrix} 0 & 0 \\ 0 & 1 \end{bmatrix}$$

(4.9)

For the given problem, the terms used in the above equation are defined and calculated.

as shown below:

k = thermal conductivity of the element = $1 \dfrac{W}{cm^2.°C}$

h = heat transfer coefficient on the fin surface = $0.03 \dfrac{W}{cm^2.°C}$

A = cross- sectional area of the fin = cm^2

A_e = area of the fin end = $A = 1.227 cm^2$

L = each element length = 3 cm

p = fin perimeter = $\pi\, d = \pi\,(1.25) = 3.927$ cm

$[K]$ = The global stiffness matrix

$$[k^{(e)}] = \left(\frac{kA}{L}\right)^{(e)} \begin{bmatrix} 1 & -1 \\ -1 & 1 \end{bmatrix} + \left(\frac{hpL}{6}\right)^e \begin{bmatrix} 2 & 1 \\ 1 & 2 \end{bmatrix} + h_e A \begin{bmatrix} 0 & 0 \\ 0 & 1 \end{bmatrix}$$

where the last matrix is to be used with element (3) only.

$$[k^{(1)}] = [k^{(2)}] = \left(\frac{1 \times 1.227}{3}\right) \begin{bmatrix} 1 & -1 \\ -1 & 1 \end{bmatrix} + \left(\frac{(0.03) \times 3.927 \times 3}{6}\right)^e \begin{bmatrix} 2 & 1 \\ 1 & 2 \end{bmatrix}$$

$$= \begin{bmatrix} 0.409 & -0.409 \\ -0.409 & 0.409 \end{bmatrix} + \begin{bmatrix} 0.1178 & 0.0589 \\ 0.0589 & 0.1178 \end{bmatrix} = \begin{bmatrix} 0.5268 & -0.3501 \\ -0.3501 & 0.5268 \end{bmatrix}$$

$$[k^{(3)}] = \begin{bmatrix} 0.5268 & -0.3501 \\ -0.3501 & 0.5268 \end{bmatrix} + \begin{bmatrix} 0 & 0 \\ 0 & 0.07362 \end{bmatrix} = \begin{bmatrix} 0.5268 & -0.3501 \\ -0.3501 & 0.6000 \end{bmatrix}$$

$$\{f_Q^{(1)}\} = \frac{h\,p\,T_f\,L}{2} \begin{Bmatrix} 1 \\ 1 \end{Bmatrix} \begin{matrix} 1 \\ 2 \end{matrix} = \frac{(0.03)\,(3.927)\,(5)\,(3)}{2} \begin{Bmatrix} 1 \\ 1 \end{Bmatrix} = \begin{Bmatrix} 0.8837 \\ 0.8837 \end{Bmatrix} \begin{matrix} 1 \\ 2 \end{matrix}$$

$$\{f_Q^{(2)}\} = \frac{h\,p\,T_f\,L}{2} \begin{Bmatrix} 1 \\ 1 \end{Bmatrix} \begin{matrix} 2 \\ 3 \end{matrix} = \frac{(0.03)\,(3.927)\,(5)\,(3)}{2} \begin{Bmatrix} 1 \\ 1 \end{Bmatrix} = \begin{Bmatrix} 0.8837 \\ 0.8837 \end{Bmatrix} \begin{matrix} 2 \\ 3 \end{matrix}$$

$$\{f_Q^{(3)}\} = \frac{h\,p\,T_f\,L}{2} \begin{Bmatrix} 1 \\ 1 \end{Bmatrix} \begin{matrix} 3 \\ 4 \end{matrix} = \frac{(0.03)\,(3.927)\,(5)\,(3)}{2} \begin{Bmatrix} 1 \\ 1 \end{Bmatrix} = \begin{Bmatrix} 0.8837 \\ 0.8837 \end{Bmatrix} \begin{matrix} 3 \\ 4 \end{matrix}$$

$$\{f_S^{(3)}\} = \begin{Bmatrix} 0 \\ h_e A T_f \end{Bmatrix} = \begin{Bmatrix} 0 \\ 0.3681 \end{Bmatrix} \begin{matrix} 3 \\ 4 \end{matrix}$$

The complete element 3 force vector is,

$$\{f^{(3)}\} = \begin{Bmatrix} 0.8837 \\ 0.8837 + 0.3681 \end{Bmatrix} \begin{matrix} 3 \\ 4 \end{matrix} = \begin{Bmatrix} 0.8837 \\ 1.2518 \end{Bmatrix} \begin{matrix} 3 \\ 4 \end{matrix}$$

Assembly of element matrcies gives,

$$[K] = \begin{bmatrix} 0.5268 & -0.3501 & 0 & 0 \\ -0.3501 & 1.0536 & -0.3501 & 0 \\ 0 & -0.3501 & 1.0536 & -0.3501 \\ 0 & 0 & -0.3501 & 0.6000 \end{bmatrix} \begin{Bmatrix} T_1 \\ T_2 \\ T_3 \\ T_4 \end{Bmatrix} = \begin{Bmatrix} 0.8837 \\ 1.7674 \\ 1.7674 \\ 1.2518 \end{Bmatrix} \begin{matrix} 1 \\ 2 \\ 3 \\ 4 \end{matrix}$$

T_1 = 80 *deg C as given, we eliminate row* 1 *and column* 1 *and modify the remaining equtions, we get,*

$$\begin{bmatrix} 1.0536 & -0.3501 & 0 \\ -0.3501 & 1.0536 & -0.3501 \\ 0 & -0.3501 & 0.6000 \end{bmatrix} \begin{Bmatrix} T_2 \\ T_3 \\ T_4 \end{Bmatrix} = \begin{Bmatrix} 29.7754 \\ 1.1782 \\ 1.2518 \end{Bmatrix}$$

Or

$$1.0536\, T_2 - 0.3501\, T_3 = 29.7754$$

$$-0.3501 T_2 + 1.0536\, T_3 - 0.3501\, T_4 = 1.7674$$

$$-0.3501\, T_3 + 0.6\, T_4 = 1.2518$$

Solution of the above set of 3 algebraic equations by the Gaussian Elimination Method

Let us first write the augmented coefficient matrix as

$$\begin{bmatrix} 1.0536 & -0.3501 & 0 & 29.7754 \\ -0.3501 & 1.0536 & -0.3501 & 1.7674 \\ 0 & -0.3501 & 0.6 & 1.2518 \end{bmatrix}$$

Multiply the first row by

$$F_{21} = -\left(\frac{-0.3506}{1.0536}\right) = 0.3323$$

and add to the second row. We get a new second row shown below:

$$(0.3323)(1.0536 \quad -0.3501 \quad 0 \quad 9.8944) + (-0.3501 \quad 1.0536 \quad -0.3501 \quad 1.7674)$$

$$= (0.3501 \quad -0.1163 \quad 0 \quad 9.8944) + (-3501 \quad 1.0536 \quad -0.3501 \quad 1.7674)$$

$$= (0 \quad 0.9373 \quad -0.3501 \quad 11.6618)$$

Now the augmented coefficient matrix is,

$$\begin{bmatrix} 1.0536 & -0.3501 & 0 & 29.7754 \\ 0 & 0.9373 & -0.3501 & 11.6618 \\ 0 & -0.3501 & 0.6 & 1.2518 \end{bmatrix}$$

Multiply the second row by

$$F_{31} = -\left(\frac{-0.3506}{0.9374}\right) = 0.3735$$

and add to the third row. We get a new third row as shown below:

$$\begin{bmatrix} 0 & -0.3501 & 0.6 & 1.2518 \end{bmatrix} + (0.3735)\begin{bmatrix} 0 & 0.9373 & -0.3501 & 11.6618 \end{bmatrix} = \begin{bmatrix} 0 & 0 & 0.4693 & 5.6075 \end{bmatrix}$$

Thus, new augmented coefficient matrix will become

$$\begin{bmatrix} 1.0536 & -0.3501 & 0 & 29.7754 \\ 0 & 0.9373 & -0.3501 & 11.6618 \\ 0 & 0 & 0.4692 & 5.6075 \end{bmatrix}$$

From the third row, we get,

$$0.4692 \, T_3 = 5.6075$$

$$\text{or } T_3 = \frac{5.6075}{0.4692} = 11.95$$

From the second row we get,

$$0.9373 \, T_2 - 0.3501 \, T_3 = 11.6618$$

$$0.9373 \, T_2 - 0.3501 \, (11.95) = 11.6618$$

$$T_2 = \frac{0.3501(11.95) + 11.6618}{0.9373} = 16.91$$

By substituting the values of

T_2 and T_3 in the first row we get,

$$1.0536 \, T_1 - 0.3501 \, T_2 + 0 = 29.7754$$

$$Therefore, \ T_1 = \frac{29.7754 + 0.3501(16.91) + 0}{1.0536} = 33.88$$

$$T_2 = 33.88, \ T_3 = 16.91, \ T_4 = 11.95 \ deg \ C$$

Example 4.3: Consider a cylindrical rod of diameter 0.4 cm and length 0.02 m. This rod has its base at 85°C. Its other end is insulated. The ambient fluid is at 25°C. The thermal conductvity of the rod material is 400 $\dfrac{W}{m.K}$. *The convective heat transfer coefficient is* 150 $\dfrac{W}{m^2.K}$. Find the nodal temperatures by using 2 elements with 3 nodes.

Solution:

The heat conduction equation that applies here is, $k \, A \dfrac{d^2T}{dx^2} - h \, p \, L \, T + h \, p \, L \, T_f = 0$

We first calculate element matrices.

$$L = 0.01 \text{ m}$$

$$\left[k^{(1)} \right] = \frac{k \, A}{L} \begin{bmatrix} 1 & -1 \\ -1 & 1 \end{bmatrix} + \frac{hPL}{6} \begin{bmatrix} 2 & 1 \\ 1 & 2 \end{bmatrix}$$

$$= \frac{400 \, \pi \, (0.002)^2}{0.01} \begin{bmatrix} 1 & -1 \\ -1 & 1 \end{bmatrix} + \frac{150 \times \pi \times 0.004 \times 0.01}{6} \begin{bmatrix} 2 & 1 \\ 1 & 2 \end{bmatrix}$$

$$= \begin{bmatrix} 0.50265 & -0.50265 \\ -0.50265 & 0.50265 \end{bmatrix} + \begin{bmatrix} 0.00628 & 0.00314 \\ 0.00314 & 0.00628 \end{bmatrix}$$

$$= \begin{bmatrix} \overset{1}{0.50893} & \overset{2}{-0.49951} \\ -0.49951 & 0.50893 \end{bmatrix} \begin{matrix} 1 \\ 2 \end{matrix}$$

$$\left[k^{(2)}\right] = \begin{bmatrix} \overset{2}{0.50893} & \overset{3}{-0.49951} \\ -0.49951 & 0.50893 \end{bmatrix} \begin{matrix} 2 \\ 3 \end{matrix}$$

$$[K] = \begin{bmatrix} \overset{1}{0.50893} & \overset{2}{-0.49951} \\ -0.49951 & 0.50893 \end{bmatrix} \begin{matrix} 1 \\ 2 \end{matrix} + \begin{bmatrix} \overset{2}{0.50893} & \overset{3}{-0.49951} \\ -0.49951 & 0.50893 \end{bmatrix} \begin{matrix} 2 \\ 3 \end{matrix}$$

Thus, Stiffness matrix, $[K] = \begin{bmatrix} \overset{1}{0.50893} & \overset{2}{-0.49951} & \overset{3}{0} \\ -0.49951 & 1.01786 & -0.49951 \\ 0 & -0.49951 & 0.50893 \end{bmatrix} \begin{matrix} 1 \\ 2 \\ 3 \end{matrix}$

$$\{f^{(1)}\} = \frac{h\,P\,L\,T_f}{2} \begin{Bmatrix} 1 \\ 1 \end{Bmatrix} \begin{matrix} 1 \\ 2 \end{matrix}$$

$$\frac{150 \times \pi \times 0.004 \times 0.01 \times 25}{2} \begin{Bmatrix} 1 \\ 1 \end{Bmatrix} = \begin{Bmatrix} 0.23561 \\ 0.23561 \end{Bmatrix} \begin{matrix} 1 \\ 2 \end{matrix}$$

$$\{f^{(2)}\} = \frac{h\,P\,L\,T_f}{2} \begin{Bmatrix} 1 \\ 1 \end{Bmatrix} \begin{matrix} 2 \\ 3 \end{matrix}$$

$$\frac{150 \times \pi \times 0.004 \times 0.01 \times 25}{2} \begin{Bmatrix} 1 \\ 1 \end{Bmatrix} = \begin{Bmatrix} 0.23561 \\ 0.23561 \end{Bmatrix} \begin{matrix} 2 \\ 3 \end{matrix} \quad F = \frac{h\,P\,L\,T_f}{2} \begin{Bmatrix} 1 \\ 2 \\ 1 \end{Bmatrix} = \begin{Bmatrix} 0.23561 \\ 0.47722 \\ 0.23561 \end{Bmatrix} \begin{matrix} 1 \\ 2 \\ 3 \end{matrix}$$

Using the global equation, $[K]\{T\} = \{F\}$, we get

$$\begin{bmatrix} 0.50893 & -0.49951 & 0 \\ -0.49951 & 1.01786 & -0.49951 \\ 0 & -0.49951 & 0.50893 \end{bmatrix} \begin{Bmatrix} T_1 \\ T_2 \\ T_3 \end{Bmatrix} = \begin{Bmatrix} 0.232561 \\ 0.47722 \\ 0.23561 \end{Bmatrix}$$

Since the base of the rod is maintained at 85°C, we may write,

$$\begin{bmatrix} 0.50893 & -0.49951 & 0 \\ -0.49951 & 1.01786 & -0.49951 \\ 0 & -0.49951 & 0.50893 \end{bmatrix} \begin{Bmatrix} T_1 \\ T_2 \\ T_3 \end{Bmatrix} = \begin{Bmatrix} 0.232561 \\ 0.47722 \\ 0.23561 \end{Bmatrix}$$

Since T_1 is to be maintained at 85°C, we modify the first row as shown below:

$$\begin{bmatrix} 1 & 0 & 0 \\ -0.49951 & 1.01786 & -0.49951 \\ 0 & -0.49951 & 0.50893 \end{bmatrix} \begin{Bmatrix} T_1 \\ T_2 \\ T_3 \end{Bmatrix} = \begin{Bmatrix} 85 \\ 0.47722 \\ 0.23561 \end{Bmatrix}$$

Now we shift column 1 by shifting column 2 as shown below:

$$\begin{bmatrix} 1 & 0 & 0 \\ 0 & 1.01786 & -0.49951 \\ 0 & -0.49951 & 0.50893 \end{bmatrix} \begin{Bmatrix} T_1 \\ T_2 \\ T_3 \end{Bmatrix} = \begin{Bmatrix} 1 \\ 0.47722 - (-0.47722 \times 85) \\ 0.23561 - (0 \times 85) \end{Bmatrix} \begin{Bmatrix} T_1 \\ T_2 \\ T_3 \end{Bmatrix}$$

$$= \begin{Bmatrix} 85 \\ 42.930 \\ 0.23561 \end{Bmatrix}$$

$$\begin{bmatrix} 1 & 0 & 0 \\ 0 & 1.01786 & -0.49951 \\ 0 & -0.49951 & 0.50893 \end{bmatrix} \begin{Bmatrix} T_1 \\ T_2 \\ T_3 \end{Bmatrix}$$

Solution of the set of the above 3 algebraic equations gives,

$$T_1 = 85, \quad T_2 = 81.8, \quad T_3 = 80.8 \,^{\circ}C$$

Example 4.4 Approximate the temperatures T_2, T_3 and T_4 of a large, composite wall of cross-section shown in Fig. 4.3. The temperature at surface 1 is given as 30°C. The heat transfer coefficient at surface 4 is $12 \dfrac{W}{m^2.K}$. The thermal conductivities are:

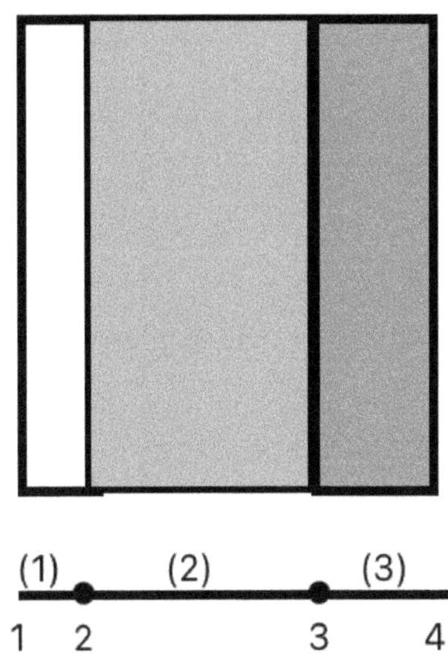

Fig 4.4

$$k_1 = 1.5 \; \frac{W}{m \, ^\circ C}, \quad k_2 = 12 \; \frac{W}{m \, ^\circ C}, \quad k_3 = 2.5 \frac{W}{m \, ^\circ C}$$

Heat transfer coefficient on surface 4 (or node 4) is,

$$h = \frac{12 \; W}{m^2 \, ^\circ C}$$

Solution: The fluid in contact with surface 4 (or node 4) is at $T_f = 10 \, ^\circ C$

Applicable heat trander equation in this case i.e. no internal heat generation case, is,

$$D \frac{d^2 T}{dx^2} = 0$$

or

$$k \frac{d^2 T}{dx^2} = 0$$

Since there is no constant term such as Q in the applicable equation, there is no

element force vector such as $\{f_Q^{(e)}\}$. Convection at surface 1, however, adds

one matrix $\left[k_M^{(e)} \right] = h \, A \begin{bmatrix} 1 & 0 \\ 0 & 0 \end{bmatrix}$ and one force vector $\{f_S^{(e)}\} = h \, A \, T_f \begin{Bmatrix} 1 \\ 0 \end{Bmatrix}$ *to the element force vector.*

Here we choose 3 elements with 4 nodes. $\{T\} = \begin{Bmatrix} T_1 \\ T_2 \\ T_3 \\ T_4 \end{Bmatrix} \quad \{F\} = \begin{Bmatrix} 0 \\ 0 \\ 0 \\ 100 \end{Bmatrix}$

Thus, the global stiffness matrix equation is,

$$[K] = \begin{bmatrix} 100 & -100 & 0 & 0 \\ -100 & 100+200 & -200 & 0 \\ 0 & -200 & 200+100 & -100 \\ 0 & 0 & -100 & 110 \end{bmatrix} \begin{Bmatrix} T_1 \\ T_2 \\ T_3 \\ T_4 \end{Bmatrix} = \begin{Bmatrix} 0 \\ 0 \\ 0 \\ 100 \end{Bmatrix}$$

It is given that, $T_1 = 30^\circ C$

Thus, we eliminate the first row and the first column in the matrix equation and before doing that, we shift
(-100) (30) to F2. Thus, F2 = 0 + (100) (30) = 3000.

Now the remaining matrix equation is,

$$\begin{bmatrix} 300 & -200 & 0 \\ -200 & 300 & -100 \\ 0 & -100 & 110 \end{bmatrix} \begin{Bmatrix} T_2 \\ T_3 \\ T_4 \end{Bmatrix} = \begin{Bmatrix} 3000 \\ 0 \\ 100 \end{Bmatrix}$$

We can now write 3 algebraic equations corresponding to the above matrix equation. These 3 equations are:

$$300\,T_2 - 200\,T_3 = 3000$$

$$-200\,T_2 + 300\,T_3 - 100\,T_4 = 0$$

$$-100\,T_3 + 110\,T_4 = 100$$

By using **Gauss's elimination method**, the solution is,

$$T_2 = 28.4°\,C;\ \ T_3 = 27.6°\,C;\ \ T_4 = 26°\,C$$

Example 4.5 A boiler consists of a fire brick wall, 0.5 m thick with a layer of insulation, 0.1 m thick. Atmospheric air in contact with the insulation layer is m thick. The thermal conductivity of the wall is 0.2 $\dfrac{W}{m\,°C}$ and that of the insulation layer is 0.01 $\dfrac{W}{m\,°C}$. The heat transfer coefficient is 5 $\dfrac{W}{m^2.°C}$. Temperature at the inner surface of the wall 1000°C. Find the remaining nodal temperatures.

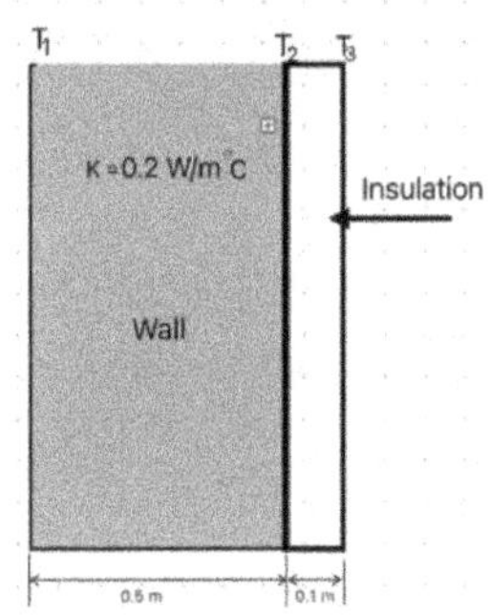

Fig. 4.5

Solution: Heat conduction equation that applies is, $k\,A\,\dfrac{d^2T}{dx^2} = 0.$

We will take a grid of two elements with three nodes as in Fig. 3.4.

$$[k^{(1)}] = \frac{k_1 A}{L_1}\begin{bmatrix} 1 & -1 \\ -1 & 1 \end{bmatrix} = \frac{(0.2)(1)}{0.5}\begin{bmatrix} 1 & -1 \\ -1 & 1 \end{bmatrix} = \begin{bmatrix} 0.4 & -0.4 \\ -0.4 & 0.4 \end{bmatrix} \{f^{(1)}\} = \begin{Bmatrix} 0 \\ 0 \end{Bmatrix}$$

$$[k^{(2)}] = \frac{k_2 A}{L_2}\begin{bmatrix} 1 & -1 \\ -1 & 1 \end{bmatrix} = \frac{(0.01)(1)}{0.1}\begin{bmatrix} 1 & -1 \\ -1 & 1 \end{bmatrix} = \begin{bmatrix} 0.1 & -0.1 \\ -0.1 & 0.1 \end{bmatrix} \{f^{(2)}\} = \begin{Bmatrix} 0 \\ 0 \end{Bmatrix}$$

$$[k_M] = h\,A\begin{bmatrix} 0 & 0 \\ 0 & 1 \end{bmatrix} = (5)(1)\begin{bmatrix} 0 & 0 \\ 0 & 1 \end{bmatrix} = \begin{bmatrix} 0 & 0 \\ 0 & 5 \end{bmatrix} \{f_s\} = h\,A\,T_f\begin{Bmatrix} 0 \\ 1 \end{Bmatrix} = (5)(1)(20)\begin{Bmatrix} 0 \\ 1 \end{Bmatrix} = \begin{Bmatrix} 0 \\ 100 \end{Bmatrix}$$

Thus, we will get complete element matrix,

$$[k^{(2)}] = \begin{bmatrix} 0.1 & -0.1 \\ -0.1 & 0.1 \end{bmatrix} + \begin{bmatrix} 0 & 0 \\ 0 & 5 \end{bmatrix}$$

and complete force vector $\{f^{(2)}\} = \begin{Bmatrix} 0 \\ 100 \end{Bmatrix}$

Thus, the assembled matrix,

$$[K] = \begin{bmatrix} 0.4 & -0.4 \\ -0.4 & 0.4 \end{bmatrix} \begin{matrix} 1 \\ 2 \end{matrix} + \begin{bmatrix} 0.1 & -0.1 \\ -0.1 & 5.1 \end{bmatrix} \begin{matrix} 2 \\ 3 \end{matrix} = \begin{bmatrix} 0.4 & -0.4 & 0 \\ -0.4 & 0.5 & -0.1 \\ 0 & -0.1 & 5.1 \end{bmatrix} \begin{matrix} 1 \\ 2 \\ 3 \end{matrix}$$

Assembled force vector,

$$\{F\} = \begin{Bmatrix} 0 \\ 0 \\ 100 \end{Bmatrix}$$

Now we will solve the matrix equation,

$$[K\,T] = \{F\}$$

or

$$\begin{bmatrix} 0.4 & -0.4 & 0 \\ -0.4 & 0.5 & -0.1 \\ 0 & -0.1 & 5.1 \end{bmatrix} \begin{Bmatrix} T_1 \\ T_2 \\ T_3 \end{Bmatrix} = \begin{Bmatrix} 0 \\ 0 \\ 100 \end{Bmatrix}$$

Since we know that $T_1 = 1000$, we will eliminate row 1 and column 1 after shifting (-0.4) (1000) to the second row of last column where it will add to zero existing there.

$$\begin{bmatrix} 0.5 & -0.1 \\ -0.1 & 5 \end{bmatrix} \begin{Bmatrix} T_2 \\ T_3 \end{Bmatrix} = \begin{Bmatrix} 400 \\ 100 \end{Bmatrix}$$

This matrix equation gives two algebraic equations:

$$0.5\,T_2 - 0.1\,T_3 = 400$$

$$-0.1\,T_2 + 5\,T_3 = 100$$

Solution of these two equations gives,
$T_3 = 36.14$

and $T_2 = 807.22$

Example 4.6 A plane wall is 4 cm thick and has a thermal conductivity of 0.5 W/cm. K. Its right surface is at 10 deg. C and its left surface is in contact with a fluid of temperature 5 deg C. Heat transfer coefficient on this surface is 1.5 W/sq.cm. K. Find the temperature of this surface. Take the wall as a single element.

Solution: Here,

$$[k^{(e)}] = [k_D^{(e)}] + [k_M^{(e)}] = \frac{kA}{L}\begin{bmatrix} 1 & -1 \\ -1 & 1 \end{bmatrix} + \begin{bmatrix} 1.5 & 0 \\ 0 & 0 \end{bmatrix} = \frac{0.5 \times 1}{4}\begin{bmatrix} 1 & -1 \\ -1 & 1 \end{bmatrix} + \begin{bmatrix} 1.5 & 0 \\ 0 & 0 \end{bmatrix} = \begin{bmatrix} 1.625 & -0.125 \\ -0.125 & 0.125 \end{bmatrix}$$

$$\{f^{(e)}\} = h\,AT_f \begin{Bmatrix} 1 \\ 0 \end{Bmatrix} = 1.5 \times 1 \times 5 \begin{Bmatrix} 1 \\ 0 \end{Bmatrix} = \begin{Bmatrix} 7.5 \\ 0 \end{Bmatrix}$$

$[K]\{T\} = \{F\}$ *gives,*

$$\begin{bmatrix} 1.625 & -0.125 \\ -0.125 & 0.125 \end{bmatrix} \begin{Bmatrix} T_1 \\ T_2 \end{Bmatrix} = \begin{Bmatrix} 7.5 \\ 0 \end{Bmatrix}$$

or

$$\begin{bmatrix} 1.625 \end{bmatrix} \{T_1\} = 7.5 + 10 \times 0.125 = 8.75$$

or

$$T_1 = \frac{8.25}{1.625} = 5.38 \ deg \ C.$$

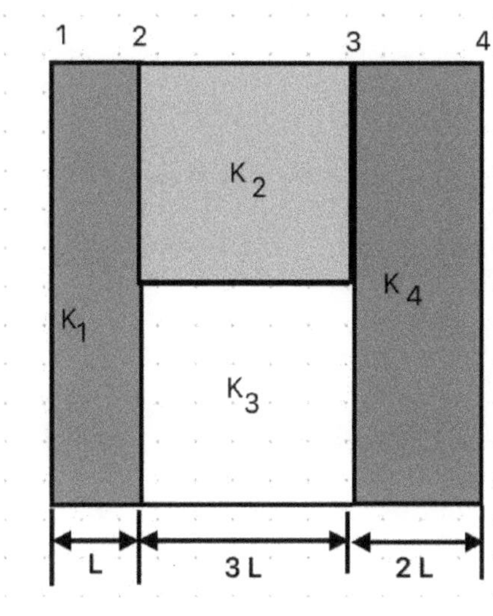

Fig. 4.6

Example 4.7 In a composite wall, the following data is known:

$$k_1 = 15\,a, \ k_2 = 3a, \ k_3 = 7a \ and \ k_4 = 5a, \ where \ a = \frac{10 \ W}{m. \,°C},$$

$$L = 0.025 \ m, \ T_1 = 350 \ °C, \ T_4 = 50 \ °C.$$

Find the temperatures where unknown. Also, calculate the rate heat transfer through the wall.

Solution:

The differential that applies here is, $k\dfrac{d^2T}{dx^2} = 0.$

The element matrices will be, $k^{(1)} = \dfrac{150(1)}{0.025} = 6000 \begin{bmatrix} 1 & -1 \\ -1 & 1 \end{bmatrix}$

$$\begin{bmatrix} k^{(1)} \end{bmatrix} = \frac{150(1)}{0.025} = 6000 \begin{bmatrix} 1 & -1 \\ -1 & 1 \end{bmatrix} = 1000 \begin{bmatrix} 6 & -6 \\ -6 & 6 \end{bmatrix}$$

$$\begin{bmatrix} k^{(2)} \end{bmatrix} = \frac{30(1)}{0.075} = 1000 \begin{bmatrix} 0.4 & -0.4 \\ -0.4 & 0.4 \end{bmatrix}$$

$$\begin{bmatrix} k^{(3)} \end{bmatrix} = \frac{70(1)}{0.075} = 1000 \begin{bmatrix} 0.9333 & -0.9333 \\ -0.9333 & 0.9333 \end{bmatrix}$$

$$\left[k^{(4)}\right] = \frac{50(1)}{0.050} = 1000 \begin{bmatrix} 1 & -1 \\ -1 & 1 \end{bmatrix} \frac{W}{m.\,^\circ C}$$

$$[F] = 1000 \begin{bmatrix} 6 & -6 & 0 & 0 \\ -6 & 6+0.4+0.9333 & -0.4-0.9333 & 0 \\ 0 & -0.4-0.9333 & 0.4+0.9333+1.0 & -1.0 \\ 0 & 0 & -1.0 & 1.0 \end{bmatrix}$$

$$\{f^{(1)}\} = \{f^{(1)}\} = \{f^{(1)}\} = \{f^{(1)}\} = \begin{Bmatrix} 0 \\ 0 \end{Bmatrix}$$

Thus, $\{F\} = \begin{Bmatrix} 0 \\ 0 \\ 0 \\ 0 \end{Bmatrix}$.

Thus, the global matrix equation may be written as, $[K]\{T\} = \{F\}$

Or

$$[F] = 1000 \begin{bmatrix} 6 & -6 & 0 & 0 \\ -6 & 7.333 & -1.333 & 0 \\ 0 & -1.3333 & 2.333 & -1.0 \\ 0 & 0 & -1.0 & 1.0 \end{bmatrix} \begin{Bmatrix} 350 \\ T_2 \\ T_3 \\ 50 \end{Bmatrix} = \begin{Bmatrix} 0 \\ 0 \\ 0 \\ 0 \end{Bmatrix}$$

$$[F] = 1000 \begin{bmatrix} \cdots\cdots\cdots & \cdots\cdots\cdots & \cdots\cdots\cdots & \cdots\cdots\cdots \\ \cdots\cdots & 7.333 & -1.333 & \cdots\cdots \\ \cdots\cdots & -1.3333 & 2.333 & \cdots\cdots \\ \cdots\cdots & \cdots\cdots\cdots & \cdots\cdots\cdots\cdots & \cdots\cdots \end{bmatrix} \begin{Bmatrix} \cdots \\ T_2 \\ T_3 \\ \cdots \end{Bmatrix} = \begin{Bmatrix} \cdots \\ 0+350(6) \\ 50000 \\ \cdots \end{Bmatrix}$$

Therefore, $7.333\,T_2 - 1.333\,T_3 = 2100$

$$-1.333T_2 + 2.333\,T_3 = 50000$$

$$-\left(\frac{-1.333}{7.333}\right)\left(7.333\,T_2 - 1.333\,T_3\right) + \left(-1.333\,T_2 + 2.333\,T_3\right) = 371.78 + 50 = 431.78$$

or $0.1818\left(7.333\,T_2 - 1.333\,T_3\right) + \left(-1.333\,T_2 + 2.333\,T_3\right) = 431.78$

or $\left(1.333\,T_2 - 0.2424\,T_3\right) + \left(-1.333\,T_2 + 2.333\,T_3\right) = 431.78$

or $2.09068\,T_3 = 431.78$

or $T_3 = \dfrac{431.78}{2.09068} = 206.53$

Substituting
$T_3 = 206.53$ *in the second equation, we get,*

$$-1.333T_2 + 2.333\,(206.53) = 50$$

$$-1.333\,T_2 = 50 - 2.333(206.53) = 431.834$$

or $T_2 = \dfrac{431.834}{1.333} = 323.96\,^\circ C$

Example 4.8 For the rectangular element shown below, calculate the shape functions for the point (3, 2). Calculate the interpolated temperature at point (3, 2) if the temperatures at points i and m are 50 deg C each and those at points j and are 20 deg C each.

$$N_i = \frac{1}{4ab}\left(x_j - x\right)\left(y_m - y\right) = (1/20)\ (7\text{-}3)\ (5\text{-}2) = 12/20$$

$$N_j = \frac{1}{4ab}\left(x - x_i\right)\left(y_m - y\right) = (1/20)\ (3\text{-}2)\ (5\text{-}2) = 3/20$$

$$N_m = \frac{1}{4ab}\left(x_j - x\right)\left(y - y_i\right) = (1/20)\ (3\text{-}2)\ (2\text{-}1) = 1/20$$

$$= (1/20)\ (7\text{-}3)\ (2\text{-}1) = 4/20$$

We may note that the sum of all shape functions of an element equals 1.

The interpolated temperature at the point (3,2), which lies inside the rectangle is,

$$T = N_i T_i + N_j T_j + N_k T_k + N_m T_m$$

$$= \frac{12}{20}(50) + \frac{3}{20}(20) + \frac{1}{20}(20) + \frac{4}{20}(50) = 44\ deg\ C$$

Shape functions and their derivatives are used in deriving element matrices.

We have seen that for a line element,

$$[N] = [N_i \quad N_j] = \left[\frac{X_j - x}{L} \quad \frac{x - X_i}{L}\right]$$

We may take derivatives of the above.

$$\frac{d}{dx}[N] = [B] = \left[-\frac{1}{L} \quad \frac{1}{L}\right]$$

$$[k^{(e)}] = \int_{x}^{X_j} D\,[B]^T[B]\,dx = \int_{X_i}^{X_j}(1)\begin{bmatrix}-\dfrac{1}{L}\\[6pt]\dfrac{1}{L}\end{bmatrix}\left[-\dfrac{1}{L}\quad\dfrac{1}{L}\right]dx = \frac{1}{L^2}\begin{bmatrix}1 & -1\\-1 & 1\end{bmatrix}\int_{X_i}^{X_j}dx$$

$$= \frac{1}{L^2}\begin{bmatrix}1 & -1\\-1 & 1\end{bmatrix}L = \frac{1}{L}\begin{bmatrix}1 & -1\\-1 & 1\end{bmatrix}$$

Example 4.9 Find the temperature at the center of a long cylinder with its data given as follows:

$$k = 20\ W\!/m.K,\ r_1 = 0,\ r_2 = 0.01\ m,\ Q = 2\times 10^8\ W\!/m^3,\ T\ ar\ r_2 = 100^{\circ}C.$$

Solution: The applicable equation here is,

$$\frac{k}{r}\frac{d}{dr}\left(r\frac{dT}{dr} + Q\right) = 0$$

The element matrices for the above differential equation have been derived as follows:

$$[k^{(e)}] = \frac{k}{L}\frac{r_1+r_2}{2}\begin{bmatrix} 1 & -1 \\ -1 & 1 \end{bmatrix} = \frac{20}{0.01}\frac{0+0.01}{2}\begin{bmatrix} 1 & -1 \\ -1 & 1 \end{bmatrix} = \begin{bmatrix} 10 & -10 \\ -10 & 10 \end{bmatrix}$$

$$\{f^{(e)}\} = \frac{QL}{6}\begin{Bmatrix} 2r_1+r_2 \\ r_1+2r_2 \end{Bmatrix} = \frac{2\times10^8\times0.01}{6}\begin{Bmatrix} 0.01 \\ 0.02 \end{Bmatrix} = \begin{Bmatrix} 10^4/3 \\ 2\times10^4/3 \end{Bmatrix}$$

Since we are using one element, the global equation $[K]\{T\} = \{F\}$ becomes,

$$\begin{bmatrix} 10 & -10 \\ -10 & 10 \end{bmatrix}\begin{Bmatrix} T_1 \\ T_2 \end{Bmatrix} = \begin{Bmatrix} \dfrac{10^4}{3} \\ \dfrac{2\times10^4}{3} \end{Bmatrix}$$

Since $T_2 = 100$, we will eliminate equation 2 and substitute $T_2 = 100$ in equation 1.

Thus,

$$10\,T_1 - 10(100) = \frac{10^4}{3}$$

or

$$T_1 = 433.3$$

Example 4.10 Shown in Fig. (1.3) is a grid of line elements. There are three line elements in this grid.

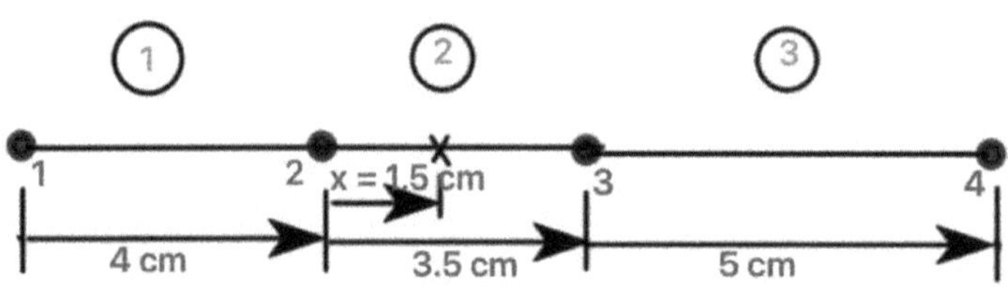

Fig. 4.7

with 4 nodes numbered as shown. Expressions for shape functions for a linear line element (e) with nodes i and j are written down below:

$$N_i = \frac{x_j - x}{x_j - x_i}\qquad N_j = \frac{x - x_i}{x_j - x_i}$$

Heat Transfer Equation in a Two-dimensional Fin

Following is the form of a two-dimensional equation which has several variants:

$$D_x\frac{\partial^2 T}{\partial x^2} + D_y\frac{\partial^2 T}{\partial y^2} - GT + Q = 0 \tag{4.10}$$

For heat conduction in a two-dimensional fin, the above equation takes the form,

$$k_x t \frac{\partial^2 T}{\partial x^2} + k_y t \frac{\partial^2 T}{\partial y^2} - 2hT + 2hT_f = 0 \tag{4.11}$$

where, t is the fin thickness,

G = 2 h, where h is the heat transfer coefficient on each surface of the fin

Q = rate of heat generation per unit volume of the fin = $2h\,T_f$ (t is the fin thickness)

Only some simple problems can be solved manually. We always to use a computer to solve more difficult, real engineering problems. We write and run computer programs for such problems. Commercial computer programs such as ANSYS'S and FLUENT are available for education, training, and design. This author has written a computer program which solves many types of one- and two-dimensional problems including axis-symmetric and time-dependent field problems.

For a triangular element in two-dimensional heat transfer, the element matrices are,

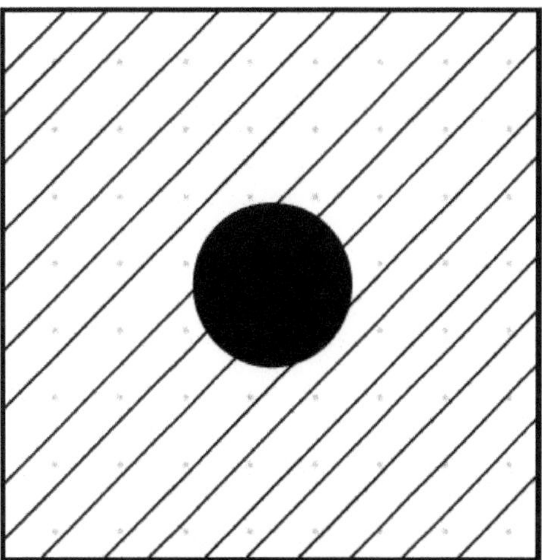

Fig. 4.8 Two-dimensional Fin fixed on a rod

$$\frac{k_x}{4A} \begin{bmatrix} b_i^2 & b_i b_j & b_i b_k \\ b_i b_j & b_j^2 & b_j b_k \\ b_i b_k & b_j b_k & b_k^2 \end{bmatrix} + \frac{k_y}{4A} \begin{bmatrix} c_i^2 & c_i c_j & c_i c_k \\ c_i c_j & c_j^2 & c_j c_k \\ c_i c_k & c_j c_k & c_k^2 \end{bmatrix}$$

$$+ \frac{2hA}{12t} \begin{bmatrix} 2 & 1 & 1 \\ 1 & 2 & 1 \\ 1 & 1 & 2 \end{bmatrix}$$

$$and \quad \{f^{(e)}\} = \frac{2h\,A\,T_f}{3t} \begin{Bmatrix} 1 \\ 1 \\ 1 \end{Bmatrix}$$

Example 4.11 Calculate the element matrices for which the following data are available:

$$k_x = k_y = 1.0 \ \frac{W}{m.K}; \ h = 0.02 \ \frac{W}{m^2.K}; \ t = 1.0 \ cm; \ T_f = 15 \ deg. \ C.$$

$$b_i = -4.5, \ b_j = 5, \ b_k = -0.5$$

$$c_i = -2, \ c_j = -2, \ c_k = 5$$

Area of the triangular element $= A = 9.5 \ cm^2$.

$$\frac{k_x}{4A} = \frac{k_y}{4A} = \frac{1.0}{4 \times 9.5} = 0.0263$$

Solution:

$$\frac{2hA}{12t} = \frac{2 \times 0.02 \times 9.5}{12 \times 1} = 0.0317$$

$$\frac{2 \times h \times A \times T_f}{3t} = \frac{2 \times 0.02 \times 9.5 \times 15}{3 \times 1} = 1.9$$

Substituting the given data, we get,

$$[k^{(e)}] = 0.0263 \begin{bmatrix} 20.3 & -22.5 & 2.25 \\ -22.5 & 25 & -2.50 \\ 2.25 & -2.50 & 0.250 \end{bmatrix} + 0.0263 \begin{bmatrix} 4 & 4 & -8 \\ 4 & 4 & -8 \\ -8 & -8 & 16 \end{bmatrix} + 0.0317 \begin{bmatrix} 2 & 1 & 1 \\ 1 & 2 & 1 \\ 1 & 1 & 2 \end{bmatrix}$$

or

$$[k^{(e)}] = \begin{bmatrix} 0.384 & -0.213 & -0.0442 \\ -0.213 & 0.446 & -0.107 \\ -0.0442 & -0.107 & 0.278 \end{bmatrix}$$

and $\{f^{(e)}\} = \dfrac{2h \, A \, T_f}{3t} \begin{Bmatrix} 1 \\ 1 \\ 1 \end{Bmatrix} = \begin{Bmatrix} 1.9 \\ 1.9 \\ 1.9 \end{Bmatrix}$

Suppose side i j of the triangular element is undergoing convection heat transfer from its area $L_{ij} \times t$.
Then, $-k \, L_{ij} \, t \, \dfrac{dT}{dn} = h \, L_{ij} \, t \left(T_{ij} - T_f \right)$

where n is normal to this edge area $Li \, j \times t$. From the equation

$$-k \, L_{ij} \, t \, \frac{dT}{dn} = h \, L_{ij} \, t \left(T_{ij} - T_f \right), \text{ we get, } -k \, \frac{dT}{dn} = .\left(h \, T_{ij} - h \, T_f \right).$$

Thus, M = h and S = h T_f. Please note that convection heat transfer from the edge is small and is usually neglected. Main convection, from both sides of the two-dimensional fin is already included in the applicable equation.

Solving a Second Order Differential Equation using a Line Element

Example 4.12 A differential equation, $5\dfrac{d^2T}{dx^2} + 200 = 0$, with the boundary conditions are given. Solve this equation using the Finite Element Method. Use 3 elements of length 1 cm each.

Solution: We see from the given problem that the thermal conductivity k = 5 in any consistent system of units and the heat generation rate per unit volume is, Q = 200.

The transfer area A = 1 unit.

The element stiffness matrices are,

$$\left[k_D^{(1)}\right] = \left[k_D^{(2)}\right] = \left[k_D^{(3)}\right]$$

$$= \frac{kA}{L}\begin{bmatrix} 1 & -1 \\ -1 & 1 \end{bmatrix} = \frac{(5)(1)}{1}\begin{bmatrix} 1 & -1 \\ -1 & 1 \end{bmatrix} = \begin{bmatrix} 5 & -5 \\ -5 & 5 \end{bmatrix}$$

The **global stiffness matrix** can now be written down:

$$[K] = \begin{bmatrix} 5 & -5 & 0 & 0 \\ -5 & 5+5 & -5 & 0 \\ 0 & -5 & 5+5 & -5 \\ 0 & 0 & -5 & 5 \end{bmatrix} = \begin{bmatrix} 5 & -5 & 0 & 0 \\ -5 & 10 & -5 & 0 \\ 0 & -5 & 10 & -5 \\ 0 & 0 & -5 & 5 \end{bmatrix}$$

The element force vectors are,

$$\left\{f_Q^{(1)}\right\} = \frac{QL}{2}\begin{Bmatrix} 1 \\ 1 \end{Bmatrix} = \frac{(200)(1)}{2}\begin{Bmatrix} 1 \\ 1 \end{Bmatrix} = \begin{Bmatrix} 100 \\ 100 \end{Bmatrix}$$

$$\left\{f_Q^{(2)}\right\} = \frac{QL}{2}\begin{Bmatrix} 1 \\ 1 \end{Bmatrix} = \frac{(200)(1)}{2}\begin{Bmatrix} 1 \\ 1 \end{Bmatrix} = \begin{Bmatrix} 100 \\ 100 \end{Bmatrix}$$

$$\left\{f_Q^{(2)}\right\} = \frac{QL}{2}\begin{Bmatrix} 1 \\ 1 \end{Bmatrix} = \frac{(200)(1)}{2}\begin{Bmatrix} 1 \\ 1 \end{Bmatrix} = \begin{Bmatrix} 100 \\ 100 \end{Bmatrix}$$

The global force vector can now be written down:

$$\{F\} = \begin{Bmatrix} 100 \\ 100+100 \\ 100+100 \\ 100 \end{Bmatrix} = \begin{Bmatrix} 100 \\ 200 \\ 200 \\ 100 \end{Bmatrix}$$

We now solve the global equation, $[K]\{T\} = \{F\}$

$$\begin{bmatrix} 5 & -5 & 0 & 0 \\ -5 & 10 & -5 & 0 \\ 0 & -5 & 10 & -5 \\ 0 & 0 & -5 & 5 \end{bmatrix}\begin{Bmatrix} T_1 \\ T_2 \\ T_3 \\ T_4 \end{Bmatrix} = \begin{Bmatrix} 100 \\ 200 \\ 200 \\ 100 \end{Bmatrix}$$

$$\begin{bmatrix} 5 & -5 & 0 & 0 \\ -5 & 10 & -5 & 0 \\ 0 & -5 & 10 & -5 \\ 0 & 0 & -5 & 5 \end{bmatrix} \begin{Bmatrix} 100 \\ T_2 \\ T_3 \\ 10 \end{Bmatrix} = \begin{Bmatrix} 100 \\ 200 \\ 200 \\ 100 \end{Bmatrix}$$

Since T1 and T4 are given, we eliminate rows and columns 1 and 4 after shifting and adding as per the norms.

Thus, $\begin{bmatrix} 10 & -5 \\ -5 & 10 \end{bmatrix} \begin{Bmatrix} T_2 \\ T_3 \end{Bmatrix} = \begin{Bmatrix} 700 \\ 250 \end{Bmatrix}$

We get, $(10)\, T_2 - (5)\, T_3 = 700$

and $-(5)\, T_2 + 10\, T_3 = 250$

$15 T_3 = 1200$

Thus, $T_3 = 1200/15 = 80$

and $10\, T_2 = 700 + 400 = 1100$

or $T_2 = 1100/10 = 110$

Example 4.13 Solve $2\left(\dfrac{\partial^2 T}{\partial x^2} + \dfrac{\partial^2 T}{\partial y^2}\right) + 4\left(x^2 + y^2\right) = 0,\ 0 \le x \le 1;\ 0 \le y \le 1$

The boundary conditions are, $T = 10$ on the side $x = 0$ and the side $y = 0$.

$-k\dfrac{dT}{dx} = -4\,T + 40$ *at surface,* $x = 1$ *and* $-k\dfrac{dT}{dy} = -4T + 40$ *on surface* $y = 1$.

Solution: *We now follow the same procedure as we did for every problem before it.*

For a rectangular element, the element stiffness matrix is,

$$\left[k_b^{(e)}\right] = \frac{D_x a}{6\,b}\begin{bmatrix} 2 & -2 & -1 & 1 \\ -2 & 2 & 1 & -1 \\ -1 & 1 & 2 & -2 \\ -1 & -1 & -2 & 2 \end{bmatrix} + \frac{D_y b}{6\,a}\begin{bmatrix} 2 & 1 & -1 & -2 \\ 1 & 2 & -2 & -1 \\ -1 & -2 & 2 & 1 \\ -2 & -1 & 1 & 2 \end{bmatrix}$$

In this problem, $D_x = D_y = 2$. Thus,

$$\left[k_b^{(e)}\right] = \frac{(2)(1)}{6(1)}\begin{bmatrix} 2 & -2 & -1 & 1 \\ -2 & 2 & 1 & -1 \\ -1 & 1 & 2 & -2 \\ 1 & -1 & -2 & 2 \end{bmatrix} + \frac{(2)(1)}{6(1)}\begin{bmatrix} 2 & 1 & -1 & -2 \\ 1 & 2 & -2 & -1 \\ -1 & -2 & 2 & 1 \\ -2 & -1 & 1 & 2 \end{bmatrix}$$

Or

$$[k_D^{(e)}] = \begin{bmatrix} \dfrac{4}{3} & \dfrac{-1}{3} & \dfrac{-2}{3} & \dfrac{-1}{3} \\[2mm] \dfrac{-1}{3} & \dfrac{4}{3} & \dfrac{-1}{3} & \dfrac{-2}{3} \\[2mm] \dfrac{-2}{3} & \dfrac{-1}{3} & \dfrac{4}{3} & \dfrac{-1}{3} \\[2mm] \dfrac{-1}{3} & \dfrac{-2}{3} & \dfrac{-1}{3} & \dfrac{4}{3} \end{bmatrix}$$

We note that the given expression $4\left(x^2 + y^2\right)$ does not have T in it. Thus, it can contribute to the element force vector only. If we write $4\left(x^2 + y^2\right) = Q$, then we get,

$$\{f_Q^{(e)}\} = \int_A Q\,[N]^T dA = \int_A \begin{bmatrix} N_i & N_j & N_k & N_m \end{bmatrix} \begin{Bmatrix} Q_i \\ Q_j \\ Q_k \\ Q_m \end{Bmatrix} \begin{Bmatrix} N_i \\ N_j \\ N_k \\ N_m \end{Bmatrix} dA$$

$$= \int_A \begin{bmatrix} N_i Q_i & N_j Q_j & N_k Q_k & N_m Q_m \end{bmatrix} \begin{Bmatrix} N_i \\ N_j \\ N_k \\ N_m \end{Bmatrix} dA$$

$$= \int_A \begin{bmatrix} N_i^2 & N_i N_j & N_i N_k & N_i N_m \\ N_j N_i & N_j^2 & N_j N_k & N_j N_k \\ N_k N_i & N_k N_j & N_k^2 & N_k N_m \\ N_m N_i & N_m N_j & N_m N_k & N_m^2 \end{bmatrix} \begin{Bmatrix} 4\left(x^2 + y^2\right)_i \\ 4\left(x^2 + y^2\right)_j \\ 4\left(x^2 + y^2\right)_k \\ 4\left(x^2 + y^2\right)_m \end{Bmatrix} dA$$

Substituting the given values of A and Q, we get,

$$\{f_Q^{(e)}\} = = \frac{A}{36} \begin{bmatrix} 4 & 2 & 1 & 2 \\ 2 & 4 & 2 & 1 \\ 1 & 2 & 4 & 2 \\ 2 & 1 & 2 & 4 \end{bmatrix} \begin{Bmatrix} 0 \\ 4 \\ 8 \\ 4 \end{Bmatrix} = \frac{1}{36} \begin{bmatrix} 4 & 2 & 1 & 2 \\ 2 & 4 & 2 & 1 \\ 1 & 2 & 4 & 2 \\ 2 & 1 & 2 & 4 \end{bmatrix} \begin{Bmatrix} 0 \\ 4 \\ 8 \\ 4 \end{Bmatrix} = \begin{Bmatrix} 0.667 \\ 1 \\ 1.334 \\ 1 \end{Bmatrix}$$

The derivative boundary conditions (dbcs) on the sides jk and km are,

$$-k\frac{dT}{dx} = -4T + 40 = MT - S \ on \ side \ jk$$

$$-k\frac{dT}{dy} = -4T + 40 = MT - S$$

Thus, $M = -4$ and $S = -40$ on the side jk in this problem.

On side km, $-k\dfrac{dT}{dy} = MT - S = -4T + 40$

Thus, $M = -4$ and on the side km $S = 40$

Thus, M on each side $= -4$ and S on side is -40

Each dbc contributes one matrix $\left[k_M^{(e)}\right]$ to complete the element matrix $[k^{(e)}]$ and one vector $\{f_S^{(e)}\}$ to complete its force vector $\{f_Q^{(e)}\}$..

The boundary condition on the side jk gives,

$$\left[k_M^{(e)}\right] = \frac{M\,L_{jk}}{6}\begin{bmatrix} 0 & 0 & 0 & 0 \\ 0 & 2 & 1 & 0 \\ 0 & 1 & 2 & 0 \\ 0 & 0 & 0 & 0 \end{bmatrix} = \frac{-4\,(1)}{6}\begin{bmatrix} 0 & 0 & 0 & 0 \\ 0 & 2 & 1 & 0 \\ 0 & 1 & 2 & 0 \\ 0 & 0 & 0 & 0 \end{bmatrix}$$

$$\{f_S^{(e)}\} = \frac{S\,L_{jk}}{2}\begin{Bmatrix} 0 \\ 1 \\ 1 \\ 0 \end{Bmatrix} = \frac{-40\,(1)}{2}\begin{Bmatrix} 0 \\ 1 \\ 1 \\ 0 \end{Bmatrix} = \begin{Bmatrix} 0 \\ -20 \\ -20 \\ 0 \end{Bmatrix}$$

The boundary condition on the side km gives,

$$\left[k_M^{(e)}\right] = \frac{M\,L_{km}}{6}\begin{bmatrix} 0 & 0 & 0 & 0 \\ 0 & 0 & 0 & 0 \\ 0 & 0 & 2 & 1 \\ 0 & 0 & 1 & 2 \end{bmatrix} = \frac{-4\,(1)}{6}\begin{bmatrix} 0 & 0 & 0 & 0 \\ 0 & 0 & 0 & 0 \\ 0 & 0 & 2 & 1 \\ 0 & 0 & 1 & 2 \end{bmatrix}$$

$$\{f_S^{(e)}\} = \frac{S\,L_{km}}{2}\begin{Bmatrix} 0 \\ 0 \\ 1 \\ 1 \end{Bmatrix} = \frac{-40(1)}{2}\begin{Bmatrix} 0 \\ 0 \\ 1 \\ 1 \end{Bmatrix} = \begin{Bmatrix} 0 \\ 0 \\ -20 \\ -20 \end{Bmatrix}$$

Thus, the complete element matrix $[k^{(e)}]$ is given

$$[k^{(e)}] = \begin{bmatrix} \dfrac{4}{3} & \dfrac{-1}{3} & \dfrac{-2}{3} & \dfrac{-1}{3} \\ \dfrac{-1}{3} & \dfrac{4}{3} & \dfrac{-1}{3} & \dfrac{-2}{3} \\ -2 & -1 & \dfrac{-4}{3} & -1 \\ \dfrac{-1}{3} & \dfrac{-2}{3} & \dfrac{-1}{3} & \dfrac{4}{3} \end{bmatrix} - \frac{4\,(1)}{6}\begin{bmatrix} 0 & 0 & 0 & 0 \\ 0 & 2 & 1 & 0 \\ 0 & 1 & 2 & 0 \\ 0 & 0 & 0 & 0 \end{bmatrix} - \frac{4(1)}{6}\begin{bmatrix} 0 & 0 & 0 & 0 \\ 0 & 0 & 0 & 0 \\ 0 & 0 & 2 & 1 \\ 0 & 0 & 1 & 2 \end{bmatrix}$$

Or

$$[K] = \begin{bmatrix} \dfrac{4}{3} & \dfrac{-1}{3} & \dfrac{-2}{3} & \dfrac{-1}{3} \\ \dfrac{-1}{3} & 0 & -1 & \dfrac{-2}{3} \\ \dfrac{-2}{3} & -1 & \dfrac{-4}{3} & -1 \\ \dfrac{-1}{3} & \dfrac{-2}{3} & -1 & 0 \end{bmatrix}$$

$$\{F\} = \{f_Q^{(e)}\} + \frac{S\,L_{jk}}{2}\left\{\begin{array}{c} \\ \\ \\ \end{array}\right\} + \frac{S\,L_{jk}}{2}\left\{\begin{array}{c} 0 \\ -20 \\ -20 \\ 0 \end{array}\right\} = \left\{\begin{array}{c} 0.667 \\ 1 \\ 1.334 \\ 1 \end{array}\right\} + \left\{\begin{array}{c} 0 \\ -20 \\ -20 \\ 0 \end{array}\right\} + \left\{\begin{array}{c} 0 \\ 0 \\ -20 \\ -20 \end{array}\right\} = \left\{\begin{array}{c} 0.667 \\ -19 \\ -38.666 \\ -19 \end{array}\right\}$$

Thus, the global equation $[K]\{T\} = \{F\}$ becomes,

$$[K] = \begin{bmatrix} \dfrac{4}{3} & \dfrac{-1}{3} & \dfrac{-2}{3} & \dfrac{-1}{3} \\[2mm] \dfrac{-1}{3} & 0 & -1 & \dfrac{-2}{3} \\[2mm] \dfrac{-2}{3} & -1 & \dfrac{-4}{3} & -1 \\[2mm] \dfrac{-1}{3} & \dfrac{-2}{3} & -1 & 0 \end{bmatrix} \left\{\begin{array}{c} T_1 \\ T_2 \\ T_3 \\ T_4 \end{array}\right\} = \left\{\begin{array}{c} 0.667 \\ -19 \\ -38.666 \\ -19 \end{array}\right\}$$

There is only one element given in this problem. The temperatures,

$T_1 = T_2 = T_3 = 10 \; deg \;$ are given in the problem.

$$\text{Thus, } [K] = \begin{bmatrix} \dfrac{4}{3} & \dfrac{-1}{3} & \dfrac{-2}{3} & \dfrac{-1}{3} \\[2mm] \dfrac{-1}{3} & 0 & -1 & \dfrac{-2}{3} \\[2mm] \dfrac{-2}{3} & -1 & \dfrac{-4}{3} & -1 \\[2mm] \dfrac{-1}{3} & \dfrac{-2}{3} & -1 & 0 \end{bmatrix} \left\{\begin{array}{c} 10 \\ 10 \\ T_3 \\ 10 \end{array}\right\} = \left\{\begin{array}{c} 0.667 \\ -19 \\ -38.666 \\ -19 \end{array}\right\}$$

Thus, because three temperatures are already known, we need to write only one equation, namely, equation number 3, namely,

$$\frac{-2}{3}(10) - (1)(10) - \frac{4}{3}T_3 - (1)(10) = -38.666$$

we get, $T_3 = \dfrac{-12}{-4/3} = 9 \; deg.$

Two-dimensional Heat Conduction in a Long Body

Let us consider a body which is long in z- direction and whose cross-section is rectangular, i, j, k, m as shown in Fig. 3.7. This rectangular area may be divided into triangular elements or rectangular elements or a combinaion of both as shown in Fig.3.7. Heat conduction equation applicable is

$$D_x \frac{\partial^2 T}{\partial x^2} + D_y \frac{\partial^2 T}{\partial y^2} + Q = 0$$

where Q is heat generation per unit volume.

Element Matrices of a Triangular Element (e) with Nodes i, j, k, and Area A

Equation to be solved, $D_x \dfrac{\partial^2 T}{\partial x^2} + D_y \dfrac{\partial^2 T}{\partial y^2} + Q = 0$

$$[k_D^{(e)}] = \frac{D_x}{4A} \begin{bmatrix} b_i^2 & b_i b_j & b_i b_k \\ b_i b_j & b_j^2 & b_j b_k \\ b_i b_k & b_j b_k & b_k^2 \end{bmatrix} + \frac{D_y}{4A} \begin{bmatrix} c_i^2 & c_i c_j & c_i c_k \\ c_i c_j & c_j^2 & c_j c_k \\ c_i c_k & c_j c_k & c_k^2 \end{bmatrix}$$

where,

$$b_i = y_j - y_k, \quad c_i = x_k - x_j$$
$$b_j = y_k - y_i, \quad c_i = x_j - x_k$$
$$b_k = y_i - y_j, \quad c_k = x_j - x_i$$

For derivative boundary conditions or dbcs existing on the side ij,

$$[k_M^{(e)}] = \frac{M L_{ij}}{6} \begin{bmatrix} 2 & 1 & 0 \\ 1 & 2 & 0 \\ 0 & 0 & 0 \end{bmatrix}$$

M and S are found by equating the exiting heat by convection to MT − S.

For derivative boundary conditions or dbc existing on the side jk,

$$[k_M^{(e)}] = \frac{M L_{jk}}{6} \begin{bmatrix} 0 & 0 & 0 \\ 0 & 2 & 1 \\ 0 & 1 & 2 \end{bmatrix}$$

For derivative boundary conditions or dbc existing on the side ik

$$[k_M^{(e)}] = \frac{M L_{ik}}{6} \begin{bmatrix} 2 & 0 & 1 \\ 0 & 0 & 0 \\ 1 & 0 & 2 \end{bmatrix}$$

Element force vector, $\{f_Q^{(e)}\} = \dfrac{Q A}{3} \begin{Bmatrix} 1 \\ 1 \\ 1 \end{Bmatrix}$

$$\{f_S^{(e)}\} = \frac{S L_{ij}}{2} \begin{Bmatrix} 1 \\ 1 \end{Bmatrix}$$

The complete stiffness matrix, $[k^{(e)}]$ is given by,

$$[k^{(e)}] = [k_D^{(e)}] + [k_M^{(e)}]$$

The complete element force vector $\{f^{(e)}\}$ is given by,

$$\{f^{(e)}\} = \{f_Q^{(e)}\} + \{f_S^{(e)}\}$$

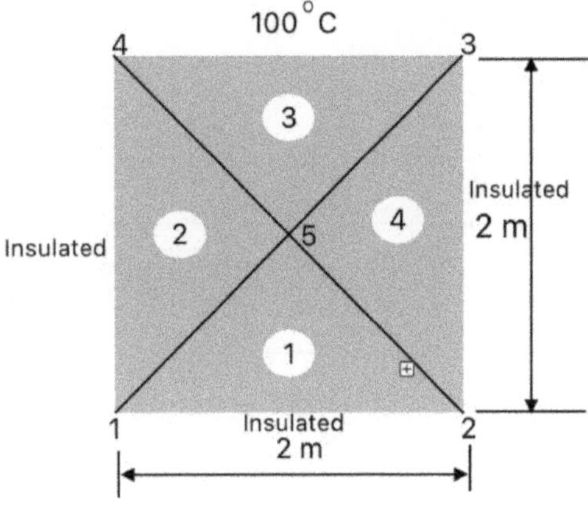

Fig. 4.9

Example 4.14 A block 2 m x 2 m x 10 m is shown below:Three surfaces of this block are insulated as shown. The top surface of this block is maintained at a constant temperature of 100°C. Uniform Heat generation occurs in the block at the rate of 1000 $W/_{m^3}$ .. Make a grid of 4 triangular elements as shown here. Take $k_x = k_y = 25 \dfrac{W}{m.°C}$. Find the temperatures at nodes 1, 2 and 5 using the finite element method.

Solution: This is a long body in z direction. Area of each element, A $= (2\times 2)/_4 = 1\, m^2$.

Thus, it may be assumed that there is no heat conduction in the z-direction. Heat conduction occurs in x and y directions only.

Equation to be solved, $D_x \dfrac{\partial^2 T}{\partial x^2} + D_y \dfrac{\partial^2 T}{\partial y^2} + Q = 0$

$$\left[k_D^{(e)}\right] = \frac{D_x}{4A}\begin{bmatrix} b_i^2 & b_i b_j & b_i b_k \\ b_i b_j & b_j^2 & b_j b_k \\ b_i b_k & b_j b_k & b_k^2 \end{bmatrix} + \frac{D_y}{4A}\begin{bmatrix} c_i^2 & c_i c_j & c_i c_k \\ c_i c_j & c_j^2 & c_j c_k \\ c_i c_k & c_j c_k & c_k^2 \end{bmatrix}$$

where,

$b_i = Y_j - Y_k, \quad c_i = X_k - X_j$

$b_j = Y_k - Y_i, \quad c_i = X_j - X_k$

$b_k = Y_i - Y_j, \quad c_k = X_j - X_i$

Element 1, $b_1 = -1, b_2 = 1;, b_5 = 0: c_1 = -1, c_2 = -1, c_5 = 2.$

Element 2, $b_1 = -1, b_5 = 2;, b_4 = -1: c_1 = -1, c_5 = 0, c_4 = 1.$

Element 3, $b_4 = -1, b_5 = 0;, b_3 = 1: c_4 = 1, c_5 = -2, c_3 = 1.$

Element 4, $b_2 = 1, b_3 = 1;, b_5 = -2: c_2 = -1, c_3 = 1, c_5 = 0.$

Table 4.1: Global Node Numbers corresponding to Local Node Numbers i, j, k

Element Number	i	j	k
1	1	2	5
2	1	5	4
3	4	5	3
4	2	3	5

$$\left[k^{(1)}\right] = \frac{25}{4}\begin{bmatrix} 1 & -1 \\ -1 & 1 \end{bmatrix} + \frac{25}{4}\begin{bmatrix} 1 & 1 & -2 \\ 1 & 1 & -2 \\ -2 & -2 & 4 \end{bmatrix} = \frac{25}{4}\begin{bmatrix} 2 & 0 & -2 \\ 0 & 2 & -2 \\ -2 & -2 & 4 \end{bmatrix}$$

$$= \begin{matrix} & 1 & 2 & 5 & \\ \end{matrix} \begin{bmatrix} 12.5 & 0 & -12.5 \\ 0 & 12.5 & -12.5 \\ -12.5 & -12.5 & 25 \end{bmatrix} \begin{matrix} 1 \\ 2 \\ 5 \end{matrix}$$

$$\left[k^{(2)}\right] = \begin{matrix} & 1 & 5 & 4 & \\ \end{matrix} \begin{bmatrix} 12.5 & -12.5 & 0 \\ -12.5 & 25 & -12.5 \\ 0 & -12.5 & 12.5 \end{bmatrix} \begin{matrix} 1 \\ 5 \\ 4 \end{matrix}$$

$$\left[k^{(3)}\right] = \begin{matrix} & 4 & 5 & 3 & \\ \end{matrix} \begin{bmatrix} 12.5 & -12.5 & 0 \\ -12.5 & 25 & -12.5 \\ 0 & -12.5 & 12.5 \end{bmatrix} \begin{matrix} 4 \\ 5 \\ 3 \end{matrix}$$

$$\left[k^{(4)}\right] = \begin{matrix} & 2 & 3 & 5 & \\ \end{matrix} \begin{bmatrix} 12.5 & 0 & -12.5 \\ 0 & 12.5 & -12.5 \\ -12.5 & -12.5 & 25 \end{bmatrix} \begin{matrix} 2 \\ 3 \\ 5 \end{matrix}$$

$$\text{Thus, } [K] = \begin{bmatrix} 25 & 0 & 0 & 0 & -25 \\ 0 & 25 & 0 & 0 & -25 \\ 0 & 0 & 25 & 0 & -25 \\ 0 & 0 & 0 & 25 & -25 \\ -25 & -25 & -25 & -25 & 100 \end{bmatrix}$$

$$\{f^{(1)}\} = \frac{Q\,A}{3}\begin{Bmatrix} 1 \\ 1 \\ 1 \end{Bmatrix} = \frac{1000 \times 1}{3}\begin{Bmatrix} 1 \\ 1 \\ 2 \end{Bmatrix} = \begin{Bmatrix} 333.33 \\ 333.33 \\ 333.33 \end{Bmatrix} \begin{matrix} 1 \\ 2 \\ 5 \end{matrix}$$

$$\{f^{(2)}\} = \frac{QA}{3}\begin{Bmatrix}1\\1\\1\end{Bmatrix} = \frac{1000\times 1}{3}\begin{Bmatrix}1\\1\\1\end{Bmatrix} = \begin{Bmatrix}333.33\\333.33\\333.33\end{Bmatrix}\begin{matrix}1\\5\\4\end{matrix}$$

$$\{f^{(3)}\} = \frac{QA}{3}\begin{Bmatrix}1\\1\\1\end{Bmatrix} = \frac{1000\times 1}{3}\begin{Bmatrix}1\\1\\2\end{Bmatrix} = \begin{Bmatrix}333.33\\333.33\\333.33\end{Bmatrix}\begin{matrix}4\\5\\3\end{matrix}$$

$$\{f^{(4)}\} = \frac{QA}{3}\begin{Bmatrix}1\\1\\1\end{Bmatrix} = \frac{1000\times 1}{3}\begin{Bmatrix}1\\1\\2\end{Bmatrix} = \begin{Bmatrix}333.33\\333.33\\333.33\end{Bmatrix}\begin{matrix}2\\3\\5\end{matrix}$$

Similarly, $\{F\} = \begin{Bmatrix}666.67\\666.67\\666.67\\666.67\\1333.34\end{Bmatrix}$

We may now write the matrix equation, $[K]\{T\} = \{F\}$

or

$$\begin{bmatrix}25 & 0 & 0 & 0 & -25\\0 & 25 & 0 & 0 & -25\\0 & 0 & 25 & 0 & -25\\0 & 0 & 0 & 25 & -25\\-25 & -25 & -25 & -25 & 100\end{bmatrix}\begin{Bmatrix}T_1\\T_2\\T_3\\T_4\\T_5\end{Bmatrix} = \begin{Bmatrix}666.67\\666.67\\666.67\\666.67\\1333.34\end{Bmatrix}$$

In terms of algebraic equations, we now write the above equation as,

$25\,T_1 - 25\,T_5 = 666.67$

$25\,T_2 - 25\,T_5 = 666.67$

$25\,T_3 - 25\,T_5 = 666.67$

$25\,T_4 - 25\,T_5 = 666.67$

$-25\,T_1 - 25\,T_2 - 25\,T_3 - 25\,T_4 + 100\,T_5 = 1333.34$

Since $T_3 = T_4 = 100$ as given, we eliminate rows 3 and 4 and

Substitute these values in the remaining equations, we get,

$25\,T_1 - 25\,T_5 = 666.67$

$25\,T_2 - 25\,T_5 = 666.67$

$-50\,T_2 + 100\,T_5 = 6333.34$

Solution of the above three equations gives,

$T_1 = T_2 = 180\,^{\circ}C \ and \ T_5 = 153.3\,^{\circ}C.$

Example 4.15 Calculate $[k^{(e)}]$ and $\{f^{(e)}\}$ for the thin triangular element shown below.

Assume the applicable equation as,

$$k_x \frac{\partial^2 T}{\partial x^2} + k_y \frac{\partial^2 T}{\partial y^2} - G\,T + Q = 0$$

Take *thermal conductivities* $k_x = k_y = 2\ \dfrac{W}{cm.\,^\circ C}$ *and* $h = \dfrac{0.2\ W}{cm^2.\,^\circ C}$.

The fluid temperature in contact with surface i k is $15\ ^\circ C$. *The surfaces i j and j k are insulated.*

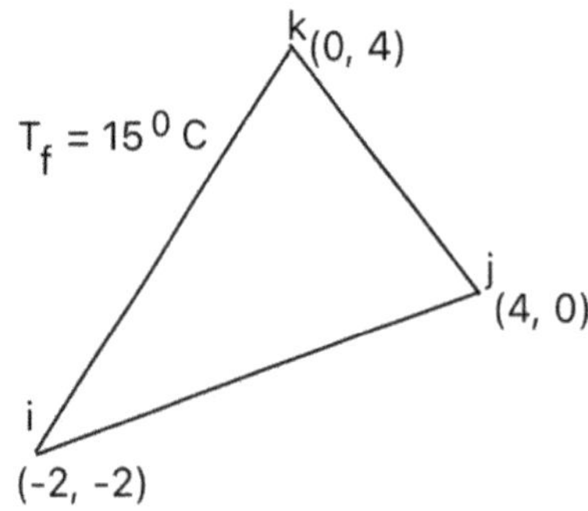

Fig. 4.10

Solution: corresponding to the given triangular element equation,

$$[k_D^{(e)}] = \frac{D_x}{4A}\begin{bmatrix} b_i^2 & b_i b_j & b_i b_k \\ b_i b_j & b_j^2 & b_j b_k \\ b_i b_k & b_j b_k & b_k^2 \end{bmatrix} + \frac{D_y}{4A}\begin{bmatrix} c_i^2 & c_i c_j & c_i c_k \\ c_i c_j & c_j^2 & c_j c_k \\ c_i c_k & c_j c_k & c_k^2 \end{bmatrix}$$

Un

$$[k_G] = \frac{GA}{12}\begin{bmatrix} 2 & 1 & 1 \\ 1 & 2 & 1 \\ 1 & 1 & 2 \end{bmatrix},$$

$$[k_M] = \frac{M L_{ik}}{6}\begin{bmatrix} 2 & 0 & 1 \\ 0 & 0 & 0 \\ 1 & 0 & 2 \end{bmatrix},$$

$$\{f_Q^{(e)}\} = \frac{QA}{3}\begin{Bmatrix} 1 \\ 0 \\ 1 \end{Bmatrix}, \quad \{f_S^{(e)}\} = \frac{M L_{ik} T_f}{2}\begin{Bmatrix} 1 \\ 0 \\ 1 \end{Bmatrix},$$

$$2A = \det\begin{bmatrix} 1 & X_i & Y_i \\ 1 & X_j & Y_j \\ 1 & X_k & X_k \end{bmatrix}$$

For a triangular element,

$$N_i = \frac{1}{2A}\left(a_i + b_i\, x + c_i\, y\right)$$

$$N_j = \frac{1}{2A}\left(a_j + b_j\, x + c_j\, y\right)$$

$$N_k = \frac{1}{2A}\left(a_k + b_k\, x + c_k\, y\right)$$

where

$$a_i = X_j Y_k - X_k Y_j;\ \ a_j = X_k Y_i - X_i Y_k;\ \ a_k = X_i Y_j - X_j Y_i$$

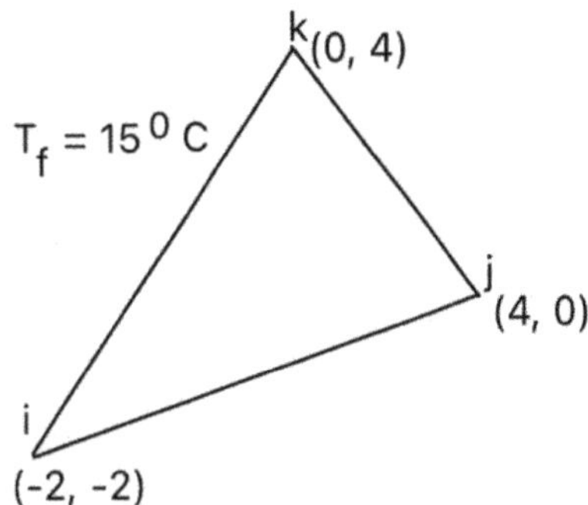

Fig. 4.10 (repeated)

CHAPTER 5

SOME RELATIONS AND DEFINITIONS

Integration of products of shape functions over a line element length L

$$\int_0^L N_i^a \, N_j^b \, dx = \frac{a! \, b!}{(a+b+1)!} \, L$$

Integration of products of shape functions over a triangular element area A

$$\int_A N_i^a \, N_j^b \, N_k^c \, dA = \frac{a! \, b! \, c!}{(a+b+c+2)!} \, 2A$$

Residual contribution of Q to force vector for a line element, when Q is constant,

$$\{f_Q^{(e)}\} = \int_0^L Q \, [N]^T \, dx$$

$$= \frac{QL}{2} \begin{Bmatrix} 1 \\ 1 \end{Bmatrix}.$$

For a line element, when Q is variable,

$$\{f_Q^{(e)}\} = \int_0^L Q \, [N]^T \, dx$$

$$= \begin{bmatrix} N_i^2 & N_i N_j \\ N_j N_i & N_j^2 \end{bmatrix} \begin{Bmatrix} Q_i \\ Q_j \end{Bmatrix}$$

$$= \frac{L}{6} \begin{bmatrix} 2 & 1 \\ 1 & 2 \end{bmatrix} \begin{Bmatrix} Q_i \\ Q_j \end{Bmatrix}$$

Residual contribution of Q For a triangular element, when Q is constant,

$$\{f_Q^{(e)}\} = \int_0^L Q\,[N]^T\,dx$$

$$= \frac{QA}{3}\begin{Bmatrix} 1 \\ 1 \\ 1 \end{Bmatrix}$$

For a triangular element, when Q is variable,

$$\{f_Q^{(e)}\} = \int_A Q\,[N]^T\,dA$$

$$= 2A\begin{bmatrix} N_i^2 & N_iN_j & N_iN_k \\ N_jN_i & N_j^2 & N_jN_k \\ N_kN_i & N_kN_j & N_k^2 \end{bmatrix}\begin{Bmatrix} Q_i \\ Q_j \\ Q_k \end{Bmatrix}$$

$$= \frac{A}{12}\begin{bmatrix} 2 & 1 & 1 \\ 1 & 2 & 1 \\ 1 & 1 & 2 \end{bmatrix}\begin{Bmatrix} Q_i \\ Q_j \\ Q_k \end{Bmatrix}$$

For a rectangular element, when Q is constant,

$$\{f_Q^{(e)}\} = \int_A Q\,[N]^T\,dA$$

$$= \frac{QA}{4}\begin{Bmatrix} 1 \\ 1 \\ 1 \\ 1 \end{Bmatrix}$$

For a rectangular element, when Q is variable,

$$\{f_Q^{(e)}\} = \int_A Q\,[N]^T\,dA$$

$$\int_A Q\begin{bmatrix} N_i^2 & N_iN_j & N_iN_k & N_iN_m \\ N_iN_j & N_j^2 & N_jN_k & N_jN_m \\ N_iN_k & N_jN_k & N_k^2 & N_kN_m \\ N_iN_m & N_jN_m & N_kN_m & N_m^2 \end{bmatrix}dA = \frac{A}{36}\begin{bmatrix} 4 & 2 & 1 & 2 \\ 2 & 4 & 2 & 1 \\ 1 & 2 & 4 & 2 \\ 2 & 1 & 2 & 4 \end{bmatrix}\begin{Bmatrix} Q_i \\ Q_j \\ Q_k \\ Q_m \end{Bmatrix}$$

One-dimensional Elasticity

Stress-Strain Relation

$$\frac{stress}{strain} = Young's\ Modulus\ of\ Elasticity$$

Or

$$\sigma = E\ \varepsilon$$

More generally, E is written as D and is called material property relation

Thus, $\sigma = D\ \varepsilon$

Displacement u inside this element can be written in terms of the nodal values U_i and U_j

$$u = [N]\{U^{(e)}\} = \begin{bmatrix} N_i & N_j \end{bmatrix} \begin{Bmatrix} U_i \\ U_j \end{Bmatrix}$$

Strain-Displacement relation

$$\varepsilon = \frac{du}{dx}$$

$$\varepsilon = \frac{du}{dx} = \begin{bmatrix} \dfrac{dN_i}{dx} & \dfrac{dN_j}{dx} \end{bmatrix} \begin{Bmatrix} U_i \\ U_j \end{Bmatrix} = \begin{bmatrix} -\dfrac{1}{L} & \dfrac{1}{L} \end{bmatrix} \begin{Bmatrix} U_i \\ U_j \end{Bmatrix} = \frac{U_j - U_i}{L}$$

Note that in one-dimensional elasticity, there is one displacement at each node.

Two-dimensional Elasticity.

Displacements u and v at a point in element i j k can be written in terms of the nodal values.In two-dimension elasticity, there are two displacements at each node – one in horizontal direction and the other in the vertical direction.

At node i the horizontal displacement is denoted by U_{2i-1} and the vertical displacement is denoted by U_{2i}.

In a triangular element, we may write the displacements u and v at a point inside the triangular element as,

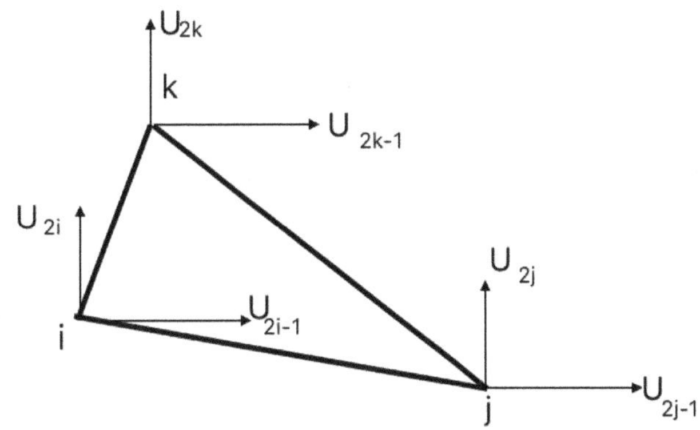

$$\begin{Bmatrix} u \\ v \end{Bmatrix} = [N]\{U^{(e)}\}$$

Or

$$u = \begin{bmatrix} N_i & N_j & N_k \end{bmatrix} \begin{Bmatrix} U_{2i-1} \\ U_{2i} \\ U_{2j-1} \\ U_{2j} \\ U_{2k-1} \\ U_{2k} \end{Bmatrix} = \begin{bmatrix} N_i & 0 & N_j & 0 & N_k & 0 \end{bmatrix} \begin{Bmatrix} U_{2i-1} \\ U_{2i} \\ U_{2j-1} \\ U_{2j} \\ U_{2k-1} \\ U_{2k} \end{Bmatrix}$$

$$v = \begin{bmatrix} N_i & N_j & N_k \end{bmatrix} \begin{Bmatrix} U_{2i-1} \\ U_{2i} \\ U_{2j-1} \\ U_{2j} \\ U_{2k-1} \\ U_{2k} \end{Bmatrix} = \begin{bmatrix} 0 & N_i & 0 & N_j & 0 & N_k \end{bmatrix} \begin{Bmatrix} U_{2i-1} \\ U_{2i} \\ U_{2j-1} \\ U_{2j} \\ U_{2k-1} \\ U_{2k} \end{Bmatrix}$$

Combining the last two equations, we get,

$$\begin{Bmatrix} u \\ v \end{Bmatrix} = \begin{bmatrix} N_i & 0 & N_j & 0 & N_k & 0 \\ 0 & N_i & 0 & N_j & 0 & N_k \end{bmatrix} \begin{Bmatrix} U_{2i-1} \\ U_{2i} \\ U_{2j-1} \\ U_{2j} \\ U_{2k-1} \\ U_{2k} \end{Bmatrix}$$

In two dimensional elasticity, there are three strains at a point in the element. These three strains are related to the 6 displacements for a triangular element as written below:

$$\begin{Bmatrix} \varepsilon_{xx} \\ \varepsilon_{yy} \\ \varepsilon_{xy} \end{Bmatrix} = \frac{1}{2A} \begin{bmatrix} b_i & 0 & b_j & 0 & b_k & 0 \\ 0 & c_i & 0 & c_j & 0 & c_k \\ c_i & b_i & c_j & b_j & c_k & b_k \end{bmatrix} \begin{Bmatrix} U_{2i-1} \\ U_{2i} \\ U_{2j-1} \\ U_{2j} \\ U_{2k-1} \\ U_{2k} \end{Bmatrix} = [B] \begin{Bmatrix} U_{2i-1} \\ U_{2i} \\ U_{2j-1} \\ U_{2j} \\ U_{2k-1} \\ U_{2k} \end{Bmatrix}$$

$$[B] = \frac{1}{2A} \begin{bmatrix} b_i & 0 & b_j & 0 & b_k & 0 \\ 0 & c_i & 0 & c_j & 0 & c_k \\ c_i & b_i & c_j & b_j & c_k & b_k \end{bmatrix}$$ *is called the gradient matrix or the strain displacement relation.*

A being the area of the the triangular element and can be found using the relation.

$$2A = det \begin{bmatrix} 1 & X_i & Y_i \\ 1 & X_j & Y_j \\ 1 & X_k & Y_k \end{bmatrix}$$

$$b_i = Y_j - Y_k,$$
$$c_i = X_k - X_j$$
$$b_j = Y_k - Y_i,$$
$$c_j = X_i - X_k$$
$$b_k = Y_i - Y_j, \quad c_k = X_j - X_i$$

Material Property relationships

Plane Stress case

Plain stress and Plain Strain Problems

A plane strain problem is one in which strains at any point on it occur in x and y directions but none in the z direction. This means that $\tau_{xz} = 0$, $\tau_{yz} = 0$. However, σ_x, σ_y, σ_z and τ_{xy}

Plane strain occurs in the x, y plane (or a thin sheet). Shear strains, ε_x, ε_y, ε_z *and shear strain* γ_{xy} *may not be zero*.

a. For the problems, where the stress can be described as plane stress type, **the Stress-Strain Relation is,**

$$[D] = \frac{E}{1 - \mu^2} \begin{bmatrix} 1 & \mu & 0 \\ \mu & 1 & 0 \\ 0 & 0 & \dfrac{1 - \mu}{2} \end{bmatrix}$$

b. For the problems, where the strain can be described as plane strain type, **the Stress-Strain Relation is,**

$$[D] = \frac{E}{1 + \mu} \begin{bmatrix} \dfrac{1 - \mu}{1 - 2\mu} & \dfrac{\mu}{1 - 2\mu} & 0 \\ \dfrac{\mu}{1 - 2\mu} & \dfrac{1 - \mu}{1 - 2\mu} & 0 \\ 0 & 0 & \dfrac{1}{2} \end{bmatrix}$$

Modification of a Set of Algebraic Equations

Suppose in set of equations, one variable, say u_1 is known

All the coefficients in row 1 are set to equal to zero except the diagonal term which is left unaltered. The diagonal term is multiplied by u_1 and this product is used to replace the first term in the right-most column.

The remaining terms in column 1 are each multiplied by the given value u_1 and subtracted from the corresponding term in the right-most column. As an example, suppose we need to solve the global equation given below:

$$10^5 \times \begin{bmatrix} 4 & -4 & 0 & 0 \\ -4 & 4+4 & -4 & 0 \\ 0 & -4 & 4+1.33 & -1.33 \\ 0 & 0 & -1.33 & 1.33 \end{bmatrix} \begin{Bmatrix} u_1 \\ u_2 \\ u_3 \\ u_4 \end{Bmatrix} = \begin{Bmatrix} P_1 \\ P_2 \\ P_3 \\ P_4 \end{Bmatrix}$$

It is given that $u_1 = 0$. *Then, after the first step,*

$$10^5 \times \begin{bmatrix} 4 & 0 & 0 & 0 \\ -4 & 4+4 & -4 & 0 \\ 0 & -4 & 4+1.33 & -1.33 \\ 0 & 0 & -1.33 & 1.33 \end{bmatrix} \begin{Bmatrix} 0 \\ u_2 \\ u_3 \\ u_4 \end{Bmatrix} = \begin{Bmatrix} (4)(0) \\ P_2 \\ P_3 \\ P_4 \end{Bmatrix}$$

After the second step,

$$10^5 \times \begin{bmatrix} 4 & 0 & 0 & 0 \\ 0 & 8 & -4 & 0 \\ 0 & -4 & 5.33 & -1.33 \\ 0 & 0 & -1.33 & 1.33 \end{bmatrix} \begin{Bmatrix} 0 \\ u_2 \\ u_3 \\ u_4 \end{Bmatrix} = \begin{Bmatrix} 0 \\ P_2 + (4)(0) \quad transfer \\ P_3 - (0)(0) \quad transfer \\ P_4 - (0)(0) \quad transfer \end{Bmatrix}$$

CHAPTER 6

SOLVING STRUCTURAL PROBLEMS

Bars, Springs, Trusses, Shafts and Beams

Applied nodal forces acting on a structural element let us determine the displacements $\{u\}$ in that element using the resistance of the element represented by its element matrix, $[k^{(e)}]$ *and its force vector represented by* $\{f^{(e)}\}$. If there are more elements than just one, then we need to assemble these element matrices and force vectors into a global matrix equation $[K]\{U\} = \{P\}$ and solve this matrix equation to determine $\{U\}$.

Analysis of a Single Bar

Example 6.1 Consider a straight bar as shown below. The following data concerns this bar.

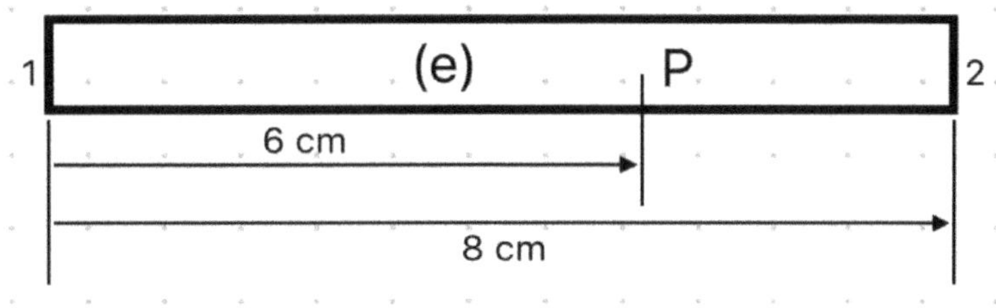

Fig. 6.1

Area of cross-section, A = 7.5 cm^2.

Young's modulus, E = $20 \times 10^9\,N/cm^2$

$u_1 = 0.05\,cm$, $u_2 = 0.0875\,cm$.

Write down the shape functions and their values at point P.

1. Find the displacement at point P
2. Write down the symbols for the strain and stress
3. Calculate the strain at point P
4. Calculate the stress at point P
5. Write down the element stiffness matrix for this element
6. Find the value of the strain energy of the element.

Solution: The purpose of this problem is to know and use the basic relationships of displacement, strain, stress, element stiffness matrix and strain energy.

We first calculate the shape functions at point P.

$$N_1 = \frac{L-x}{L} = \frac{8-6}{8} = 0.25$$

$$N_2 = \frac{x}{L} = \frac{6}{8} = 0.75$$

The rest of the required calculations are now completed.

1. Displacement at point $P = u = N_1 u_1 + N_2 u_2 = 0.25 \times 0.05 + 0.75 \times 0.0875 = 0.078125\ cm$
2. The symbol for strain is, ε *and that for stress is* σ.

3. $\varepsilon = \begin{bmatrix} \dfrac{dN_1}{dx} & \dfrac{dN_2}{dx} \end{bmatrix} \begin{Bmatrix} u_1 \\ u_2 \end{Bmatrix} = \dfrac{1}{L}(-u_1 + u_2) = \dfrac{1}{8}(-0.05 + 0.0875) = 0.004688\ cm$

4. Stress = Young's modulus of elasticity x strain

   Or $\sigma = E\varepsilon = (20 \times 10^9)(0.004688) = 0.09375 \times 10^9\ N/cm^2$

5. Element stiffness matrix, $[k^{(e)}] = \dfrac{A E}{L}\begin{bmatrix} 1 & -1 \\ -1 & 1 \end{bmatrix} = \dfrac{7.5 \times 20 \times 10^9}{8} = 18.75\begin{bmatrix} 1 & -1 \\ -1 & 1 \end{bmatrix}$

6. *Strain energy of the element* $= \dfrac{1}{2}\{u\}^T[k^{(e)}]\{u\}$

$$= \dfrac{1}{2}\{0.05 \quad 0.0875\} \times 18.75 \times 10^9 \begin{bmatrix} 1 & -1 \\ -1 & 1 \end{bmatrix} \begin{Bmatrix} 0.05 \\ 0.0875 \end{Bmatrix} =$$

$$10^9\begin{bmatrix} 0.46875 & 0.82031 \end{bmatrix}\begin{bmatrix} 1 & -1 \\ -1 & 1 \end{bmatrix}\begin{Bmatrix} 0.5 \\ 0.875 \end{Bmatrix} = 10^9\begin{bmatrix} -0.35156 & 0.35156 \end{bmatrix}\begin{Bmatrix} 0.5 \\ 0.875 \end{Bmatrix}$$

$$= = 0.132 \times 10^9\ N\,cm/cm^3$$

Example 6.2 Three elements with nodes 1, 2, 3 and 4 are shown in Fig. A load of 10000 N is applied at node 2. Nodes 1 and 4 are fixed. We will now find internal resistances R1, R2, R3 and R4 after first finding displacements at nodes 2 and 3.

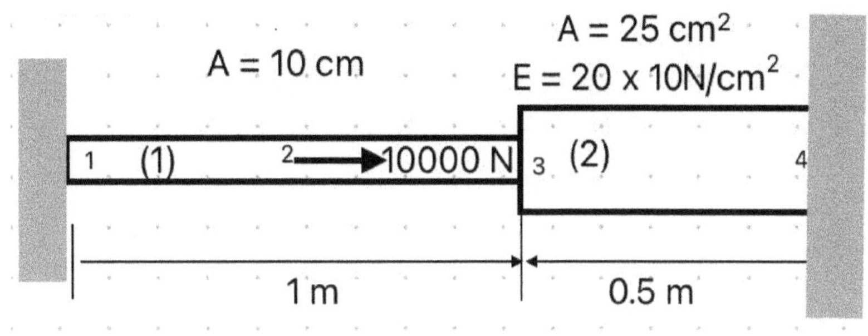

Fig. 6.2

$$\left[k^{(1)}\right] = \frac{A\,E}{L}\begin{bmatrix} 1 & -1 \\ -1 & 1 \end{bmatrix} = \frac{10\times 20\times 10^6}{100}\begin{bmatrix} 1 & -1 \\ -1 & 1 \end{bmatrix} = 2\times 10^6\begin{bmatrix} 1 & -1 \\ -1 & 1 \end{bmatrix}$$

$$= 10^6\begin{bmatrix} 2 & -2 \\ -2 & 2 \end{bmatrix}$$

$$\left[k^{(2)}\right] = \frac{A\,E}{L}\begin{bmatrix} 1 & -1 \\ -1 & 1 \end{bmatrix} = \frac{10\times 20\times 10^6}{100}\begin{bmatrix} 1 & -1 \\ -1 & 1 \end{bmatrix} = 2\times 10^6\begin{bmatrix} 1 & -1 \\ -1 & 1 \end{bmatrix}$$

$$= 10^6\begin{bmatrix} 2 & -2 \\ -2 & 2 \end{bmatrix}$$

$$\left[k^{(3)}\right] = \frac{A\,E}{L}\begin{bmatrix} 1 & -1 \\ -1 & 1 \end{bmatrix} = \frac{25\times 20\times 10^6}{50}\begin{bmatrix} 1 & -1 \\ -1 & 1 \end{bmatrix} = 10\times 10^6\begin{bmatrix} 1 & -1 \\ -1 & 1 \end{bmatrix}$$

$$= 10^6\begin{bmatrix} 10 & -10 \\ -10 & 10 \end{bmatrix}$$

$$\{f^{(1)}\} = \begin{Bmatrix} 0 \\ 0 \end{Bmatrix},\ \{f^{(2)}\} = \begin{Bmatrix} 10000 \\ 0 \end{Bmatrix}.\ \{f^{(3)}\} = \begin{Bmatrix} 0 \\ 0 \end{Bmatrix}$$

Using the direct stiffness procedure, we now assemble the element Matrix and the global force vector.

$$[K] = 10^6\begin{bmatrix} 2 & -2 & 0 & 0 \\ -2 & 2+2 & -2 & 0 \\ 0 & -2 & 2+10 & -10 \\ 0 & 0 & -10 & 10 \end{bmatrix} = 10^6\begin{bmatrix} 2 & -2 & 0 & 0 \\ -2 & 4 & -2 & 0 \\ 0 & -2 & 12 & -10 \\ 0 & 0 & -10 & 0 \end{bmatrix}$$

$$\{F\} = \begin{Bmatrix} 0 \\ 0 \end{Bmatrix}\begin{matrix}1\\2\end{matrix} + \begin{Bmatrix} 10000 \\ 0 \end{Bmatrix}\begin{matrix}2\\3\end{matrix} + \begin{Bmatrix} 0 \\ 0 \end{Bmatrix}\begin{matrix}3\\4\end{matrix} = \begin{Bmatrix} 0 \\ 0+10000 \\ 0+0 \\ 0 \end{Bmatrix} = \begin{Bmatrix} 0 \\ 10000 \\ 0 \\ 0 \end{Bmatrix}$$

The global equation $[K]\,\{U\} = \{P\}$ becomes,

$$10^6 \begin{array}{cccc} 1 & 2 & 3 & 4 \end{array}$$

$$10^6 \begin{bmatrix} 2 & -2 & 0 & 0 \\ -2 & 4 & -2 & 0 \\ 0 & -2 & 12 & -10 \\ 0 & 0 & -10 & 0 \end{bmatrix} \begin{Bmatrix} U_1 \\ U_2 \\ U_3 \\ U_4 \end{Bmatrix} = \begin{Bmatrix} 0 \\ 10000 \\ 0 \\ 0 \end{Bmatrix} \begin{array}{c} 1 \\ 2 \\ 3 \\ 4 \end{array}$$

Since it is known that $U_1 = U_4 = 0$, we get,

$$10^6 \begin{bmatrix} 2 & -2 & 0 & 0 \\ -2 & 4 & -2 & 0 \\ 0 & -2 & 12 & -10 \\ 0 & 0 & -10 & 0 \end{bmatrix} \begin{Bmatrix} 0 \\ U_2 \\ U_3 \\ 0 \end{Bmatrix} = \begin{Bmatrix} 0 \\ 10000 \\ 0 \\ 0 \end{Bmatrix}$$

Now we may eliminate row 1, column 1, row 4 and column 4, we get,

$$10^6 \begin{bmatrix} 4 & -2 \\ -2 & 12 \end{bmatrix} \begin{Bmatrix} U_2 \\ U_3 \end{Bmatrix} = \begin{Bmatrix} 10000 \\ 0 \end{Bmatrix}$$

Or

$$4U_2 - 2U_3 = \frac{10000}{10^6}$$

$$-2U_2 + 12U_3 = 0$$

Solution of the above two equations is,

$$U_2 = 0.003\ cm$$

$$U_3 = 0.0005\ cm$$

Internal forces (or resistance forces)

To find internal forces, we can use the displacements. The internal forces at nodes 1, 2, 3 and 4 are named as R_1, R_2, R_3 and R_4 respectively.

Substituting displacements in the global equation, we get,

$$10^6 \begin{bmatrix} 2 & -2 & 0 & 0 \\ -2 & 4 & -2 & 0 \\ 0 & -2 & 12 & -10 \\ 0 & 0 & -10 & 0 \end{bmatrix} \begin{Bmatrix} 0 \\ 0.003 \\ 0.0005 \\ 0 \end{Bmatrix} = \begin{Bmatrix} R_1 \\ R_2 \\ R_3 \\ R_4 \end{Bmatrix} = \begin{Bmatrix} R_i^{(1)} = internal\ force\ in\ element\ (1)\ at\ its\ node\ i \\ R_j^{(1)} = internal\ force\ in\ element\ (1)\ at\ its\ node\ j \\ R_i^{(2)} = internal\ force\ in\ element\ (2)\ at\ its\ node\ i \\ R_j^{(2)} = internal\ force\ in\ element\ (2)\ at\ its\ node\ j \end{Bmatrix}$$

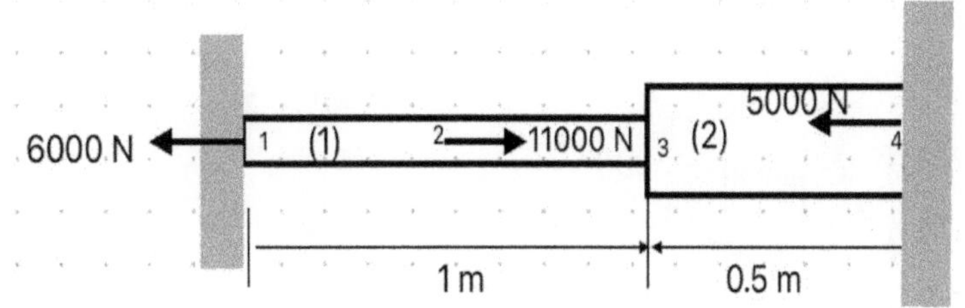

Fig. 6.3: Internal forces in a bar

$(-0.006) \times 10^6 = R_1 = -6000\ N$

$(0.012 - 0.001) \times 10^6 = R_2 = 11000\ N$

$(-0.006 + 0.006) \times 10^6 = R_3 = 0$

$-005 \times 10^6 = R_4 = -5000\ N$

If the there is change in temperature between that for which it was designed and that at which it is used, we need to take into account an additional applied force, $\{f^{(e)}\} = \begin{Bmatrix} -A\,E\,\alpha\,\delta T \\ A\,E\,\alpha\,\delta T \end{Bmatrix}$.

Thus, the global force equation will become, $[K]\{U\} = \{P\} + \{F.\}$

Example 6.2 In the analysis of a bar, $\{P\} = \begin{Bmatrix} 0 \\ 10000 \\ -20000 \\ 0 \end{Bmatrix}$, $\{F\} = \begin{Bmatrix} -33000 \\ -33000 + 330000 \\ -33000 - 52800 \\ 52800 \end{Bmatrix} = \begin{Bmatrix} -33000 \\ 0 \\ -19800 \\ 52800 \end{Bmatrix}$

$$[K] = 4 \times 10^6 \begin{bmatrix} 1 & -1 & 0 & 0 \\ -1 & 1 & 0 & 0 \\ 0 & 0 & 0 & 0 \\ 0 & 0 & 0 & 0 \end{bmatrix} + 4 \times 10^6 \begin{bmatrix} 0 & 0 & 0 & 0 \\ 0 & 1 & -1 & 0 \\ 0 & -1 & 1 & 0 \\ 0 & 0 & 0 & 0 \end{bmatrix} + 4 \times 10^6 \begin{bmatrix} 0 & 0 & 0 & 0 \\ 0 & 0 & 0 & 0 \\ 0 & 0 & 2 & -2 \\ 0 & 0 & -2 & 2 \end{bmatrix}$$

$$[K] = 4 \times 10^6 \begin{bmatrix} 1 & -1 & 0 & 0 \\ -1 & 2 & -1 & 0 \\ 0 & -1 & 3 & -2 \\ 0 & 0 & -2 & 2 \end{bmatrix}$$

Substituting in the global equation, $[K]\{U\} = \{P\} + \{F\}$, we get,

$$4 \times 10^6 \begin{bmatrix} 1 & -1 & 0 & 0 \\ -1 & 2 & -1 & 0 \\ 0 & -1 & 3 & -2 \\ 0 & 0 & -2 & 2 \end{bmatrix} \begin{Bmatrix} U_1 \\ U_2 \\ U_3 \\ U_4 \end{Bmatrix} = \begin{Bmatrix} 0 \\ 10000 \\ -20000 \\ 0 \end{Bmatrix} + \begin{Bmatrix} -33000 \\ 0 \\ -19800 \\ 52800 \end{Bmatrix} = \begin{Bmatrix} -33000 \\ 10000 \\ -39800 \\ 52800 \end{Bmatrix}$$

Using the conditions that $U_1 = U_4 = 0$, we get,

$u_1 = 0$ and $u_4 = 0$, we get,

$$4 \times 10^6 \begin{bmatrix} 1 & -1 & 0 & 0 \\ -1 & 2 & -1 & 0 \\ 0 & -1 & 3 & -2 \\ 0 & 0 & -2 & 2 \end{bmatrix} \begin{Bmatrix} 0 \\ U_2 \\ U_3 \\ 0 \end{Bmatrix} = \begin{Bmatrix} -33000 \\ 10000 \\ -39800 \\ 52800 \end{Bmatrix}$$

Eliminating, row 1, column 1 and row 4, column 4, we get,

$$2U_2 - U_3 = \frac{10000}{4 \times 10^6} = 0.0025$$

$$-U_2 + 3U_3 = \frac{-39800}{4 \times 10^6} = -0.00995$$

The solution of these two algebraic equations is,

$$U_3 = -0.00348 \ cm \text{ and } U_2 = -0.00049$$

Analysis of a Single Spring

Let us consider a spring in tension T. It means that a force of magnitude T is pulling node 2 of the spring in the positive x-direction and a force of magnitude T is pulling at node 1 of the spring in the negative x-direction.

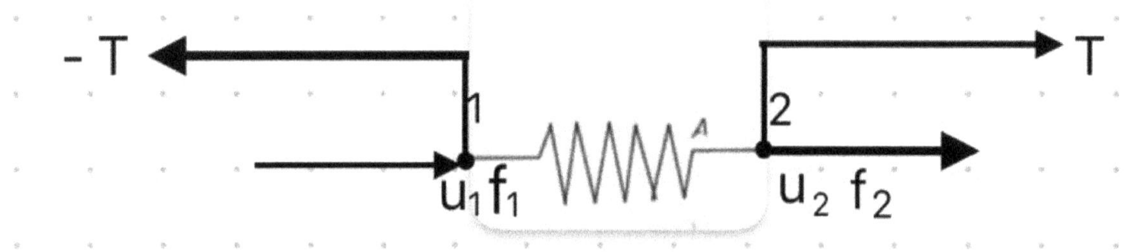

Fig. 6.4

We may replace internal force T in the spring, by two forces at the two spring ends:

one force at node 1 denoted by $f_1^{(e)}$ .and the other force at node 2 denoted by $f_2^{(e)}$.

Forces $f_1^{(e)}$ and $f_2^{(e)}$ are assumed to be positive in the positive x direction.

Displacement of the spring at node 1 is denoted by u_1.

Displacement of the spring at node 2 is denoted by u_2.

Displacements u_1 and u_2 are assumed to be positive in the positive x direction.

$T = k\delta$, where k is siffness of the spring and δ is the deflection of the spring.

Force at node 1, $f_1^{(e)} = k\left(u_1 - u_2\right)$.

Force at node 2, $f_2^{(e)} = k\left(u_2 - u_1\right)$.

We notice that the above two forces are equal in magnitude but opposite in direction.

We may write the two equations as one matrix equation: l

$$\left\{ \begin{array}{c} f_1^{(e)} \\ f_2^{(e)} \end{array} \right\} = k \left[\begin{array}{cc} 1 & -1 \\ -1 & 1 \end{array} \right] \left\{ \begin{array}{c} u_1 \\ u_2 \end{array} \right\}$$

Example 6.4 Three springs are connected in series as shown in the figure below. The ends of this assemblage are both fixed. The springs have stiffness of 20 N/mm, 30 N/mm, and 40 N/mm respectively. A force P of 50 N is applied at node 4. Find the displacements of nodes 3 and 4 and reactions at nodes 1 and 2.

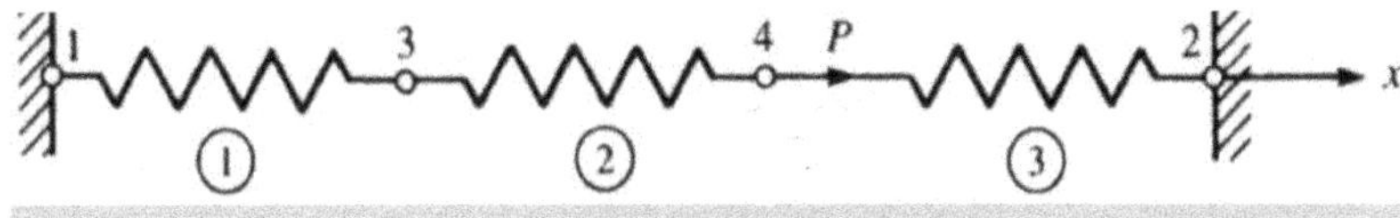

Fig. 6.5

Solution: The element stiffnesses are,

$$[k^{(1)}] = \begin{array}{cc} & \begin{array}{cc} 1 & 3: \end{array} \\ \begin{array}{c} 1 \\ 3, \end{array} & \left[\begin{array}{cc} 20 & -20 \\ -20 & 20 \end{array} \right] \end{array} \quad [k^{(2)}] = \begin{array}{cc} & \begin{array}{cc} 3 & 4 \end{array} \\ \begin{array}{c} 3 \\ 4, \end{array} & \left[\begin{array}{cc} 30 & -30 \\ -30 & 30 \end{array} \right] \end{array} \quad [k^{(3)}] = \begin{array}{cc} & \begin{array}{cc} 4 & 3 \end{array} \\ \begin{array}{c} 4 \\ 2 \end{array} & \left[\begin{array}{cc} 40 & -40 \\ -40 & 40 \end{array} \right] \end{array}$$

$f_3 = 0 \; and \; f_4 = 50$

$$\begin{array}{cccc} 1 & 2 & 3 & 4 \end{array}$$
$$\left[\begin{array}{cccc} 20 & 0 & -20 & 0 \\ 0 & 40 & 0 & -40 \\ -20 & 0 & 20+30 & -30 \\ 0 & -40 & -30 & 70 \end{array} \right] \left\{ \begin{array}{c} u_1 \\ u_2 \\ u_3 \\ u_4 \end{array} \right\} = \left\{ \begin{array}{c} f_1 \\ f_2 \\ f_3 \\ f4 \end{array} \right\}$$

$$\begin{array}{cccc} 1 & 2 & 3 & 4 \end{array}$$
$$\left[\begin{array}{cccc} 20 & 0 & -20 & 0 \\ 0 & 40 & 0 & -40 \\ -20 & 0 & 50 & -30 \\ 0 & -40 & -30 & 70 \end{array} \right] \left\{ \begin{array}{c} u_1 \\ u_2 \\ u_3 \\ u_4 \end{array} \right\} = \left\{ \begin{array}{c} f_1 \\ f_2 \\ f_3 \\ f_4 \end{array} \right\}$$

Substituting the known values of u and f, we get

$$\begin{array}{cccc} 1 & 2 & 3 & 4 \end{array}$$
$$\left[\begin{array}{cccc} 20 & 0 & -20 & 0 \\ 0 & 40 & 0 & -40 \\ -20 & 0 & 50 & -30 \\ 0 & -40 & -30 & 70 \end{array} \right] \left\{ \begin{array}{c} 0 \\ 0 \\ u_3 \\ u_4 \end{array} \right\} = \left\{ \begin{array}{c} f_1 \\ f_2 \\ 0 \\ 50 \end{array} \right\}$$

Since we are given that $u_1 = 0$, we remove the first row and first column

after shifting $k_{21} u_1 = 0$ to the right hand last column at second row.

Thus,
$$\begin{array}{ccc} 2 & 3 & 4 \end{array}$$
$$\begin{bmatrix} 40 & 0 & -40 \\ 0 & 50 & -30 \\ -40 & -30 & 70 \end{bmatrix} \begin{Bmatrix} 0 \\ u_2 \\ u_3 \end{Bmatrix} = \begin{Bmatrix} f_2 \\ 0 \\ 50 \end{Bmatrix}$$

Since we are given that $u_2 = 0$, we remove the second row and the second column after shifting $k_{32} u_2 = 0$ to the right-hand last column at the third row.

$$\begin{array}{cc} 3 & 4 \end{array}$$
$$\begin{bmatrix} 50 & -30 \\ -30 & 70 \end{bmatrix} \begin{Bmatrix} u_3 \\ u_4 \end{Bmatrix} = \begin{Bmatrix} 0 \\ 50 \end{Bmatrix} \begin{array}{c} 3 \\ 4 \end{array}$$

Thus, we are left with two algebraic equations,
$$50\, u_3 - 30\, u_4 = 0$$

$$-30\, u_3 + 70\, u_4 = 50$$

Solution of the above set of two equations gives,
$$u_3 = \frac{15}{26}\ mm \text{ and } u_4 = \frac{25}{26}\ mm$$

Let us go back to the first equation and the second equation.
$$20\, u_1 - 20\, u_3 = f_1$$

$$or\ -(40)\left(\frac{25}{26}\right) = f_2$$

$$or\ f_2 = -38.46\ N$$

Note that the reaction forces f_1 and f_3 = 11.54 N + 38.46 N = 50 N both act in the

negative x direction and balance the applied force P_4 = 50 N which is in the

positive x direction.

Example 6.5 Consider a spring system as shown below:
$$k_1 = \frac{30\ N}{mm},\ k_2 = \frac{50\ N}{mm} \text{ and } k_3 = \frac{70\ N}{mm},\ P_2 = -120\ N$$

Find the displacement of node 2 and Reactions at nodes 1 and 3.

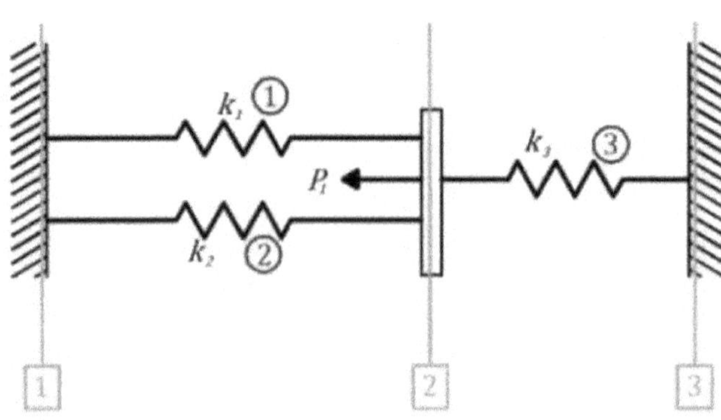

Fig. 6.6

Solution: Here, we see that

$$\left[k^{(1)}\right] = \begin{matrix} & 1 & 2 \\ & \begin{bmatrix} 30 & -30 \\ -30 & 30 \end{bmatrix} & \begin{matrix} 1 \\ 2 \end{matrix} \end{matrix}$$

$$\left[k^{(2)}\right] = \begin{matrix} & 1 & 2 \\ & \begin{bmatrix} 50 & -50 \\ -50 & 50 \end{bmatrix} & \begin{matrix} 1 \\ 2 \end{matrix} \end{matrix}$$

$$\left[k^{(3)}\right] = \begin{matrix} & 2 & 3 \\ & \begin{bmatrix} 80 & -80 \\ -80 & 80 \end{bmatrix} & \begin{matrix} 2 \\ 3 \end{matrix} \end{matrix}$$

$f_2 = -120 \ N, \ u_1 = 0, \ and \ u_3 = 0.$

Global stiffness matrix

First add stiffnesses of elements (1) and (2). Then add the element stiffness of element (3)

$$\begin{matrix} & 1 & 2 & 3 \\ & \begin{bmatrix} 30+50 & -30-50 & 0 \\ -30-50 & 30+50+70 & -70 \\ 0 & -70 & 70 \end{bmatrix} & & \begin{matrix} 1 \\ 2 \\ 3 \end{matrix} \end{matrix}$$

$$[K] = \begin{matrix} & 1 & 2 & 3 \\ & \begin{bmatrix} 80 & -80 & 0 \\ -80 & 150 & -70 \\ 0 & -70 & 70 \end{bmatrix} & & \begin{matrix} 1 \\ 2 \\ 3 \end{matrix} \end{matrix}$$

<u>Now write down the matrix equation and solve it.</u>

$[K]\{U\} = \{F\} \ gives$

$$\begin{bmatrix} 80 & -80 & 0 \\ -80 & 150 & -70 \\ 0 & -70 & 70 \end{bmatrix} \begin{Bmatrix} 0 \\ u_2 \\ 0 \end{Bmatrix} = \begin{Bmatrix} f_1 \\ -120 \\ f_3 \end{Bmatrix}$$

Since $u_1 = 0$ *and* $u_3 = 0$, *we eliminate rows and columns* 1 *and* 3 *and shift* -70×0 *and* -80×0

on the right hand column.

$150 \ u_2 = -120 + 0 + 0$

Thus,

$$150\, u_2 = -120 \ or \ u_2 = \frac{-120}{150} = -0.8 \ mm$$

Substituting u_2 in the first row, we get,

$$f_1 = -80\, u_2 = -80 \times (-0.8) = 64 \ N$$

Substituting u_2 in the third row we get,

$$f_3 = u_2 = -70 \times (-0.8) = 56 \ N$$

Note that the reaction forces f_1 and f_3 = 64 N + 56 N = 120 N both act in the positive x direction and balance the applied force f_2 = −120 N which is in the negative x direction.

Bar Elements

A loaded step.

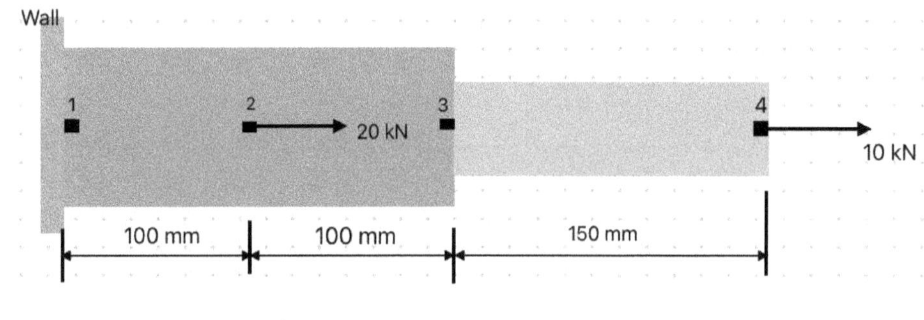

Fig. 6.7

$A_1 = 200 \ mm^2; A_2 = 200 \ mm^2; A_3 = 100 \ mm^2.$

Young's modulus, $E = \dfrac{200000 \ N}{mm^2}$, $P_2 = 20 \ kN$, $P_4 = 10 \ kN$.

$\Delta T = 0.$

$$[k^{(e)}] = \frac{AE}{L}\begin{bmatrix} 1 & -1 \\ -1 & 1 \end{bmatrix}$$

$$[k^{(1)}] = \frac{(200)(200000)}{100}\begin{bmatrix} 1 & -1 \\ -1 & 1 \end{bmatrix} = 4\times 10^5 \begin{matrix} & 1 & 2 \\ & \begin{bmatrix} 1 & -1 \\ -1 & 1 \end{bmatrix} & \begin{matrix} 1 \\ 2 \end{matrix} \end{matrix}$$

$$[k^{(2)}] = \frac{(200)(200000)}{100}\begin{bmatrix} 1 & -1 \\ -1 & 1 \end{bmatrix} = 4\times 10^5 \begin{matrix} & 2 & 3 \\ & \begin{bmatrix} 1 & -1 \\ -1 & 1 \end{bmatrix} & \begin{matrix} 2 \\ 3 \end{matrix} \end{matrix}$$

$$[k^{(3)}] = \frac{(100)(200000)}{150}\begin{bmatrix} 1 & -1 \\ -1 & 1 \end{bmatrix} = 1.33\times 10^5 \begin{matrix} & 3 & 4 \\ & \begin{bmatrix} 1 & -1 \\ -1 & 1 \end{bmatrix} & \begin{matrix} 3 \\ 4 \end{matrix} \end{matrix}$$

$$[K] = 10^5 \times \begin{matrix} & 1 & 2 & 3 & 4 \\ \begin{bmatrix} 4 & -4 & 0 & 0 \\ -4 & 4+4 & -4 & 0 \\ 0 & -4 & 4+1.33 & -1.33 \\ 0 & 0 & -1.33 & 1.33 \end{bmatrix} & \begin{matrix} 1 \\ 2 \\ 3 \\ 4 \end{matrix} \end{matrix}$$

$$[K]\{U\}=\{P\} \text{ gives } 10^5 \times \begin{bmatrix} 4 & -4 & 0 & 0 \\ -4 & 4+4 & -4 & 0 \\ 0 & -4 & 4+1.33 & -1.33 \\ 0 & 0 & -1.33 & 1.33 \end{bmatrix} \begin{Bmatrix} u_1 \\ u_2 \\ u_3 \\ u_4 \end{Bmatrix} = \begin{Bmatrix} P_1 \\ P_2 \\ P_3 \\ P_4 \end{Bmatrix}$$

$$[K]\{U\}=\{P\} \text{ gives } 10^5 \begin{bmatrix} 4 & -4 & 0 & 0 \\ -4 & 8 & -4 & 0 \\ 0 & -4 & 5.33 & -1.33 \\ 0 & 0 & -1.33 & 1.33 \end{bmatrix} \begin{Bmatrix} 0 \\ u_2 \\ u_3 \\ u_4 \end{Bmatrix} = \begin{Bmatrix} P_1 \\ 20000 \\ 0 \\ 10000 \end{Bmatrix}$$

$$[K]\{U\}=\{P\} \text{ gives } \begin{bmatrix} 4 & -4 & 0 & 0 \\ -4 & 8 & -4 & 0 \\ 0 & -4 & 5.33 & -1.33 \\ 0 & 0 & -1.33 & 1.33 \end{bmatrix} \begin{Bmatrix} 0 \\ u_2 \\ u_3 \\ u_4 \end{Bmatrix} = \begin{Bmatrix} P_1/10^5 \\ 0.2 \\ 0 \\ 0.1 \end{Bmatrix}$$

Since u_1 is given, we delete the first row and the first column and modify the last column.

Three equations that remain are,

$$10^5 \begin{bmatrix} 8 & -4 & 0 \\ -4 & 5.33 & -1.33 \\ 0 & -1.33 & 1.33 \end{bmatrix} \begin{Bmatrix} u_2 \\ u_3 \\ u_4 \end{Bmatrix} = \begin{Bmatrix} 0.2 \\ 0 \\ 0.1 \end{Bmatrix}$$

or

$$8u_2 - 4u_3 = 0.2$$

$$-4u_2 + 5.33u_3 - 1.33u_4 = 0$$

$$-1.33u_3 + 1.33u_4 = 0.1$$

The solution is,

$$u_2 = 0.075 \, mm, \, u_3 = 0.1 \, mm, \, u_4 = 0.175 \, mm$$

From the first equation we see that,

$$-4 \times u_2 = P_1/10^5$$

or

$$P_1 = -4 \times 10^5 \times 0.075 = -30000 \, N$$

Note that the reaction force f_1 acts in the negative x direction

and balances the applied force $f_2 + f_4 = 20 + 10 = 30 \, kN$ which

act in the positive x direction.

Example 6.6 Consider a stepped bar as shown below. The bar is fixed to the walls at its ends. Loads of 5 kN and and 10 kN are applied at nodes 2 and 3. Take $E = 20 \times \dfrac{10^6\ N}{cm^2}$ and $\alpha = 11 \times \dfrac{10^{-6}}{{}^{\circ}C}$. $A_1 = 24\ cm^2$, $A_2 = 15\ cm^2$. Take *Take* $\Delta T = 12\ {}^{\circ}C$.

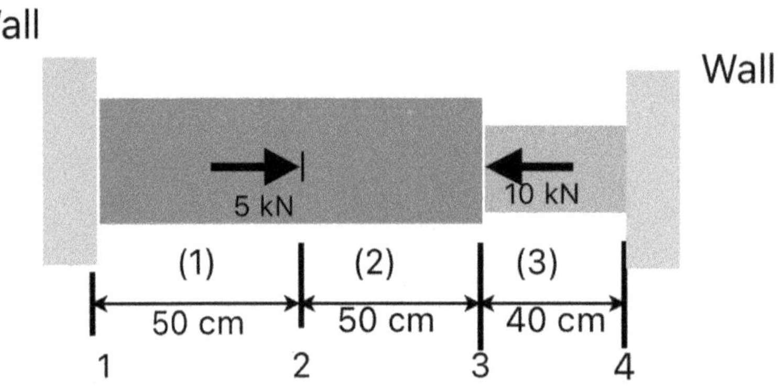

Fig. 6.9

Solution:

$$[k^{(e)}] = \frac{A\,E}{L}\begin{bmatrix} 1 & -1 \\ -1 & 1 \end{bmatrix}$$

$$[k^{(1)}] = \frac{(24)\,(20)\times 10^6}{50}\begin{bmatrix} 1 & -1 \\ -1 & 1 \end{bmatrix} = 10^6 \begin{bmatrix} 9.6 & -9.6 \\ -9.6 & 9.6 \end{bmatrix}\begin{matrix} 1 \\ 2 \end{matrix}$$

$$[k^{(2)}] = \frac{(24)\,(20)\times 10^6}{50}\begin{bmatrix} 1 & -1 \\ -1 & 1 \end{bmatrix} = 10^6 \begin{bmatrix} 9.6 & -9.6 \\ -9.6 & 9.6 \end{bmatrix}\begin{matrix} 2 \\ 3 \end{matrix}$$

$$[k^{(3)}] = \frac{(15)\,(20)\times 10^6}{50}\begin{bmatrix} 1 & -1 \\ -1 & 1 \end{bmatrix} = 10^6 \begin{bmatrix} 6 & -6 \\ -6 & 6 \end{bmatrix}\begin{matrix} 3 \\ 4 \end{matrix}$$

$$[K] = 10^6 \begin{bmatrix} 9.6 & -9.6 & & \\ -9.6 & 9.6+9.6 & -9.6 & \\ & -9.6 & 9.6+6 & -6 \\ & & -6 & 6 \end{bmatrix} \quad \text{or}\quad [K] = 10^6 \begin{bmatrix} 9.6 & -9.6 & 0 & 0 \\ -9.6 & 19.2 & -9.6 & 0 \\ 0 & -9.6 & 15.6 & -6 \\ 0 & 0 & -6 & 6 \end{bmatrix}$$

$$\{f^{(e)}\} = A\,E\,\alpha\,\Delta T \begin{Bmatrix} -1 \\ 1 \end{Bmatrix}$$

$$\{f^{(1)}\} = A\,E\,\alpha\,\Delta T \begin{Bmatrix} -1 \\ 1 \end{Bmatrix} = (24)\,(20\times 10^6)\,(11\times 10^{-6})\,(12)\begin{Bmatrix} -1 \\ 1 \end{Bmatrix}\begin{matrix} 1 \\ 2 \end{matrix} = \begin{Bmatrix} -63360 \\ 63360 \end{Bmatrix}$$

$$\{f^{(2)}\} = A\,E\,\alpha\,\Delta T \begin{Bmatrix} -1 \\ 1 \end{Bmatrix} = (24)\,(20\times 10^6)\,(11\times 10^{-6})\,(12)\begin{Bmatrix} -1 \\ 1 \end{Bmatrix}\begin{matrix} 1 \\ 2 \end{matrix} = \begin{Bmatrix} -63360 \\ 63360 \end{Bmatrix}$$

$$\{f^{(3)}\} = A\,E\,\alpha\,\Delta T \begin{Bmatrix} -1 \\ 1 \end{Bmatrix} = (15)(20\times 10^6)(11\times 10^{-6})(12) \begin{Bmatrix} -1 \\ 1 \end{Bmatrix} \begin{matrix} 1 \\ 2 \end{matrix} = \begin{Bmatrix} -39600 \\ 39600 \end{Bmatrix}$$

$$\{F\} = \begin{Bmatrix} -63360 \\ 63360 - 63360 \\ 63360 - 39600 \\ 39600 \end{Bmatrix} = \begin{Bmatrix} -63360 \\ 0 \\ 23760 \\ 39600 \end{Bmatrix}$$

$$\{P\} = \begin{Bmatrix} P_1 \\ P_2 \\ P_3 \\ P_4 \end{Bmatrix} = \begin{Bmatrix} P_1 \\ 5000 \\ -10000 \\ P_4 \end{Bmatrix}$$

$[K]\{U\} = \{P\} + \{F\}$ gives

$$[K] = 10^6 \begin{bmatrix} 9.6 & -9.6 & 0 & 0 \\ -9.6 & 19.2 & -9.6 & 0 \\ 0 & -9.6 & 15.6 & -6 \\ 0 & 0 & -6 & 6 \end{bmatrix} \begin{Bmatrix} u_1 \\ u_2 \\ u_3 \\ u_4 \end{Bmatrix}$$

$$10^6 \begin{bmatrix} 9.6 & -9.6 & 0 & 0 \\ -9.6 & 19.2 & -9.6 & 0 \\ 0 & -9.6 & 15.6 & -6 \\ 0 & 0 & -6 & 6 \end{bmatrix} \begin{Bmatrix} 0 \\ u_2 \\ u_3 \\ 0 \end{Bmatrix} = \begin{Bmatrix} -63360 \\ 0 \\ 23760 \\ 39600 \end{Bmatrix} = \begin{Bmatrix} P_1 - 63360 \\ 5000 \\ 13760 \\ P_4 + 39360 \end{Bmatrix}$$

Since u_1 and u_4 are given as zero each, we remove row 1 and column 1 Also, we can remove row 4 and column 4 for the same reason.

Thus,

$$10^6 \begin{bmatrix} 19.2 & -9.6 \\ -9.6 & 15.6 \end{bmatrix} \begin{Bmatrix} u_2 \\ u_3 \end{Bmatrix} = \begin{Bmatrix} 5000 \\ -10000 \end{Bmatrix} + \begin{Bmatrix} 0 \\ 23760 \end{Bmatrix}$$

The two algebraic equations can now be written as

$$19.2\,u_2 - 9.6\,u_3 = 5000 / 10^6$$

$$-9.6\,u_2 + 15.6\,u_3 = 13760 / 10^6$$

The solution of these two equations gives,

$$u_2 = 0.00101 \ cm \ and \ u_3 = 0.001506 \ cm.$$

Substituting these values in the first algebraic equation of the matrix equation, we get

$$10^6 \left[9.6\,(0) - 9.6\,u_2 + (u_3)(0) + (0)(0) \right] = P_1 - 63360$$

or

$$10^6 \left[9.6\,(0) - 9.6\,u_2 + (u_3)(0) + (0)(0) \right] = P_1 - 63360$$

or $P_1 = 63360 - 10^6(-9.6)\,(0.00101) = 53664\ N$

Writing the fourth algebraic equation from the matrix equation,

$$10^6\big[\,(0)\,u_1 + (0)\,u_2 - 6(u_3) + (0)\,(u_4)\,\big] = P_4 + 39600$$

or $P_4 = -39600 + 10^6(-6)\,(0.001505) = -48630$

$$10^6\big[\,9.6\,(0) - 9.6\,u_2 + (u_3)(0) + (0)\,(0)\,\big] = P_1 - 63360$$

Note that the sum of positive forces on the stepped bar = 53664 + 5000 = 58664 N

Note that the sum of negative forces on the stepped bar = - 48630 - 10000 = - 58630 N

$$\left\{\begin{array}{c} R_i^{(e)} \\[6pt] R_j^{(e)} \end{array}\right\} = \frac{A\,E}{L}\begin{bmatrix} 1 & -1 \\ -1 & 1 \end{bmatrix}\left\{\begin{array}{c} u_i \\[6pt] u_j \end{array}\right\} + A\,E\,\alpha\,\Delta\,T\left\{\begin{array}{c} -1 \\[6pt] 1 \end{array}\right\}$$

$R_i^{(e)}$ is the internal force in the element at its node i.

If $R_j^{(e)}$ is positive, then it is in the direction of positive displacement, u_i

Truss Element:

2i-1 2j-1 2i 2j

$$[k^{(e)}] = \frac{A\,E}{L}\begin{bmatrix} C^2 & CS & -C^2 & -CS \\ CS & S^2 & -CS & -S^2 \\ -C^2 & -CS & C^2 & CS \\ -CS & -S^2 & CS & S^2 \end{bmatrix}\begin{array}{c} 2i-1 \\ 2j-1 \\ 2i \\ 2j \end{array}$$

$$\{f^{(e)}\} = A\,E\,\alpha\,\delta T \left\{\begin{array}{c} -1\,C \\ -1\,S \\ 1\,C \\ 1\,S \end{array}\right\}\begin{array}{c} 2i-1 \\ 2j-1 \\ 2i \\ 2j \end{array}$$

$C = \cos$

$S = \sin$

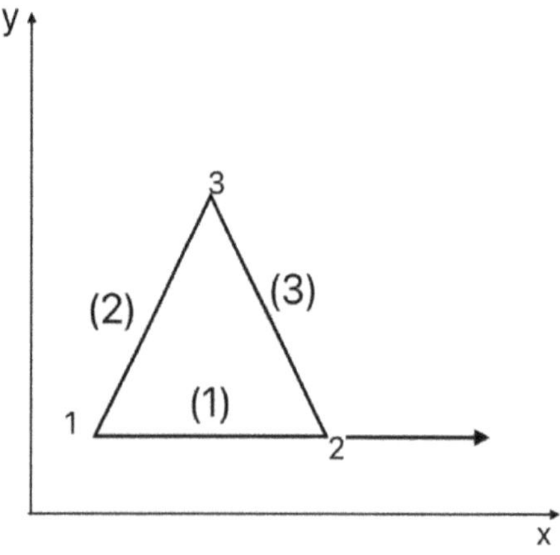

Fig. 6.10: Element and node numbering of truss triangle.

Truss Problem

TABLE II Orientation of a truss member

Connectivity and angles of members of a truss

Element number	Local node number i j	Angle between the positive x-axis and the element going from local node i to node j
1	1 2	C = cos S = sin
2	2 3	C = cos S = sin

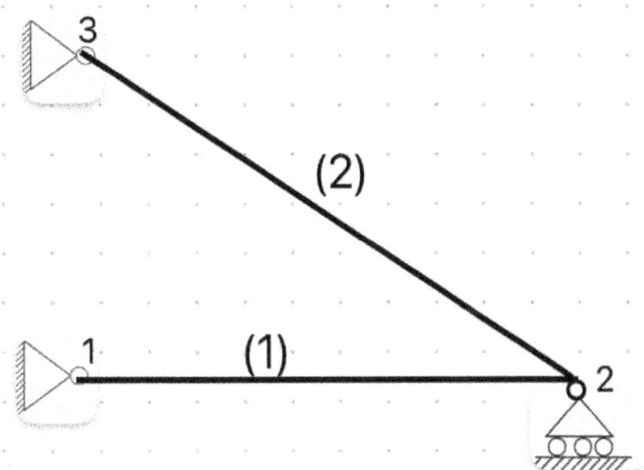

Fig. 6.11: Orientation of members of a truss as per **TABLE II**

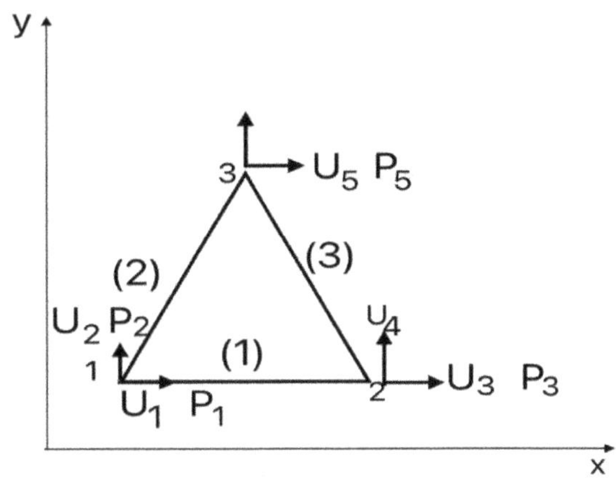

Fig. 6:12 Components of applied nodal forces and displacements

U_{2i-1} = *displacement in the horizontal direction*

U_{2i} = *displacement in the vertical direction*

P_{2i-1} = *applied force in the horizontal direction*

P_{2i} = *applied force in the vertical direction*

Example 6.7 Consider a truss which has two elements or members. Element 1 is in the horizontal direction and its length is 4 m. Element 2 makes an angle of 143.13 deg with the positive x -direction and is 5 m long. Force applied at node 2 is $P_3 = 200000\ N$

Area of cross-section of each member is 20 $cm^2.$

Young's Modulus, $E = 20\times 10^6\ N/{cm^2}.$

$$\frac{A_1 E}{L_1} = \frac{20\left(20\times 10^6\right)}{400} = 10^6$$

Th Orientation of a truss member

Connectivity and angles of members of a truss

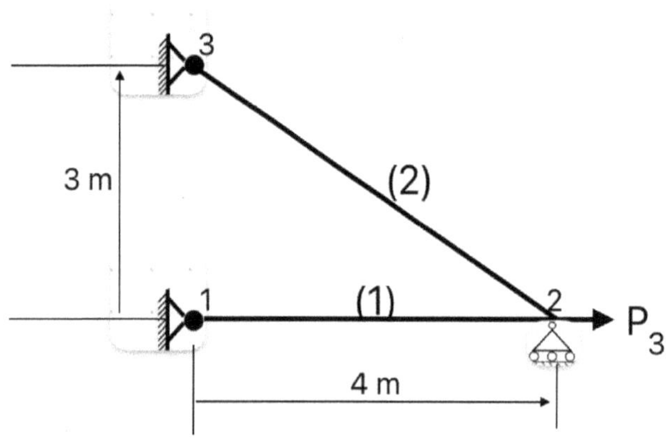

Fig. 6.13

TABLE II

Element number	Local node number i j	Angle between the positive x-axis and the element going from local node i to node j
1	1 2	C = cos S = sin
2	2 3	C = cos S = sin

$$[k^{(1)}] = \frac{A_1 E}{L_1} \begin{bmatrix} c^2 & cs & -c^2 & -cs \\ cs & s^2 & -cs & -s^2 \\ -c^2 & -cs & c^2 & cs \\ -cs & -s^2 & cs & s^2 \end{bmatrix} = 10^6 \begin{bmatrix} 1 & 0 & -1 & 0 \\ 0 & 0 & 0 & 0 \\ -1 & 0 & 1 & 0 \\ 0 & 0 & 0 & 0 \end{bmatrix}$$

$$\frac{A_2 E}{L_2} = \frac{20\left(20\times 10^6\right)}{500} = 0.8\times 10^6$$

$$\left[k^{(2)}\right] = \frac{A_2 E}{L_2}\begin{bmatrix} c^2 & cs & -c^2 & -cs \\ cs & s^2 & -cs & -s^2 \\ -c^2 & -cs & c^2 & cs \\ -cs & -s^2 & cs & s^2 \end{bmatrix} = 0.8 \times 10^6 \begin{bmatrix} 0.64 & -0.48 & -0.64 & 0.48 \\ -0.48 & 0.36 & 0.48 & -0.36 \\ -0.64 & 0.48 & 0.64 & -0.48 \\ 0.48 & -0.36 & -0.48 & 0.36 \end{bmatrix}$$

$$= 10^6 \begin{bmatrix} 1 & 0 & -1 & 0 \\ 0 & 0 & 0 & 0 \\ -1 & 0 & 1 & 0 \\ 0 & 0 & 0 & 0 \end{bmatrix}\begin{matrix} 1 \\ 2 \\ 3 \\ 4 \end{matrix} + 10^6 \begin{bmatrix} 0.512 & -0.384 & -0.512 & 0.384 \\ -0.384 & 0.288 & 0.384 & -0.288 \\ -0.512 & 0.384 & 0.512 & -0.384 \\ 0.384 & -0.288 & -0.384 & 0.288 \end{bmatrix}\begin{matrix} 3 \\ 4 \\ 5 \\ 6 \end{matrix}$$

$$[K] = 10^6 \begin{bmatrix} 1 & 0 & -1 & 0 & 0 & 0 \\ 0 & 1 & 0 & -1 & 0 & 0 \\ -1 & 0 & 1.512 & -0.384 & -0.512 & 0.384 \\ 0 & -1 & -0.384 & 0.288 & 0.384 & -0.288 \\ 0 & 0 & -0.512 & 0.384 & 0.512 & -0.384 \\ 0 & 0 & 0.384 & -0.288 & -0.384 & 0.288 \end{bmatrix}\begin{matrix} 1 \\ 2 \\ 3 \\ 4 \\ 5 \\ 6 \end{matrix}$$

Equation to solve:

where,

$$\begin{Bmatrix} u_1 \\ u_2 \\ u_3 \\ u_4 \\ u_5 \\ u_6 \end{Bmatrix} = \begin{Bmatrix} 0 \\ 0 \\ u_3 \\ 0 \\ 0 \\ 0 \end{Bmatrix} \text{ and } \begin{Bmatrix} P_1 \\ P_2 \\ P_3 \\ P_4 \\ P_5 \\ P_6 \end{Bmatrix} = \begin{Bmatrix} 0 \\ 0 \\ 200000 \\ 0 \\ 0 \\ 0 \end{Bmatrix}$$

Thus, $10^6 \begin{bmatrix} 1 & 0 & -1 & 0 & 0 & 0 \\ 0 & 1 & 0 & -1 & 0 & 0 \\ -1 & 0 & 1.512 & -0.384 & -0.512 & 0.384 \\ 0 & -1 & -0.384 & 0.288 & 0.384 & -0.288 \\ 0 & 0 & -0.512 & 0.384 & 0.512 & -0.384 \\ 0 & 0 & 0.384 & -0.288 & -0.384 & 0.288 \end{bmatrix}\begin{Bmatrix} 0 \\ 0 \\ U_3 \\ 0 \\ 0 \\ 0 \end{Bmatrix} = \begin{Bmatrix} 0 \\ 0 \\ 200000 \\ 0 \\ 0 \\ 0 \end{Bmatrix}$

Removing the 5 rows and 5 columns where element displacements are known. we get,

$$1.512 \, U_3 = \left(\frac{1}{10^6}\right)(200000)$$

$or \, U_3 = 0.132275 \, cm.$

$$\begin{Bmatrix} R_1 \\ R_2 \\ R_3 \\ R_4 \\ R_5 \\ R_6 \end{Bmatrix} = 10^6 \begin{bmatrix} 1 & 0 & -1 & 0 & 0 & 0 \\ 0 & 1 & 0 & -1 & 0 & 0 \\ -1 & 0 & 1.512 & -0.384 & -0.512 & 0.384 \\ 0 & -1 & -0.384 & 0.288 & 0.384 & -0.288 \\ 0 & 0 & -0.512 & 0.384 & 0.512 & -0.384 \\ 0 & 0 & 0.384 & -0.288 & -0.384 & 0.288 \end{bmatrix} \begin{Bmatrix} 0 \\ 0 \\ 0.132275 \\ 0 \\ 0 \\ 0 \end{Bmatrix}$$

$R_1 = -132275 \, N$

$R_2 = 0$

$R_4 = -0.384(0.132275)(1000000) = -50793.6 \, N$

$R_5 = -0.512(0.132275)(1000000) = -67724.8 \, N$

$R_6 = 0.384(0.132275)(1000000) = 50793.6 \, N$

Example 6.8 Consider a truss which has two elements or members. Element 1 is in the horizontal direction and its length is 60 cm. Element 2 makes an angle of 143.13 deg with the positive x -direction and is 100 cm long. Force applied at node 2 is $P_3 = 200000 \, N$

Area of cross-section of member (1) is $12 \, cm^2.$

Young's Modulus, $E = 20 \times 10^6 \, N/cm^2.$

$$\frac{A_1 E}{L_1} = \frac{5(20 \times 10^6)}{100} = 10^6$$

$$\frac{A_2 E}{L_2} = \frac{12(20 \times 10^6)}{60} = 4 \times 10^6$$

TABLE II Orientation of a Truss Member

Connectivity and angles of members of a truss

Element number	Local node number i j	Angle between the positive x-axis and the element going from local node i to node j
1	1 3	C = cos S = sin
2	2 3	C = cos S = sin

Applied force, $P_5 = 25000 \, N$

Applied force, $P_6 = -43301.3\ N$

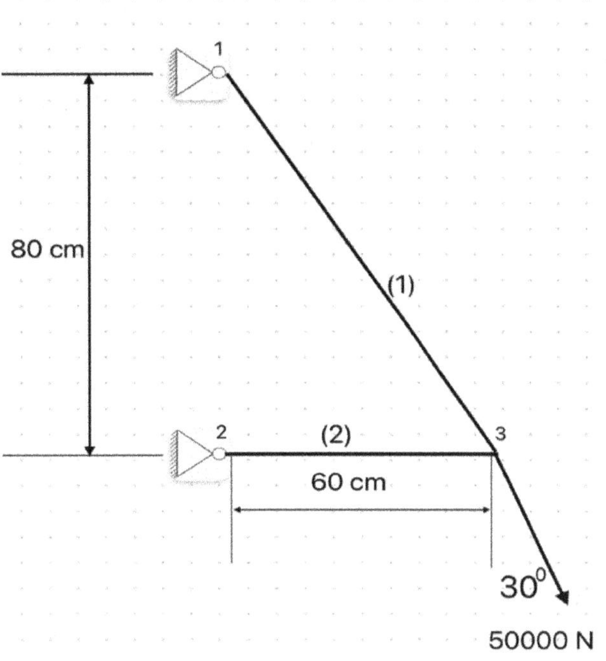

Fig. 6.13

$$\left[k^{(1)}\right] = \frac{A_1 E}{L_1}\begin{array}{cccc} 1 & 2 & 5 & 6 \end{array}\begin{bmatrix} c^2 & cs & -c^2 & -cs \\ cs & s^2 & -cs & -s^2 \\ -c^2 & -cs & c^2 & cs \\ -cs & -s^2 & cs & s^2 \end{bmatrix} = 10^6\begin{bmatrix} 1.44 & -1.92 & -1.44 & 1.92 \\ -1.92 & 2.56 & 1.92 & -2.56 \\ -1.44 & 1.92 & 1.44 & -1.92 \\ 1.92 & -2.56 & -1.92 & 2.56 \end{bmatrix}\begin{array}{c} 1 \\ 2 \\ 5 \\ 6 \end{array}$$

$$\left[k^{(2)}\right] = \frac{A_2 E}{L_2}\begin{array}{cccc} 3 & 4 & 5 & 6 \end{array}\begin{bmatrix} c^2 & cs & -c^2 & -cs \\ cs & s^2 & -cs & -s^2 \\ -c^2 & -cs & c^2 & cs \\ -cs & -s^2 & cs & s^2 \end{bmatrix} = 10^6\begin{bmatrix} 4 & 0 & -4 & 0 \\ 0 & 0 & 0 & 0 \\ -4 & 0 & 4 & 0 \\ 0 & 0 & 0 & 0 \end{bmatrix}\begin{array}{c} 3 \\ 4 \\ 5 \\ 6 \end{array}$$

$$[K] = 10^6\begin{array}{cccccc} 1 & 2 & 3 & 4 & 5 & 6 \end{array}\begin{bmatrix} 1.44 & -1.92 & -1 & 0 & 0 & 0 \\ -1.92 & 2.56 & 0 & -1 & 0 & 0 \\ -1 & 0 & 4 & 0 & -5.44 & 1.92 \\ 0 & -1 & 0 & 0 & 1.92 & -2.56 \\ -4 & 0 & -2.44 & 1.92 & 5.44 & -1.92 \\ 0 & 0 & 1.92 & -2.56 & -1.92 & 2.56 \end{bmatrix}\begin{array}{c} 1 \\ 2 \\ 3 \\ 4 \\ 5 \\ 6 \end{array}$$

Equation to solve,

where,

$$\begin{Bmatrix} U_1 \\ U_2 \\ U_3 \\ U_4 \\ U_5 \\ U_6 \end{Bmatrix} = \begin{Bmatrix} 0 \\ 0 \\ 0 \\ 0 \\ U_5 \\ U_6 \end{Bmatrix} \text{ and } \begin{Bmatrix} P_1 \\ P_2 \\ P_3 \\ P_4 \\ P_5 \\ P_6 \end{Bmatrix} = \begin{Bmatrix} 0 \\ 0 \\ 0 \\ 0 \\ 25000 \\ -43301.3 \end{Bmatrix}$$

Note that x and y coordinates are used in the determination of global stiffness matrix [K]. The displacement components {U} and applied force components {P} are also in x and y coordinates here.

Thus, the global matrix equation is,

$$10^6 \begin{bmatrix} 1.44 & -1.92 & -1 & 0 & 0 & 0 \\ -1.92 & 2.56 & 0 & -1 & 0 & 0 \\ -1 & 0 & 4 & 0 & -5.44 & 1.92 \\ 0 & -1 & 0 & 0 & 1.92 & -2.56 \\ -4 & 0 & -2.44 & 1.92 & 5.44 & -1.92 \\ 0 & 0 & 1.92 & -2.56 & -1.92 & 2.56 \end{bmatrix} \begin{Bmatrix} 0 \\ 0 \\ 0 \\ 0 \\ U_5 \\ U_6 \end{Bmatrix} = \begin{Bmatrix} 0 \\ 0 \\ 0 \\ 0 \\ 25000 \\ -43301.3 \end{Bmatrix}$$

Removing the 4 rows and 4 columns where element displacements are known. we get,

$$5.44 \, U_5 - 1..92 \, U_6 = 25000 \text{ Or } U_6 - 0.3529 \, U_5 = 4595.6/1000000$$

$$-1.92 U_5 + 2.56 \, U_6 = -43301.3 \text{ Or } -U_6 + 1.3333 \, U_5 = 22552.76/1000000$$

Thus,

$$0.9801 U_6 = (-22552.76 + 4595.6)/1000000 = -17957.16/1000000 = -0.01795716$$

Or $U_6 = -0.01795716/0.9801 = -0.01832$

$U_5 = 4595.6/1000000 + [(0.3529)(-0.01832)] = -0.001869$ cm

We will now consider the internal nodal reactions (or internal forces),

$R_1, R_2, \ldots R_6$. Thus, we may write,

$$\begin{Bmatrix} R_1 \\ R_2 \\ R_3 \\ R_4 \\ R_5 \\ R_6 \end{Bmatrix} = 10^6 \begin{bmatrix} 1.44 & -1.92 & -1 & 0 & 0 & 0 \\ -1.92 & 2.56 & 0 & -1 & 0 & 0 \\ -1 & 0 & 4 & 0 & -5.44 & 1.92 \\ 0 & -1 & 0 & 0 & 1.92 & -2.56 \\ -4 & 0 & -2.44 & 1.92 & 5.44 & -1.92 \\ 0 & 0 & 1.92 & -2.56 & -1.92 & 2.56 \end{bmatrix} \begin{Bmatrix} 0 \\ 0 \\ 0 \\ 0 \\ -0.01832 \\ -0.001869 \end{Bmatrix}$$

$$\text{Or} \quad \begin{Bmatrix} R_1 \\ R_2 \\ R_3 \\ R_4 \\ R_5 \\ R_6 \end{Bmatrix} = \begin{Bmatrix} 0 \\ 0 \\ -96072.32 \\ 30389.76 \\ 96072.32 \\ -30389.76 \end{Bmatrix}$$

where

$$\begin{Bmatrix} R_1 \\ R_2 \\ R_3 \\ R_4 \\ R_5 \\ R_6 \end{Bmatrix} = \begin{Bmatrix} R_i^{(1)} = x - \text{component of internal force in element (1) at its node } i \\ R_j^{(1)} = y - \text{compnent of internal force in element (1) at its node } j \\ R_i^{(2)} = x - \text{component of internal force in element (2) at its node } i \\ R_j^{(2)} = y - \text{component of internal force in element (2) at its node } j \\ R_i^{(3)} = x - \text{component of internal force in element (3) at its node } i \\ R_j^{(3)} = y - \text{component if internal force in element (3) at its node } j \end{Bmatrix}$$

We may also write the member internal element forces along the member as follows:

$$\overline{R}_i^{(e)} = \frac{A E}{L}\left[\left(U_{2i-1} - U_{2j-1}\right)\cos\theta + \left(U_{2i} - U_{2j}\right)\sin\theta\right] + A E \alpha \, \delta T$$

$$\overline{R}_j^{(\ )} = \frac{A E}{L}\left[\left(U_{2j-1} - U_{2i-1}\right)\cos\theta + \left(U_{2j} - U_{2i}\right)\sin\theta\right] - A E \alpha \, \delta T$$

$$= 10^6\left[\left(U_5 - U_3\right)\cos\theta + \left(U_6 - U_4\right)\sin\theta\right]$$

$$= 10^6 \times -0.0124872 = -12487 \, N$$

If $\overline{R}_j^{(e)}$ is found to be positive, then the force in the member is tension.

In the above example, member (1) has $i = 1$ and $j = 3$.

Thus, $2i = 2$ and $2j = 6$, $2i-1 = 1$ and $2j-1 = 5$.

$$\overline{R}_j^{(\ )} = \frac{A E}{L}\left[\left(U_{2j-1} - U_{2i-1}\right)\cos\theta + \left(U_{2j} - U_{2i}\right)\sin\theta\right] - A E \alpha \, \delta T$$

$$= 10^6\left[\left(U_5 - U_1\right)\cos\theta + \left(U_6 - U_2\right)\sin\theta\right]$$

$$= 10^6\left[(-0.01832 - 0)(0.6) + (-0.001869 - 0)(-0.8)\right]$$

$$= 10^6 \times -0.009497 = -9497 \, N$$

Thus, member (1) is in compression with a force of 9497 N

Solving Beam Problems

Beam Element

A simply supported beam element of length L, with nodes i and j is shown here. When loaded, the nodes undergo vertical displacements and rotation about z axis. Analysis of the beam means calculating nodal displacements and stresses in the beam. Thefollowing example illustrates the beam calculations.

Example 6.9 A beam has a length of 500 cm and has an applied load of 20000 N at its mid point. The beam is fixed at its left end and is on rollers at its right end. Calculate the nodal displacements of this beam. Calculate the internal shear force and bending moment at its nodes. Use the following expression for calculating its elements stiffnesses.

2i-1 2i 2j-1 2j

$$[k^{(e)}] = \frac{EI}{L^3} \begin{bmatrix} 12 & 6L & -12 & 6L \\ 6L & 4L^2 & -6L & 2L^2 \\ -12 & -6L & 12 & -6L \\ 6L & 2L^2 & -6L & 4L^2 \end{bmatrix} Njb \begin{matrix} 2i-1 \\ 2i \\ 2j-1 \\ 2j \end{matrix}$$

The material property values are,

$$E = 20 \times 10^6 \ ^N\!/_{cm^2}$$

$$I = 2500 \ cm^4$$

Use the notation as shown in the figure given below:

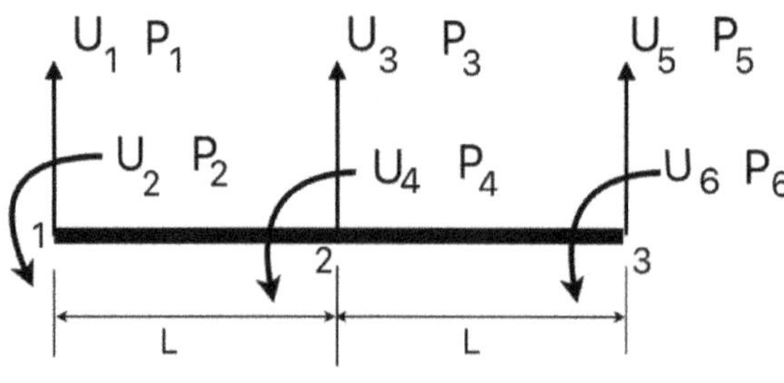

Fig. 6.14

Solution: Divide the beam into two elements. Then, we calculate the stiffness matrices of these elements,

$$
[k^{(1)}] = 400
\begin{array}{cccc}
1 & 2 & 3 & 4
\end{array}
\begin{bmatrix}
12 & 3000 & -12 & 3000 \\
3000 & 1000000 & -3000 & 500000 \\
-12 & -3000 & 12 & -3000 \\
3000 & 500000 & -3000 & 1000000
\end{bmatrix}
\begin{array}{c}
1 \\ 2 \\ 3 \\ 4
\end{array} ,
$$

$$
[k^{(2)}] = 400
\begin{array}{cccc}
3 & 4 & 5 & 6
\end{array}
\begin{bmatrix}
12 & 3000 & -12 & 3000 \\
3000 & 1000000 & -3000 & 500000 \\
-12 & -3000 & 12 & -3000 \\
3000 & 500000 & -3000 & 1000000
\end{bmatrix}
\begin{array}{c}
3 \\ 4 \\ 5 \\ 6
\end{array}
$$

We now assemble Global matrix $[K]$

$$
[K] = 400
\begin{bmatrix}
12 & 3000 & -12 & 3000 & 0 & 0 \\
3000 & 1000000 & -3000 & 500000 & 0 & 0 \\
-12 & -3000 & 12+12 & -3000+3000 & -12 & 3000 \\
3000 & 500000 & -3000+3000 & 1000000+1000000 & -3000 & 500000 \\
0 & 0 & -12 & -3000 & 12 & -3000 \\
0 & 0 & 3000 & 500000 & -3000 & 1000000
\end{bmatrix}
$$

Now use the given displacement conditions and the given loading conditions

$$
\{U\} =
\begin{Bmatrix}
0 \\ 0 \\ U_3 \\ U_4 \\ 0 \\ U_6
\end{Bmatrix}
\text{ and } \{P\} =
\begin{Bmatrix}
0 \\ 0 \\ -20000 \\ 0 \\ 0 \\ 0
\end{Bmatrix}
$$

Forces are considered positive in the positive coordinate directions. Moments are considered positive in the counterclockwise direction.

Now solve the applicable global matrix equation, $[K]\{U\} = \{P\}$

$$
400
\begin{bmatrix}
12 & 3000 & -12 & 3000 & 0 & 0 \\
3000 & 1000000 & -3000 & 500000 & 0 & 0 \\
-12 & -3000 & 12+12 & -3000+3000 & -12 & 3000 \\
3000 & 500000 & -3000+3000 & 1000000+1000000 & -3000 & 500000 \\
0 & 0 & -12 & -3000 & 12 & -3000 \\
0 & 0 & 3000 & 500000 & -3000 & 1000000
\end{bmatrix}
\begin{Bmatrix}
0 \\ 0 \\ U_3 \\ U_4 \\ 0 \\ U_6
\end{Bmatrix}
=
\begin{Bmatrix}
0 \\ 0 \\ -20000 \\ 0 \\ 0 \\ 0
\end{Bmatrix}
$$

Or

$$400 \begin{bmatrix} 24 & 0 & 3000 \\ -3000 & 2000000 & -3000 \\ 3000 & 500000 & 1000000 \end{bmatrix} \begin{Bmatrix} U_3 \\ U_4 \\ U_6 \end{Bmatrix} = \begin{Bmatrix} -20000 \\ 0 \\ 0 \end{Bmatrix}$$

Or

$$24\ U_3 + 3000\ U_6 = -500$$

$$-3000\ U_3 + 2000000\ U_4 - 3000\ U_6 = 0$$

$$3000\ U_3 + 500000\ U_4 + 1000000\ U_6 = 0$$

Solution of the above set of the algebraic equations is,

- $\quad = 0.01250$ cm
- $\quad = -0.003125$ cm

$$U_3 = -3.646\ cm$$

With the displacements known, we can rewrite the equation in terms of the reaction forces (or internal nodal forces) for the complete beam. This could also be done for each element of the beam.

$$400 \begin{bmatrix} 12 & 3000 & -12 & 3000 & 0 & 0 \\ 3000 & 1000000 & -3000 & 500000 & 0 & 0 \\ -12 & -3000 & 12+12 & -3000+3000 & -12 & 3000 \\ 3000 & 500000 & -3000+3000 & 1000000+1000000 & -3000 & 500000 \\ 0 & 0 & -12 & -3000 & 12 & -3000 \\ 0 & 0 & 3000 & 500000 & -3000 & 1000000 \end{bmatrix} \begin{Bmatrix} 0 \\ 0 \\ -3.646 \\ -0.003125 \\ 0 \\ 0.01250 \end{Bmatrix} = \begin{Bmatrix} R_1 \\ R_2 \\ R_3 \\ R_4 \\ R_5 \\ R_6 \end{Bmatrix}$$

For element (1), we write

$$R^{(1)} = 400 \begin{bmatrix} 12 & 3000 & -12 & 3000 \\ 3000 & 1000000 & -3000 & 500000 \\ -12 & -3000 & 12 & -3000 \\ 3000 & 500000 & -3000 & 1000000 \end{bmatrix} \begin{Bmatrix} 0 \\ 0 \\ -3.646 \\ -0.003125 \end{Bmatrix} = \begin{Bmatrix} R_1 \\ R_2 \\ R_3 \\ R_4 \end{Bmatrix}$$

The reactions (or internal forces) for element (1) are given by

$$V_1^{(1)} = 400\ [-12(-3.646) + 3000\ (-0.003125)] = 13750.8$$

$$M_1^{(1)} = 400\ [-3000(-3.646) + 500000\ (-0.003125)] = 3750200$$

$$V_2^{(1)} = 400\ [12(-3.646) - 3000\ (-0.003125)] = -13750.8$$

$$M_2^{(1)} = 400\ [-3000(-3.646) + 1000000\ (-0.003125)] = 3125200$$

The reactions (or internal forces) for element (2) are given by

$$R^{(2)} = 400 \begin{bmatrix} 12 & 3000 & -12 & 3000 \\ 3000 & 1000000 & -3000 & 500000 \\ -12 & -3000 & 12 & -3000 \\ 3000 & 500000 & -3000 & 1000000 \end{bmatrix} \begin{Bmatrix} -3.646 \\ -0.003125 \\ 0 \\ 0.01250 \end{Bmatrix} = \begin{Bmatrix} R_3 \\ R_4 \\ R_5 \\ R_6 \end{Bmatrix}$$

$V_2^{(2)} = 400\,[12(-3.646) + 3000\,(-0.003125) + 3000(0.01250)] = -6250.8$

$M_2^{(2)} = 400\,[3000(-3.646) + 1000000\,(-0.003125) + 500000\,(0.01250)] = -3125200$

$V_3^{(2)} = 400\,[-12(-3.646) - 3000\,(-0.003125)] = 6250.8$

$M_3^{(2)} = 400\,[3000(-3.646) + 500000\,(-0.003125) + 1000000\,(0.0125)] = 0$

Uniformly loaded simply supported beam

Example 6.10 A simply supported beam is uniformly loaded as shown below:

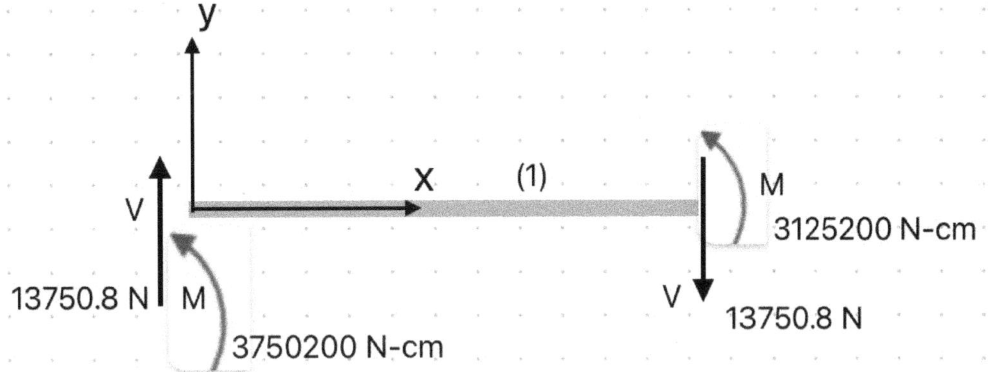

Fig. 6.15 (a)

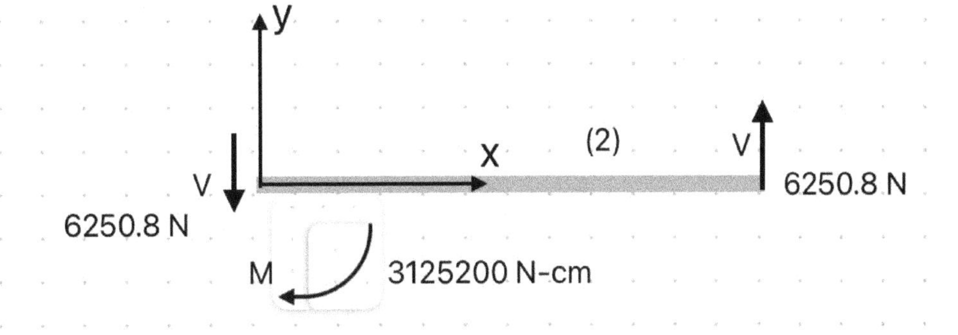

Fig. 6.15 (b)

Use two elements. Find the nodal deflections.

Solution: The equation that applies to this beam is

$$E I \frac{d^2y}{dx^2} - M(x) = 0. \text{ This equation is similar to } D\frac{d^2T}{dx^2} + Q = 0.$$

Thus, $D = E I$ *and* $Q = -M$.

$$\left[k^{(1)}\right] = \frac{10^{10}}{200}\begin{bmatrix} 1 & -1 \\ -1 & 1 \end{bmatrix}$$

$$Q = -\frac{L}{6}\begin{bmatrix} 2 & 1 \\ 1 & 2 \end{bmatrix}\begin{Bmatrix} M_1 \\ M_2 \end{Bmatrix}$$

$$= -\frac{200}{6}\begin{bmatrix} 2 & 1 \\ 1 & 2 \end{bmatrix}\begin{Bmatrix} \frac{w}{2}\left(2L\,x - x^2\right)_{x=0} \\ \frac{w}{2}\left(2L\,x - x^2\right)_{x=200} \end{Bmatrix}$$

$$= -\frac{200}{6}\begin{bmatrix} 2 & 1 \\ 1 & 2 \end{bmatrix}\begin{Bmatrix} 0 \\ \frac{500}{2}\left(200^2\right) \end{Bmatrix} = \begin{Bmatrix} \frac{500}{2}\left(200^2\right) \\ 500\left(200^2\right) \end{Bmatrix}$$

$$\left[k^{(2)}\right] = \frac{10^{10}}{200}\begin{bmatrix} 1 & -1 \\ -1 & 1 \end{bmatrix}$$

$$Q = -\frac{L}{6}\begin{bmatrix} 2 & 1 \\ 1 & 2 \end{bmatrix}\begin{Bmatrix} M_2 \\ M_3 \end{Bmatrix}$$

$$= -\frac{200}{6}\begin{bmatrix} 2 & 1 \\ 1 & 2 \end{bmatrix}\begin{Bmatrix} \frac{w}{2}\left(2L\,x - x^2\right)_{x=200} \\ \frac{w}{2}\left(2L\,x - x^2\right)_{x=400} \end{Bmatrix}$$

$$= -\frac{200}{6}\begin{bmatrix} 2 & 1 \\ 1 & 2 \end{bmatrix}\begin{Bmatrix} \frac{500}{2}\left(200\right)^2 \\ 0 \end{Bmatrix}$$

$$= -\frac{200}{6}\begin{Bmatrix} 500\left(200^2\right) \\ \frac{500}{2}\left(200^2\right) \end{Bmatrix}$$

Thus, the global equation, [K]{Y} = {M} becomes,

$$\frac{10^{10}}{200}\begin{bmatrix} 1 & -1 & 0 \\ -1 & 2 & -1 \\ 0 & -1 & 1 \end{bmatrix}\begin{Bmatrix} y_1 \\ y_2 \\ y_3 \end{Bmatrix} = -\frac{200}{6}\begin{Bmatrix} 0 \\ \frac{500}{2}\left(200^2\right) + 500\left(200^2\right) \\ \frac{500}{2}\left(200^2\right) \end{Bmatrix}$$

$$\begin{bmatrix} 1 & -1 & 0 \\ -1 & 2 & -1 \\ 0 & -1 & 1 \end{bmatrix} \begin{Bmatrix} 0 \\ y_2 \\ 0 \end{Bmatrix} = -\frac{200}{6} \times \frac{200}{10^{10}} \begin{Bmatrix} 0 \\ 500(200^2) + 500(200^2) \\ \dfrac{500}{2}(200^2) \end{Bmatrix} = -6666.67 \begin{Bmatrix} 0 \\ \dfrac{1000(200^2)}{10^{100}} \\ \dfrac{250(200^2)}{10^{10}} \end{Bmatrix}$$

Therefore,

$$2\,y_2 = -\frac{6666.67 \times 1000(200^2)}{10^{10}} = 26.66$$

or

$$y_2 = \frac{26.66}{2} = 13.33 \ cm.$$

Alternative Method

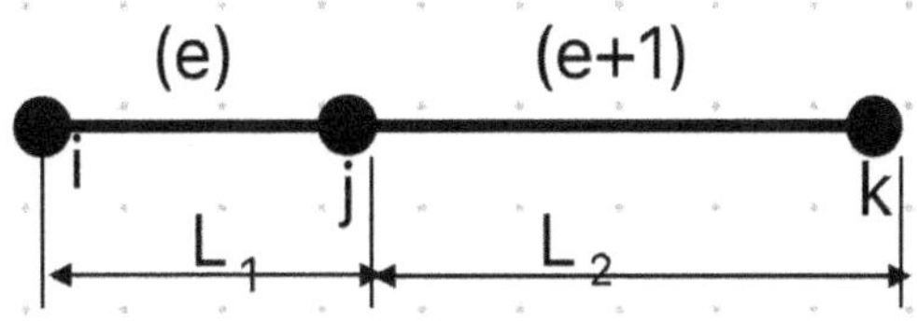

Fig. 6.16

Nodal relation applicable here is,

$$D\frac{d^2T}{dx^2} + Q = 0, \text{ the nodal (algebraic) equation at node j is}$$

$$R_j = \left(D\frac{dT}{dX}\right)_j^{(e+1)} - \left(D\frac{dT}{dx}\right)_j^{(e)} - \left(\frac{D}{L}\right)_i^{(e)} T_i + \left[\left(\frac{D}{L}\right)^{(e)} + \left(\frac{D}{L}\right)^{(e+1)}\right] T_j - \left(\frac{D}{L}\right)^{(e+1)} T_k - \left(\frac{QL}{2}\right)^{(e)} - \left(\frac{QL}{2}\right)^{(e+1)} = 0$$

The derivative boundary conditions are left out since there are no derivative boundary condition given in this problem.

The differential equation that applies to the problem given here is,

$$D\frac{d^2T}{dx^2} - M(x) = 0,$$

$$R_s = \frac{-D^{(e)}\,y_{s-1} + \left[D^{(e)} + D^{(e+1)}\right]y_s - D^{(e+1)}\,y_{s+1}}{L} - \frac{L}{6}\left[M_{s-1} + 4M_s + M_{s+1}\right] = 0$$

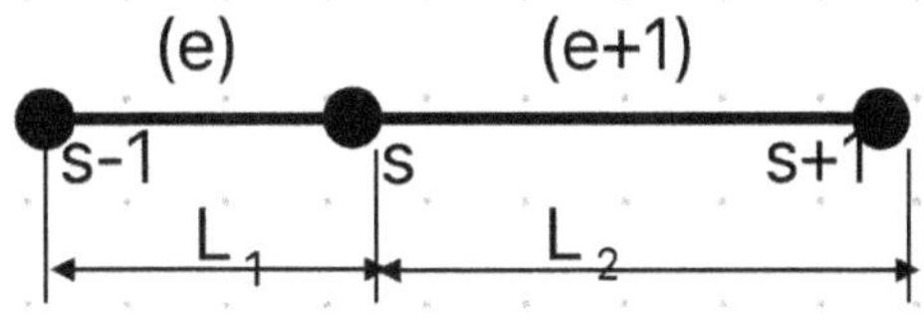

Fig. 6.17

where,

$$M_{s-1} = \frac{w^{(e)}}{2}\left(2Lx - x^2\right)_{x=0} = 0$$

$$M_s = \frac{w}{2}\left(2Lx - x^2\right)_{x=L} = \frac{wL^2}{2} = \frac{500}{2}(200)^2$$

$$4\,M_s = 2(500)\left(200^2\right) = 1000\left(200^2\right)$$

$$4\,M_s \times \frac{L}{6} = 4\,M_s \times \frac{200}{6} = \frac{1000 \times \left(200^3\right)}{6}$$

$$M_{s+1} = \frac{w}{2}\left(2Lx - x^2\right)_{x=2L} = 0$$

$$D^{(e)} = D^{(e+1)} = E\,I$$

$$y_{s-1} = y_{s+1} = 0$$

$$R_s = \frac{0 + \left[E\,I + E\,I\right]y_s - 0}{L} + \frac{L}{6}\left[0 + 4\,M_s + 0\right] = 0$$

or

$$\frac{2\,E\,I}{L}y_s - \frac{L}{6}\left(4\,M_s\right) = 0$$

or

$$y_s = -\frac{4\,M_s\,L}{6} \times \frac{L}{2 \times E\,I} = -\frac{1000\left(200^3\right)(200)}{6 \times 2 \times 10^{10}} = 13.33\ cm$$

Example 6.11 Consider a beam loaded shown loaded in Fig. 10.2. Find the displacements, reactions, and the element loads. Use the following information

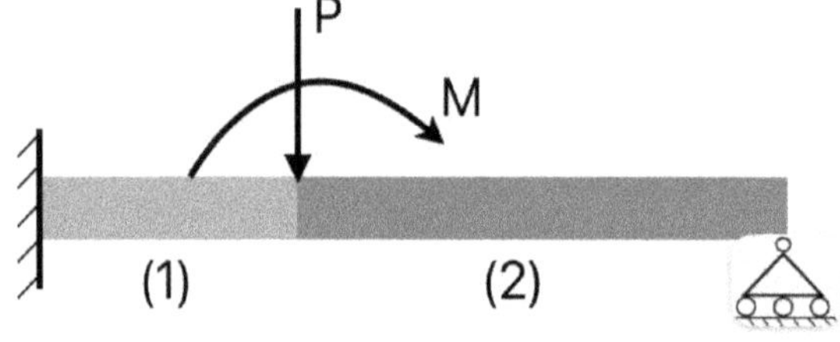

Fig. 6.18

$$E^{(1)} = 30\ Mpsi\ \ E^{(2)} = 10\ Mpsi$$

$$L^{(1)} = 100\ in\ \ L^{(2)} = 200\ in$$

$$I^{(1)} = 21.3\ in^4\ \ I^{(1)} = 21.3\ in^4$$

P = 1000 lbf M = 50 kip-in

Use the following expression for calculating its elements stiffnesses.

2i-1 2i 2j-1 2j

$$[k^{(e)}] = \frac{E\,I}{L^3}\begin{bmatrix} 12 & 6L & -12 & 6L \\ 6L & 4L^2 & -6L & 2L^2 \\ -12 & -6L & 12 & -6L \\ 6L & 2L^2 & -6L & 4L^2 \end{bmatrix}\begin{matrix} 2i-1 \\ 2i \\ 2j-1 \\ 2j \end{matrix}$$

Substituting the given values, we get,

$$[k^{(1)}] = 10^3 \begin{bmatrix} 7.67 & 383 & -7.67 & 383 \\ 383 & 25560 & -383 & 12780 \\ -7.67 & -383 & 7.67 & -383 \\ 383 & 12780 & -383 & 25560 \end{bmatrix}$$

$$[k^{(2)}] = 10^3 \begin{bmatrix} 0.320 & 31.9 & -0.320 & 31.9 \\ 31.9 & 4260 & -31.9 & 2130 \\ -0.320 & -31.9 & 0.320 & -31.9 \\ 31.9 & 2130 & -31.9 & 4260 \end{bmatrix}$$

Assembling the element matrices we get,

$$[K] = 10^3 \begin{bmatrix} 7.67 & 383 & -7.67 & 383 & & \\ 383 & 25560 & -383 & 12780 & & \\ -7.67 & -383 & 7.67+0.320 & -383+31.9 & -0.320 & 31.9 \\ 383 & 12780 & -383+31.9 & 25560+4260 & -31.9 & 2130 \\ & & -0.320 & -31.9 & 0.320 & -31.9 \\ & & 31.9 & 2130 & -31.9 & 4260 \end{bmatrix}$$

Now solve the applicable global matrix equation, $[K]\{U\} = \{P\}$ and write,

$$10^3 \begin{bmatrix} 7.67 & 383 & -7.67 & 383 & & \\ 383 & 25560 & -383 & 12780 & & \\ -7.67 & -383 & 7.67+0.320 & -383+31.9 & -0.320 & 31.9 \\ 383 & 12780 & -383+31.9 & 25560+4260 & -31.9 & \\ & & -0.320 & -31.9 & 0.320 & -31.9 \\ & & 31.9 & 2130 & -31.9 & 4260 \end{bmatrix} \begin{Bmatrix} U_1 \\ U_2 \\ U_3 \\ U_4 \\ U_5 \\ U6 \end{Bmatrix} = \begin{Bmatrix} P_1 \\ P_2 \\ P_3 \\ P_4 \\ P_5 \\ P_6 \end{Bmatrix}$$

We know from the given beam that $U_1 = U_2 = U_5 = 0,$ *and* $P_3 = 1000 \; lbf$, $P_4 = 50000 \; lb-in$, *we substitute these values in the above equation. We get,*

$$10^3 \begin{bmatrix} 7.67 & 383 & -7.67 & 383 & & \\ 383 & 25560 & -383 & 12780 & & \\ -7.67 & -383 & 7.99 & -351.1 & -0.320 & 31.9 \\ 383 & 12780 & -351.1 & 29820 & -31.9 & 2130 \\ & & -0.320 & -31.9 & 0.320 & -31.9 \\ & & 31.9 & 2130 & -31.9 & 4260 \end{bmatrix} \begin{Bmatrix} 0 \\ 0 \\ U_3 \\ U_4 \\ 0 \\ U_6 \end{Bmatrix} = \begin{Bmatrix} P_1 \\ P_2 \\ -1000 \\ -500000 \\ P_5 \\ P_6 \end{Bmatrix}$$

Deleting the rows and columns corresponding to the known values of displacements, we get

$$10^3 \begin{bmatrix} 7.99 & -351.1 & 31.9 \\ -351.1 & 29820 & 2130 \\ 31.9 & 2130 & 4260 \end{bmatrix} \begin{Bmatrix} U_3 \\ U_4 \\ U_6 \end{Bmatrix} = \begin{Bmatrix} -1000 \\ -50000 \\ 0 \end{Bmatrix}$$

Or

$$7.99 \, U_2 - 351.1 \, U_4 + 31.9 \, U_6 = -1$$

$$-351.1 \, U_2 + 29820 \, U_4 + 2130 \, U_6 = -50$$

$$31.9 \, U_2 + 2130 \, U_4 + 4260 \, U_6 = 0$$

The solution to the system of equations is approximately:

$$U_2 = -0.5344 \; in$$

$$U_4 = -0.00856 \; rad$$

$$U_6 = 0.00828 \; rad$$

Thus, $\{U\}^T = \left\{ 0 \quad 0 \quad -0.5344 \quad -0.00856 \quad 0 \quad 0.00828 \right\}$

To get internal reactions of element (1), we write,

$$\begin{Bmatrix} V_1^{(1)} \\ M_1^{(1)} \\ V_2^{(1)} \\ M_2^{(1)} \end{Bmatrix} = 10^3 \begin{bmatrix} 7.67 & 383 & -7.67 & 383 \\ 383 & 25560 & -383 & 12780 \\ -7.67 & -383 & 7.67 & -383 \\ 383 & 12780 & -383 & 25560 \end{bmatrix} \begin{Bmatrix} 0 \\ 0 \\ -0.5344 \\ -0.00856 \end{Bmatrix} = \begin{Bmatrix} 820.4 \; lbf \\ 95.3 \; kip - in \\ -820.4 \; lbf \\ -14.1 \; kip - in \end{Bmatrix}$$

To get internal reactions of element (), we write,

$$\begin{Bmatrix} V_2^{(2)} \\ M_2^{(2)} \\ V_3^{(2)} \\ M_3^{(2)} \end{Bmatrix} = 10^3 \begin{bmatrix} 0.320 & 31.9 & -0.320 & 31.9 \\ 31.9 & 4260 & -31.9 & 2130 \\ -0.320 & -31.9 & 0.320 & -31.9 \\ 31.9 & 2130 & -31.9 & 4260 \end{bmatrix} \begin{Bmatrix} -0.5344 \\ -0.00856 \\ 0 \\ 0.00828 \end{Bmatrix} = \begin{Bmatrix} -180 \; lbf \\ -35.9 \; kip - in \\ 180 \; lbf \\ 0 \; kip - in \end{Bmatrix}$$

Analysis of Tapered Thin Plate

Example 6.12 A tapered thin plate, made of steel has a length of 0.5 m and a thickness of 0.02 m. Its width is 0.18 m at its fixed end and 0.08 m at its free end. In addition to its self-weight, it is subjected to a point and reaction at its support. Take E for steel as $\dfrac{2 \times 10^{11} \; N}{m^2}$ and its density as $7800 \; \dfrac{kg}{m^3}$.

Solution: Note that the cross-sectional area of the plate at the fixed end is,

$$0.18 \times 0.02 = 0.0036 \; m^2.$$

The area of the cross-section at the free end is, $0.08 \times 0.02 = 0.0016 \; m^2$. Let us create two elements, (1) and (2) with three nodes 1,2 and 3.

The cross-sectional area at point P is,

$$N_1 A_1 + N_2 A_2 = \frac{Y_2 - y}{Y_2 - Y_1} A_1 + \frac{y - Y_1}{Y_2 - Y_1} A_2$$

$$= \frac{0.5 - 0.3}{0.5}(0.0036) + \frac{0.3 - 0}{0.5}(0.0016) = 0.00144 + 0.00096 = 0.0024 \; m^2.$$

We replace the given plate with a stepped plate as shown alongside it.

Element (1) has an average cross-sectional area of $\dfrac{0.0036 + 0.0024}{2} = 0.003 \; m^2$

Similarly, element (2) has an average cross-sectional area of $\dfrac{0.0024 + 0.0016}{2} = 0.002 \; m^2$

We now create element (1) of a stepped bar with a uniform cross-sectional area of $0.003 \; m^2$

Similarly, we create element (2) of the stepped bar with a uniform cross-sectional area of $0.002\ m^2$. The lengths of the parts in the stepped bar are the same as in the tapered bar.

Now we can calculate the element matrices.

$$\left[k^{(1)}\right] = \frac{A_1 E_1}{L_1}\begin{bmatrix} 1 & -1 \\ -1 & 1 \end{bmatrix} = \frac{0.003\left(2\times 10^{11}\right)}{0.3}\begin{bmatrix} 1 & -1 \\ -1 & 1 \end{bmatrix} = 2\times 10^9\begin{bmatrix} 1 & -1 \\ -1 & 1 \end{bmatrix}$$

$$\left[k^{(2)}\right] = \frac{A_2 E_2}{L_2}\begin{bmatrix} 1 & -1 \\ -1 & 1 \end{bmatrix} = \frac{0.002\left(2\times 10^{11}\right)}{0.2}\begin{bmatrix} 1 & -1 \\ -1 & 1 \end{bmatrix} = 2\times 10^9\begin{bmatrix} 1 & -1 \\ -1 & 1 \end{bmatrix}$$

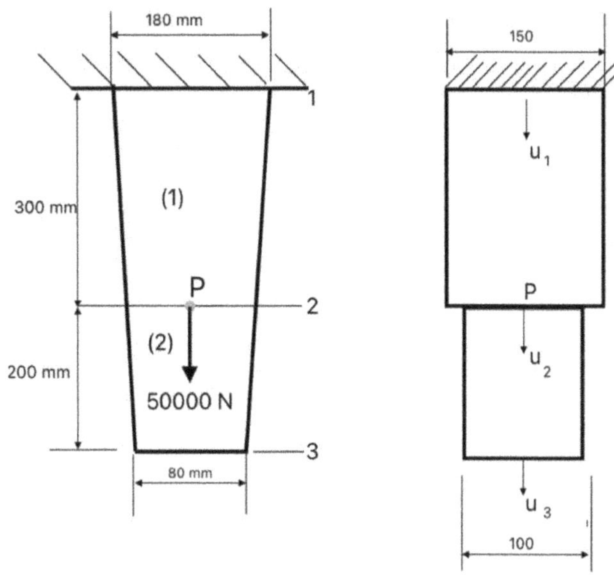

Fig. 6.18

$$[K] = 2\times 10^9\begin{bmatrix} 1 & -1 & 0 \\ -1 & 2 & -1 \\ 0 & -1 & 1 \end{bmatrix}$$

The force vectors arise from the body force (or self weight) of the plate.

$$\{f^{(1)}\} = \frac{A_1 L_1 \rho\, g}{2}\begin{Bmatrix} 1 \\ 1 \end{Bmatrix} = \frac{0.003\times 0.3\times 7800\times 9.81}{2}\begin{Bmatrix} 1 \\ 1 \end{Bmatrix} = \begin{Bmatrix} 34.433 \\ 34.433 \end{Bmatrix}$$

$$\{f^{(2)}\} = \frac{A_2 L_2 \rho\, g}{2}\begin{Bmatrix} 1 \\ 1 \end{Bmatrix} = \frac{0.002\times 0.2\times 7800\times 9.81}{2}\begin{Bmatrix} 1 \\ 1 \end{Bmatrix} = \begin{Bmatrix} 15.304 \\ 15.304 \end{Bmatrix}$$

The global matrix equation is, $[K]\{U\} = \{P\} + \{F\}$

Or

$$2\times 10^9\begin{bmatrix} 1 & -1 & 0 \\ -1 & 2 & -1 \\ 0 & -1 & 1 \end{bmatrix}\begin{Bmatrix} u_1 \\ u_2 \\ u_3 \end{Bmatrix} = \begin{Bmatrix} P_1 \\ P_2 \\ P_3 \end{Bmatrix} + \begin{Bmatrix} f_1 \\ f_2 \\ f_3 \end{Bmatrix}$$

Applying the boundary conditions,

$$2\times 10^9 \begin{bmatrix} 1 & -1 & 0 \\ -1 & 2 & -1 \\ 0 & -1 & 1 \end{bmatrix} \begin{Bmatrix} 0 \\ u_2 \\ u_3 \end{Bmatrix} = \begin{Bmatrix} P_1 \\ 50000 \\ 0 \end{Bmatrix} + \begin{Bmatrix} 34.433 \\ 34.433 + 15.304 \\ 15.304 \end{Bmatrix} = \begin{Bmatrix} P_1 + 34.433 \\ 50049.737 \\ P_3 + 15.304 \end{Bmatrix}$$

Since $u_1 = 0$, we eliminate the first row and the first column. We get,

$$2\times 10^9 \begin{bmatrix} 2 & -1 \\ -1 & 1 \end{bmatrix} \begin{Bmatrix} u_2 \\ u_3 \end{Bmatrix} = \begin{Bmatrix} 50049.737 \\ 0 + 15.304 \end{Bmatrix}$$

$$2u_2 - u_3 = 25024.87 \times 10^{-9}$$

$$-u_2 + u_3 = 7.652 \times 10^{-9}$$

Solving the above two equations, we get,

$$u_3 = 25040.204 \times 10^{-9}\, m$$

Since , $-u_2 + u_3 = 7.652 \times 10^{-9}$ we get,

$$u_2 = u_3 - 7.652 \times 10^{-9}$$

$$= (25040.204 - 7.652) \times 10^{-9}$$

$$= 25032.55 \times 10^{-9}$$

Substituting in the first equation of the matrix equation, we get,

$$-2\times 10^9\, u_2 = P_1 + 34.433$$

$$-2\times 10^9\, u_2 = P_1 + 34.433$$

$$P_1 = -2\times 10^9\, (25032.204 \times 10^{-9}) - 34.433 = -50098.8\, N$$

Writing the second equation of the global matrix equation, we get,

$$P_2 = 50000 + 49.737 = 50049.7\, N$$

Writing the third equation of the global matrix equation, we get,

$$= 0 + 15.304$$

$$(2\times 10^9)(7.652)(10^{-9}) = P_3 + 15,304$$

$$(2\times 10^9)(7.652)(10^{-9}) = P_3 + 15,304$$

Therefore, $P_3 = 0$.

Example 6.13 Find the nodal displacements in the conical bar by dividing it into two elements. Total length of the bar is 20 cm.

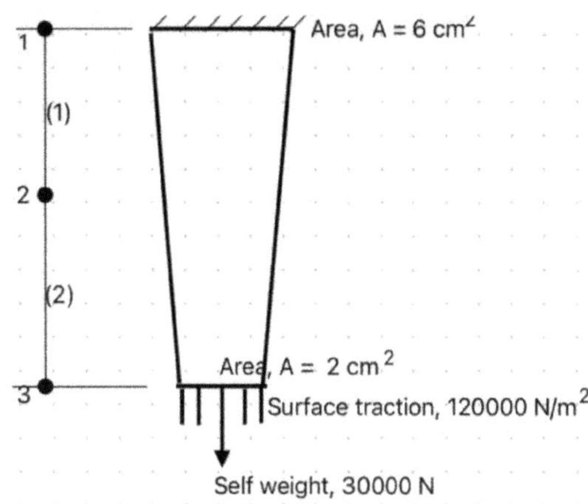

A Conical bar

Fig. 6.19

Solution:

We will take the x coordinate in the downward direction.

For element (1),

$$x_i = x_1 = 0 \ and \ x_j = 10 \ cm.$$

$$\bar{x} = \frac{x_1 + x_2}{2} = \frac{0 + 10}{2} = 5 \ cm$$

Since $Area \ A_1 = \dfrac{\pi D_1^2}{4} = 6, \ D_1 = \sqrt{\dfrac{6 \times 4}{\pi}} = 2.764 \ cm$

$Area \ A_2 = \dfrac{\pi D_2^2}{4} = 2, \ D_2 = \sqrt{\dfrac{2 \times 4}{\pi}} = 1.596 \ cm$

$$\bar{r} = \frac{1}{2}\left[D_1 - \frac{\left(D_1 - D_2\right)}{20} \times \bar{x}\right] = \frac{1}{2}\left[2.764 - \frac{2.764 - 1.596}{20} \times 5\right] = 1.236 \ cm$$

$$\bar{A}_1 = \pi \, (\bar{r})^2 = \pi (1.236)^2 = 4.799 \ cm^2$$

$$\left[k^{(1)}\right] = \frac{A\,E}{L}\begin{bmatrix} 1 & -1 \\ -1 & 1 \end{bmatrix} = \frac{4.799 \times 20 \times 10^6}{10}\begin{bmatrix} 1 & -1 \\ -1 & 1 \end{bmatrix}$$

$$= 10^6\begin{bmatrix} 9.598 & -9.598 \\ -9.598 & 9.598 \end{bmatrix}$$

$$\{f^{(1)}\} = \begin{Bmatrix} 0 \\ 0 \end{Bmatrix}$$

For element (2),

$$x_i = x_2 = 10 \ and \ x_j = x_3 = 20 \ cm.$$

$$\bar{x} = \frac{x_1 + x_2}{2} = \frac{10 + 20}{2} = 15 \ cm$$

Since $Area \ A_2 = \dfrac{\pi D_2^2}{4} = 2, \ D_2 = \sqrt{\dfrac{2 \times 4}{\pi}} = 1.596 \ cm$

$$\bar{r} = \frac{1}{2}\left[D_1 - \frac{(D_1 - D_2)}{20} \times \bar{x} \right] = \frac{1}{2}\left[2.764 - \frac{2.764 - 1.596}{20} \times 15 \right] = 1.236 \ cm$$

$$\overline{A_2} = \pi \left(\bar{r} \right)^2 = \pi(1.236)^2 = 2.799 \ cm^2$$

$$\left[k^{(2)} \right] = \frac{A E}{L}\begin{bmatrix} 1 & -1 \\ -1 & 1 \end{bmatrix} = \frac{2.799 \times 20 \times 10^6}{10}\begin{bmatrix} 1 & -1 \\ -1 & 1 \end{bmatrix}$$

$$= 10^6 \begin{bmatrix} 5.598 & -5.598 \\ -5.598 & 5.598 \end{bmatrix}$$

Surface traction = Area in $cm^2 \times$ $surf ace \ traction \ per \ cm^2$ traction per cm

$$\{f^{(2)}\} = 10^6 \begin{Bmatrix} 0.03 \\ 0.24 \end{Bmatrix}$$

$$\{F\} = 10^6 \begin{Bmatrix} 0 \\ 0.03 \\ 24 \end{Bmatrix}$$

Thus,

$$[K] = 10^6 \begin{bmatrix} 9.598 & -9.598 & 0 \\ -9.598 & 9.598 + 5.598 & = 5.598 \\ 0 & -5.598 & 5.598 \end{bmatrix}$$

$$= 10^6 \begin{bmatrix} 9.598 & -9.598 & 0 \\ -9.598 & 15.198 & -5.598 \\ 0 & -5.598 & 5.598 \end{bmatrix}$$

Using the global equation, $[K]\{U\} = \{F\}$

$$= 10^6 \begin{bmatrix} 9.598 & -9.598 & 0 \\ -9.598 & 15.198 & -5.598 \\ 0 & -5.598 & 5.598 \end{bmatrix} \begin{Bmatrix} u_1 \\ u_2 \\ u_3 \end{Bmatrix} = 10^6 \begin{Bmatrix} 0 \\ 0.03 \\ 0.24 \end{Bmatrix}$$

Since $u_1 = 0$, is specified, we get

$$= \begin{bmatrix} 1 & 0 & 0 \\ 0 & 15.198 & -5.598 \\ 0 & -5.598 & 5.598 \end{bmatrix} \begin{Bmatrix} u_1 \\ u_2 \\ u_3 \end{Bmatrix} = \begin{Bmatrix} 0 \\ 0.03 \\ 0.24 \end{Bmatrix}$$

The solution is,

$$u_1 = 0, \quad u_2 = 0.0281 \ cm, \quad u_3 = 0.0710 \ cm$$

Problems on Circular Shafts

Example 6.14 Consider a solid circular shaft of length l= 2 m, diameter D= 0.1 m and made of a material with a shear modulus $G = 80(10)^9 \ N/m^2$. The shaft is fixed at one end and subjected to a torsional moment T = 500 Nm at the other end. Determine the angle of twist at the free end of the shaft and the shear stress distribution along the radius using FEM with two elements.

Solution: To solve this problem using FEM, follow these steps:

1. **Discretization**

   Divide the shaft into 2 finite elements of equal length.

2. **Element Stiffness Matrix**

   $$G = 80(10)^9 \ N/m^2$$

   $$J = \frac{\pi D^4}{32} = \frac{\pi(0.1)^4}{32} = 9.82(10^{-7}) \ m^4$$

   L = l/2 = 2/2 = 1 m

   $$\frac{GJ}{L} = \frac{80(10^9)(9.82)(10^{-7})}{1} = 78560$$

   The torsional stiffness matrix for each element of length L and polar moment of inertia J is given by:

   $$\frac{GJ}{L}\begin{bmatrix} 1 & -1 \\ -1 & 1 \end{bmatrix} = 78560 \begin{bmatrix} 1 & -1 \\ -1 & 1 \end{bmatrix}$$

3. Assembly of Global Stiffness

$$
\begin{array}{cccc} 1 & 2 & 2 & 3 \end{array}
$$

$$
78560 \begin{bmatrix} 1 & -1 \\ -1 & 1 \end{bmatrix} \begin{matrix} 1 \\ 2 \end{matrix} \; + \; 78560 \begin{bmatrix} 1 & -1 \\ -1 & 1 \end{bmatrix} \begin{matrix} 2 \\ 3 \end{matrix}
$$

$$
[K] = 78560 \begin{bmatrix} 1 & -1 & 0 \\ -1 & 1+1 & -1 \\ 0 & -1 & 1 \end{bmatrix} \begin{matrix} 1 \\ 2 \\ 3 \end{matrix} \; or \; [K] = 78560 \begin{bmatrix} 1 & -1 & 0 \\ -1 & 2 & -1 \\ 0 & -1 & 1 \end{bmatrix} \begin{matrix} 1 \\ 2 \\ 3 \end{matrix}
$$

Apply the equation,

$[K]\{\theta\} = \{T\}$, we get

$$
78560 \begin{bmatrix} 1 & -1 & 0 \\ -1 & 2 & -1 \\ 0 & -1 & 1 \end{bmatrix} \begin{bmatrix} \theta_1 \\ \theta_2 \\ \theta_3 \end{bmatrix} = \begin{bmatrix} T_1 \\ T_2 \\ T_3 \end{bmatrix}
$$

4. Boundary Conditions

Since the end node 1 is fixed, $\theta_1 = 0.\,Thus,\;we\;delete\;row\;1\;and\;column\;1\;after\;shiftin\;it\;to\;tge\;right\;side.$

Thus,

$$
78560 \begin{bmatrix} 2 & -1 \\ -1 & 1 \end{bmatrix} \begin{bmatrix} \theta_2 \\ \theta_3 \end{bmatrix} = \begin{bmatrix} 0 \\ 500 \end{bmatrix}
$$

5. Solving the System

$$
78560 \begin{bmatrix} 2 & -1 \\ -1 & 1 \end{bmatrix} \begin{bmatrix} \theta_2 \\ \theta_3 \end{bmatrix} = \begin{bmatrix} 0 \\ 500 \end{bmatrix}
$$

We get, $\theta_3 = 0.01273\;rad$ and $\theta_2 = 0.006365\;rad$

Solve the system of equations for the nodal angles of twist

6. Shear Stress Calculation

Calculate the shear stress τ along the radius using:

$$
\tau = \frac{T\,r}{J} = \frac{500(\,0.05)}{9.82(\,10^{-7})} = 2.546(\,10^{7})\,\frac{N}{m^2}
$$

A Simply Supported Beam

Example 6.15 A simply supported beam has a total length of 3 meters. It has its left part equal to 1 m with $EI = 10^{10}\,\dfrac{N}{cm^2}$. *The next part of the beam is 1 m long and has* $EI = 2\left(\dfrac{10^{10}\,N}{cm^2}\right)$. The last part of the beam is 1 m long and has $EI = 10^{10}\,\dfrac{N}{cm^2}$. Divide this beam into three elements with four nodes. Find the the deflection under the beam's nodes.

Solution: The differential equation that applies to this beam is

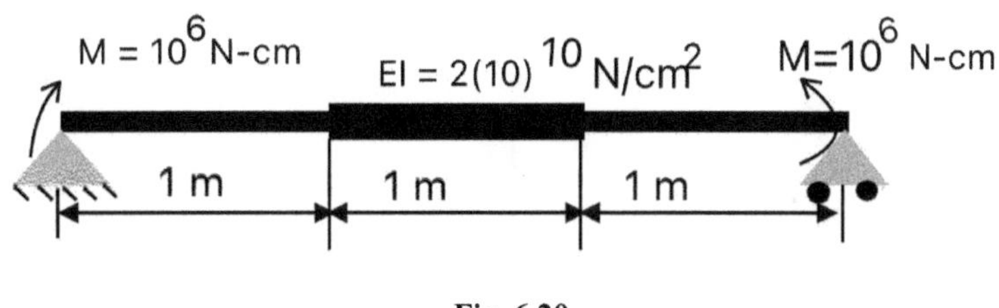

Fig. 6.20

$$EI\,\frac{d^2y}{dx^2} - M = 0.$$ In terms of the equation, we already know, we may write it as

$$D\,\frac{d^2T}{dx^2} + Q = 0,$$ with EI = D and Q = - M and T = y. Note that y stands for nodal deflection.

Note also that y = 0 at nodes 1 and 4. We may now write the nodal equations using the residual equation at the interior nodes 2 and 3.

$$R_j = -\left(\frac{D}{L}\right)^{(e)}_i T_i + \left[\left(\frac{D}{L}\right)^{(e)} + \left(\frac{D}{L}\right)^{(e+1)}\right] T_j - \left(\frac{D}{L}\right)^{(e+1)} T_k - \left(\frac{Q\,L}{2}\right)^{(e)} - \left(\frac{Q\,L}{2}\right)^{(e+1)} = 0$$

$$R_2 = -\left(\frac{10^{10}}{100}\right) y_1 + \left[\left(\frac{10^{10}}{100}\right) + \left(\frac{2\left(10^{10}\right)}{100}\right)\right] y_2 - \left(\frac{2\left(10^{10}\right)}{100}\right) y_3 - \left(\frac{-10^6\,(100)}{2}\right) - \left(\frac{-10^6\,(100)}{2}\right) = 0$$

$$R_3 = -\left(\frac{2\left(10^{10}\right)}{100}\right) y_2 + \left[\left(\frac{2\left(10^{10}\right)}{100}\right) + \left(\frac{\left(10^{10}\right)}{100}\right)\right] y_3 - \left(\frac{\left(10^{10}\right)}{100}\right) y_4 - \left(\frac{-10^6\,(100)}{2}\right) - \left(\frac{-10^6\,(100)}{2}\right) = 0.$$

$$R_2 = -\,y_1 + 3y_2 - 2y_3 + 1 = 0$$

$$R_3 = -\,2y_2 + 3y_3 - y_4 + 1 = 0.$$

Substituting $y_1 = y_4 = 0,$ *we get,*

$$3y_2 - 2y_3 + 1 = 0$$

$$-\,2y_2 + 3y_3 + 1 = 0.$$

Solution of the last two equations gives,

$$y_2 = y_3 = -1 \, cm.$$

The negative value of y indicates that the deflection is in the downward direction.

Alternatively, we could have used the global matrix equation to solve this problem. This is done below:

Element matrices are,

$$\left[k^{(1)}\right] = \frac{10^{10}}{100}\begin{bmatrix} 1 & -1 \\ -1 & 1 \end{bmatrix} = 10^8 \begin{bmatrix} 1 & -1 \\ -1 & 1 \end{bmatrix}$$

$$\left[k^{(2)}\right] = \frac{2 \times 10^{10}}{100}\begin{bmatrix} 1 & -1 \\ -1 & 1 \end{bmatrix} = 2 \times 10^8 \begin{bmatrix} 1 & -1 \\ -1 & 1 \end{bmatrix}$$

$$\left[k^{(3)}\right] = \frac{10^{10}}{100}\begin{bmatrix} 1 & -1 \\ -1 & 1 \end{bmatrix} = 10^8 \begin{bmatrix} 1 & -1 \\ -1 & 1 \end{bmatrix}$$

$$\{f^{(1)}\} = \frac{QL}{2}\begin{Bmatrix} 1 \\ 1 \end{Bmatrix} = \frac{-ML}{2}\begin{Bmatrix} 1 \\ 1 \end{Bmatrix} = \frac{-10^8}{2}\begin{Bmatrix} 1 \\ 1 \end{Bmatrix}$$

$$\{f^{(2)}\} = \frac{QL}{2}\begin{Bmatrix} 1 \\ 1 \end{Bmatrix} = \frac{-ML}{2}\begin{Bmatrix} 1 \\ 1 \end{Bmatrix} = \frac{-10^8}{2}\begin{Bmatrix} 1 \\ 1 \end{Bmatrix}$$

$$\{f^{(3)}\} = \frac{QL}{2}\begin{Bmatrix} 1 \\ 1 \end{Bmatrix} = \frac{-ML}{2}\begin{Bmatrix} 1 \\ 1 \end{Bmatrix} = \frac{-10^8}{2}\begin{Bmatrix} 1 \\ 1 \end{Bmatrix}$$

The assembled matrix [K] is a 4 x 4 matrix shown below

$$[K] = \frac{10^{10}}{100}\begin{bmatrix} 1 & -1 & 0 & 0 \\ -1 & 1+2 & -2 & 0 \\ 0 & -2 & 2+1 & -1 \\ 0 & 0 & -1 & 1 \end{bmatrix} = 10^8 \begin{bmatrix} 1 & -1 & 0 & 0 \\ -1 & 3 & -2 & 0 \\ 0 & -2 & 3 & -1 \\ 0 & 0 & -1 & 1 \end{bmatrix}$$

Similarly, assembled force vector {F} is a 4 x 1 vector

$$\{F\} = \frac{-10^8}{2}\begin{Bmatrix} 1 \\ 2 \\ 2 \\ 1 \end{Bmatrix}$$

Since we must solve $[K]\{y\} = \{F\}$, we write down,

$$10^8 \begin{bmatrix} 1 & -1 & 0 & 0 \\ -1 & 3 & -2 & 0 \\ 0 & -2 & 3 & -1 \\ 0 & 0 & -1 & 1 \end{bmatrix} \begin{Bmatrix} y_1 \\ y_2 \\ y_3 \\ y_4 \end{Bmatrix} = \frac{-10^8}{2} \begin{Bmatrix} 1 \\ 2 \\ 2 \\ 1 \end{Bmatrix}$$

Since y_1 *and* y_4 are zero each, we can remove rows 1 and 4 and also columns 1 and 4. We get the following two equations:

$$3y_2 - 2y_3 = -1$$
$$-2y_2 + 3y_3 = -1$$

Multiplying the second equation by 1.5 and adding these two equations, we get f

$$2.5y_3 = -2.5$$

$$y_3 = -1 \ cm$$

Substituting in the first equation,

$$3y_2 = 2(y_3) - 1 = 2(-1) - 1 = -3$$

Therefore, $y_2 = \dfrac{-3}{3} = -1 \ cm.$

CHAPTER 7:

FLUID FLOW AND ELECTRIC FLOW CIRCUITS

Let us consider one element of a pipe in which a fluid is flowing. The fluid is entering the element at pressure P_1 and leaving at pressure P_2. The element length is L. This element offers resistance to the fluid flowing through it. The *Pipe resistance to flow*, $R = \dfrac{128\,\mu\,L}{\pi\,d^4}$.

The element is shown in **Fig.7**. 1. Note that μ is dynamic viscosity of the fluid and d is the pipe diameter.

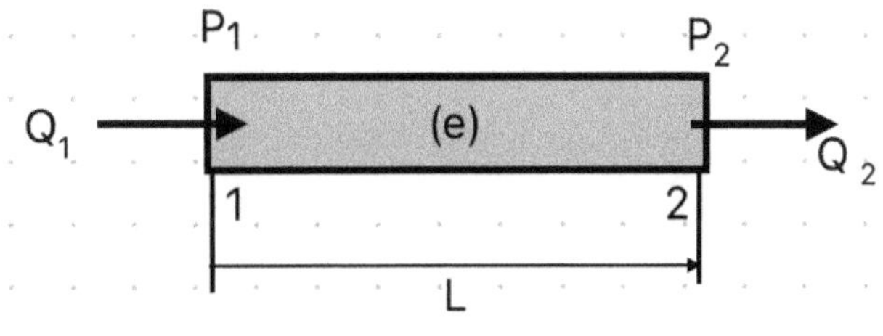

Fig. 7.1

Now we will consider the following problem of water flow:

Example 7.1 A pipe is made up of three sections, each of length 1 m. The three sections of the pipe are shown below. Data pertaining to the sections of the pipe is shown in the Fig. 7.1. given below. Find the pressure at the points where sections join. Pressure of the fluid at the entrance to the pipe is 10 m of fluid. At the exit the pressure is 1 m of fluid head. Find the pressure at the remaining joining sections.

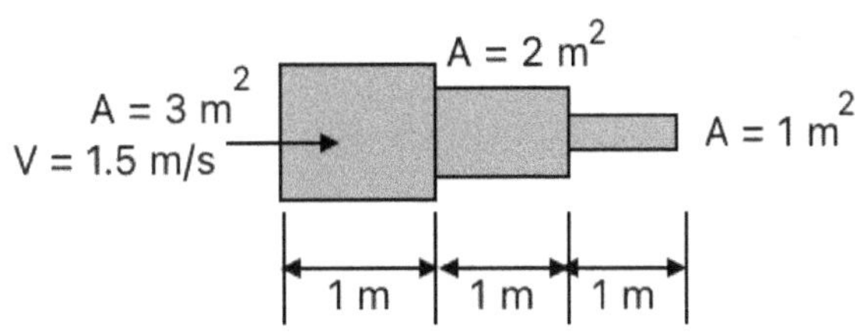

Fig. 7.1

We assume that the pipe resistance are $\dfrac{1}{3c}$, $\dfrac{1}{2c}$ and $\dfrac{1}{1c}$ respectively.

In the analysis of fluid or electric circuits, we generally use inverse of resistances. Thus,

$$\left[k^{(1)}\right] = 3\,c \begin{bmatrix} 1 & -1 \\ -1 & 1 \end{bmatrix} = c \begin{bmatrix} 3 & -3 \\ -3 & 3 \end{bmatrix},$$

$$\left[k^{(2)}\right] = 2\,c \begin{bmatrix} 1 & -1 \\ -1 & 1 \end{bmatrix} = c \begin{bmatrix} 2 & -2 \\ -2 & 2 \end{bmatrix}$$

$$\left[k^{(3)}\right] = 1\,c \begin{bmatrix} 1 & -1 \\ -1 & 1 \end{bmatrix} = c \begin{bmatrix} 1 & -1 \\ -1 & 1 \end{bmatrix}$$

$$[K] = c \begin{bmatrix} 3 & -3 & & \\ -3 & 3+2 & -2 & 0 \\ 0 & 0 & -2 & 2+1 & -1 \\ 0 & 0 & & -1 & 1 \end{bmatrix} \begin{Bmatrix} 1 \\ 2 \\ 3 \\ 4 \end{Bmatrix}$$

Or

$$[K] = c \begin{bmatrix} 3 & -3 & 0 & 0 \\ -3 & 5 & -2 & -1 \\ 0 & -2 & 3 & -1 \\ 0 & 0 & -1 & 1 \end{bmatrix}$$

The global equation $[K]\{p\} = \{Q\}$ *becomes*

$$c \begin{bmatrix} 3 & -3 & 0 & 0 \\ -3 & 5 & -2 & -1 \\ 0 & -2 & 3 & -1 \\ 0 & 0 & -1 & 1 \end{bmatrix} \begin{Bmatrix} P_1 \\ P_2 \\ P_3 \\ P_4 \end{Bmatrix} = \begin{Bmatrix} Q_2 \\ Q_2 \\ Q_3 \\ Q_4 \end{Bmatrix}$$

$$c \begin{bmatrix} 3 & -3 & 0 & 0 \\ -3 & 5 & -2 & -1 \\ 0 & -2 & 3 & -1 \\ 0 & 0 & -1 & 1 \end{bmatrix} \begin{Bmatrix} 10 \\ P_2 \\ P_3 \\ 1 \end{Bmatrix} = \begin{Bmatrix} 4.6 \\ 0 \\ 0 \\ 4.5 \end{Bmatrix}$$

Assuming that $c = 1$, *we get*

$$\begin{bmatrix} 3 & -3 & 0 & 0 \\ -3 & 5 & -2 & -1 \\ 0 & -2 & 3 & -1 \\ 0 & 0 & -1 & 1 \end{bmatrix} \begin{Bmatrix} 10 \\ P_2 \\ P_3 \\ 1 \end{Bmatrix} = \begin{Bmatrix} 4.5 \\ 0 \\ 0 \\ 4.5 \end{Bmatrix}$$

Note that at the nodes 2 and 3 the net flow rates are assumed as zero each because of steady flow. Also, it is known that the pressures are 4.5 m of fluid head and 1 m of fluid head respectively.

Since p_1 and p_4 are known, we delete rows 1 and 4 and modify

the remaining rows. we thus get,

$$\begin{bmatrix} 3 & -3 & 0 & 0 \\ -3 & 5 & -2 & -1 \\ 0 & -2 & 3 & -1 \\ 0 & 0 & -1 & 1 \end{bmatrix} \begin{Bmatrix} 10 \\ p_2 \\ p_3 \\ 1 \end{Bmatrix} = \begin{Bmatrix} 4.5 \\ 0 \\ 0 \\ 4.5 \end{Bmatrix}$$

$$\begin{bmatrix} 3 & -3 & 0 & 0 \\ -3 & 5 & -2 & -1 \\ 0 & -2 & 3 & -1 \\ 0 & 0 & -1 & 1 \end{bmatrix} \begin{Bmatrix} 10 \\ p_2 \\ p_3 \\ 1 \end{Bmatrix} = \begin{Bmatrix} 4.5 \\ 0 \\ 0 \\ 4.5 \end{Bmatrix}$$

Or

$$5p_2 - 2p_3 = 31$$

$$-2p_2 + 3p_3 = 1$$

Or

$$10p_2 - 4p_3 = 62$$

$$-10p_2 + 15p_3 = 5$$

Thus,

$$p_2 = 8.636 \, m$$

$$p_3 = 6.09 \, m$$

Example 7.2 A fluid flows steadily in the fluid circuit shown below. Find the pressure at the nodes 1,2 and 4. Fluid flow rates and flow resistances in the pipelines are given in the figure. Inverse of resistances is used in the solution. Value of c = 1.

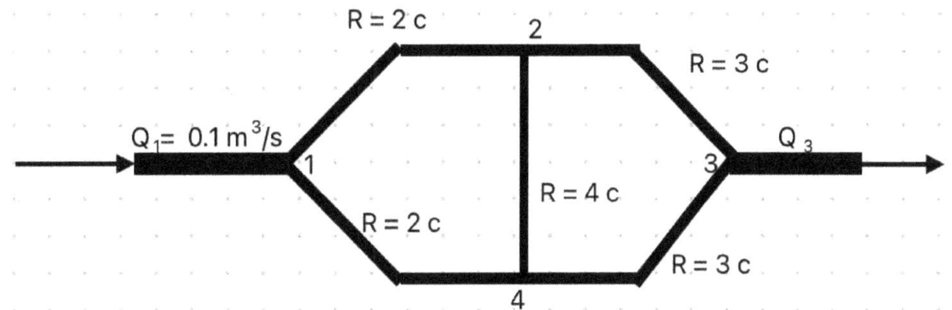

A system of pipes with fluid flowing through them

Fig. 7.2

Solution: We will use reciprocal of each resistance. There are four nodes.

$$[K] = \frac{1}{12\,c}\begin{bmatrix} \dfrac{1}{2\,c}+\dfrac{1}{2c} & -\dfrac{1}{2c} & 0 & -\dfrac{1}{2\,c} \\[2mm] -\dfrac{1}{2\,c} & \dfrac{1}{2\,c}+\dfrac{1}{4\,c}+\dfrac{1}{3\,c} & -\dfrac{1}{3\,c} & -\dfrac{1}{4\,c} \\[2mm] 0 & -\dfrac{1}{3\,c} & \dfrac{1}{3\,c}+\dfrac{1}{3\,c} & -\dfrac{1}{4\,c} \\[2mm] -\dfrac{1}{2\,c} & -\dfrac{1}{4\,c} & -\dfrac{1}{3\,c} & \dfrac{1}{2\,c}+\dfrac{1}{4\,c}+\dfrac{1}{3\,c} \end{bmatrix}$$

$$[K] = \frac{1}{12\,c}\begin{bmatrix} 6+6 & -6 & 0 & -6 \\ -6 & 6+3+4 & -4 & -3 \\ 0 & -4 & 4+4 & -4 \\ -6 & -3 & -4 & 6+3+4 \end{bmatrix}$$

$$= \frac{1}{12\,c}\begin{bmatrix} 12 & -6 & 0 & -6 \\ -6 & 13 & -4 & -3 \\ 0 & -4 & 8 & -4 \\ -6 & -3 & -4 & 13 \end{bmatrix}\begin{Bmatrix} P_1 \\ P_2 \\ P_3 \\ P_4 \end{Bmatrix} = \begin{Bmatrix} Q_1 \\ Q_2 \\ Q_3 \\ Q_4 \end{Bmatrix}$$

Using the given conditions,

$c = 1,\ p_3 = 0,\ Q_1 = 0.1,\ Q_3 = 0.1$ *and taking the flow rate as zero*

at the interior nodes 2 and 4 , we get

$$\begin{bmatrix} 12 & -6 & 0 & -6 \\ -6 & 13 & 0 & -3 \\ 0 & 0 & 8 & 0 \\ -6 & -3 & 0 & 13 \end{bmatrix}\begin{Bmatrix} P_1 \\ P_2 \\ 0 \\ P_4 \end{Bmatrix} = \begin{Bmatrix} 12(\,0.1) \\ 0 \\ 12(\,0.1) \\ 0 \end{Bmatrix}$$

The equations to solve are,

$$12\,p_1 - 6\,p_2 - 6\,p_4 = 1.2$$

$$-6\,p_1 + 13\,p_2 - 3\,p_4 = 0$$

$$-6\,p_1 - 3\,p_2 + 13\,p_4 = 0$$

The solution is,

$$p_1 = 0.25;\ p_2 = 0.15;\ p_4 = 0.15 \quad \text{(All gage pressures)}$$

Example 7.3 We are given that in the following fluid flow circuit,

$$R_1 = 2\,v,\ R_2 = 3\,v,\ R_3 = 2\,v,\ R_4 = 2\,v\ and\ R_5 = 6\,v.$$

We are asked to calculate flow rates and nodal pressures.

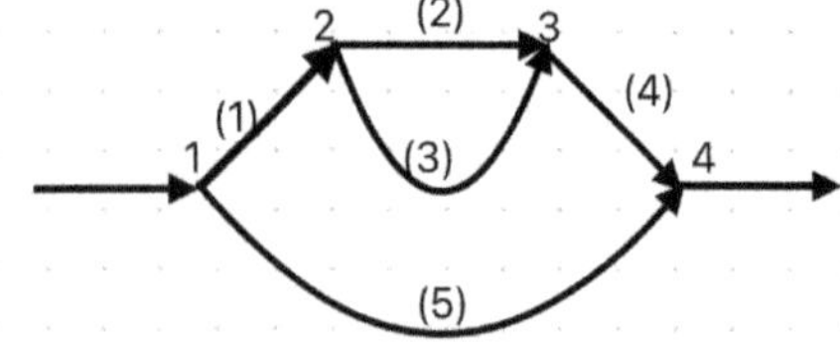

Fig. 7.3

Element matrices are,

$$
[k^{(1)}] = \frac{1}{v}
\begin{array}{cc}
\quad 1 & \quad 2 \\
\begin{bmatrix} \dfrac{1}{2} & \dfrac{-1}{2} \\[2ex] \dfrac{-1}{2} & \dfrac{1}{2} \end{bmatrix} & \begin{array}{c} 1 \\[3ex] 2 \end{array}
\end{array}
+ \frac{1}{v}
\begin{array}{cc}
\quad 1 & \quad 4 \\
\begin{bmatrix} \dfrac{1}{6} & \dfrac{-1}{6} \\[2ex] \dfrac{-1}{6} & \dfrac{1}{6} \end{bmatrix} & \begin{array}{c} 1 \\[3ex] 4 \end{array}
\end{array}
$$

$$
[k^{(2)}] = \frac{1}{v}
\begin{array}{cc}
\quad 2 & \quad 3 \\
\begin{bmatrix} \dfrac{1}{3} & \dfrac{-1}{3} \\[2ex] \dfrac{-1}{3} & \dfrac{1}{3} \end{bmatrix} & \begin{array}{c} 2 \\[3ex] 3 \end{array}
\end{array}
+ \frac{1}{v}
\begin{array}{cc}
\quad 2 & \quad 3 \\
\begin{bmatrix} \dfrac{1}{2} & \dfrac{-1}{2} \\[2ex] \dfrac{-1}{2} & \dfrac{1}{2} \end{bmatrix} & \begin{array}{c} 2 \\[3ex] 3 \end{array}
\end{array}
$$

$$
[k^{(3)}] = \frac{1}{v}
\begin{array}{cc}
\quad 3 & \quad 4 \\
\begin{bmatrix} \dfrac{1}{2} & \dfrac{-1}{2} \\[2ex] \dfrac{-1}{2} & \dfrac{1}{2} \end{bmatrix} & \begin{array}{c} 3 \\[3ex] 4 \end{array}
\end{array}
$$

Thus,

$$
[K] = \frac{1}{v}
\begin{array}{cccc}
\quad\quad 1 & \quad\quad 2 & \quad\quad 3 & \quad\quad 4 \\
\begin{bmatrix}
\dfrac{1}{2}+\dfrac{1}{6} & \dfrac{-1}{2} & 0 & \dfrac{-1}{6} \\[2.5ex]
\dfrac{-1}{2} & \dfrac{1}{2}+\dfrac{1}{3}+\dfrac{1}{2} & -\dfrac{1}{3}-\dfrac{1}{2} & 0 \\[2.5ex]
0 & \dfrac{-1}{3}-\dfrac{1}{2} & \dfrac{1}{3}+\dfrac{1}{2}+\dfrac{1}{2} & \dfrac{-1}{2} \\[2.5ex]
\dfrac{-1}{6} & 0 & \dfrac{-1}{2} & \dfrac{1}{6}+\dfrac{1}{2}
\end{bmatrix}
&
\begin{array}{c} 1 \\[3ex] 2 \\[3ex] 3 \\[3ex] 4 \end{array}
\end{array}
$$

Or

$$
[K] = \frac{1}{v}
\begin{bmatrix}
\dfrac{2}{3} & \dfrac{-1}{2} & 0 & \dfrac{-1}{6} \\[2.5ex]
\dfrac{-1}{2} & \dfrac{4}{3} & -\dfrac{5}{6} & 0 \\[2.5ex]
0 & \dfrac{-5}{6} & \dfrac{4}{3} & \dfrac{-1}{2} \\[2.5ex]
\dfrac{-1}{6} & 0 & \dfrac{-1}{2} & \dfrac{1}{3}
\end{bmatrix}
$$

We can now solve the global equation, $[K]\{P\} = \{Q\}$, if the boundary conditions are given.

$$
[K] =
\begin{bmatrix}
4 & -3 & 0 & -1 \\
-3 & 8 & -5 & 0 \\
0 & -5 & 8 & -3 \\
-1 & 0 & -3 & 2
\end{bmatrix}
\begin{Bmatrix} P_1 \\ P_2 \\ P_3 \\ P_4 \end{Bmatrix}
=
\begin{Bmatrix} 6vQ_1 \\ 6vQ_2 \\ 6vQ_3 \\ 6vQ_4 \end{Bmatrix}
$$

Applying the conditions, $P_4 = 0$; $Q_2 = 0$ and $Q_3 = 0$, we get,

$$\begin{bmatrix} 4 & -3 & 0 \\ -3 & 8 & -5 \\ 0 & -5 & 8 \end{bmatrix} \begin{Bmatrix} P_1 \\ P_2 \\ P_3 \end{Bmatrix} = \begin{Bmatrix} 6 v Q \\ 0 \\ 0 \end{Bmatrix}$$

Solution is: $P_1 = \dfrac{39}{14} v Q$, $P_2 = \dfrac{24}{14} v Q$, $P_3 = \dfrac{15}{14} v Q$.

Electrical Circuits

An electrical circuit is shown here. We will analyse this circuit using the finite element method and find the values of *voltage* V_2 *and resistance* R.

Example 7.4

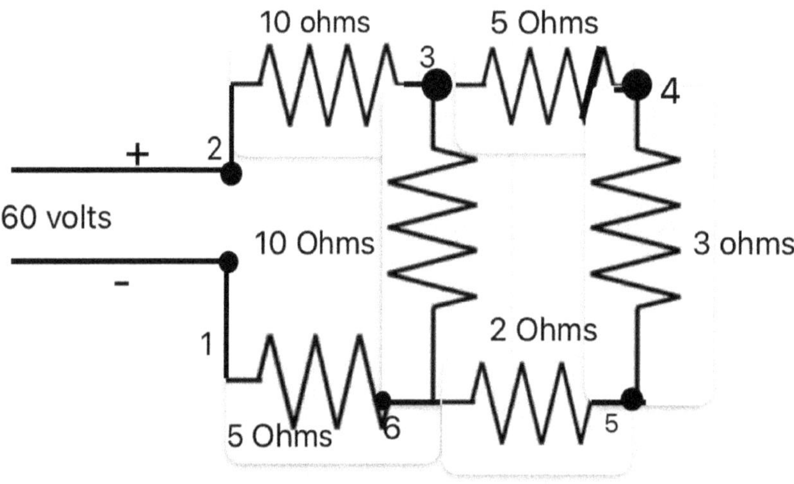

Fig. 7.4

Solution: We will use reciprocals of resistances. Let us first number the nodes as shown in the above figure. We assume the voltage at node 1 as zero and that at node 2 as 60 volts. The net nodal currents at nodal junctions 3, 4, 5 and 6 will be taken as zero.

$$\begin{bmatrix} 0.2 & 0 & 0 & 0 & 0 & -0.2 \\ 0 & 0.1 & -0.1 & 0 & 0 & 0 \\ 0 & -0.1 & 0.1+0.2+0.1 & -0.2 & 0 & -0.1 \\ 0 & 0 & -0.2 & 0.2+0.333 & -0.333 & 0 \\ 0 & 0 & 0 & -0.333 & 0.333+0.5 & -0.5 \\ -0.2 & 0 & -0.1 & 0 & -0.5 & 0.5+0.1+0.2 \end{bmatrix} \begin{Bmatrix} 0 \\ 60 \\ V_3 \\ V_4 \\ V_5 \\ V_6 \end{Bmatrix} = \begin{Bmatrix} I_1 \\ I_2 \\ 0 \\ 0 \\ 0 \\ 0 \end{Bmatrix}$$

Note in the above table that $V_1 = 0$

We thus delete row 1 and modify others as shown below:

$$\begin{bmatrix} 0.1 & -0.1 & 0 & 0 & 0 \\ -0.1 & 0.1+0.2+0.1 & -0.2 & 0 & -0.1 \\ 0 & -0.2 & 0.2+0.333 & -0.333 & 0 \\ 0 & 0 & -0.333 & 0.333+0.5 & -0.5 \\ 0 & -0.1 & 0 & -0.5 & 0.5+0.1+0.2 \end{bmatrix} \begin{Bmatrix} 60 \\ V_3 \\ V_4 \\ V_5 \\ V_6 \end{Bmatrix} = \begin{Bmatrix} I_2+0 \\ 0 \\ 0 \\ 0 \\ 0 \end{Bmatrix}$$

Note in the above table that $V_2 = 60 = 0$. We thus delete row 2 and modify others as shown below:

$$\begin{bmatrix} 0.1+0.2+0.1 & -0.2 & 0 & -0.1 \\ -0.2 & 0.2+0.333 & -0.333 & 0 \\ 0 & -0.333 & 0.333+0.5 & -0.5 \\ -0.1 & 0 & -0.5 & 0.5+0.1+0.2 \end{bmatrix} \begin{Bmatrix} V_3 \\ V_4 \\ V_5 \\ V_6 \end{Bmatrix} = \begin{Bmatrix} 6 \\ 0 \\ 0 \\ 0 \end{Bmatrix}$$

Thus, the system of equations using FEM using the above table gives,

$0.4\,x - 0.2\,y - 0.1\,w = 6$

$-0.2\,x + 0.5333\,y - 0.333\,z = 0$

$-0.333\,y + 0.8333\,z - 0.5\,w = 0$

$-0.1\,x - 0.5\,z + 0.8\,w = 0$

The solution the above system of equations is

$V_3 = x = 29.96$

$V_4 = y = 22.44$

$V_5 = z = 17.94$

$V_6 = z = 14.96$

Example 7.5 Solve the electrical circuit shown below:

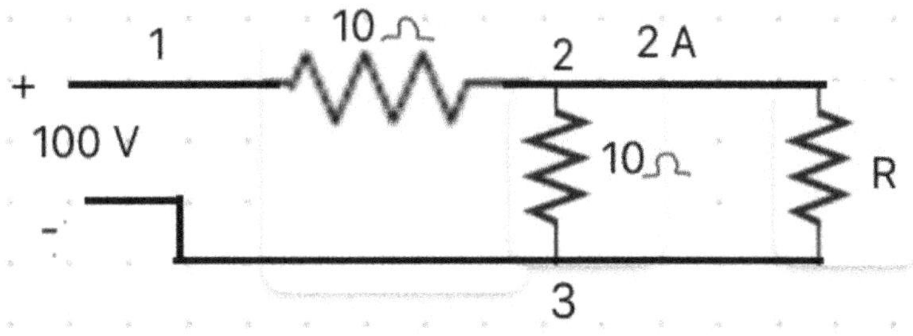

Fig.7.5

Solution: We begin by labeling the elements and the nodes. There are three elements and 3 and 3 nodes. Then we write element matrices using reciprocal resistances.

$$[k^{(1)}] = \begin{array}{cc} & \begin{array}{cc} 1 & 2 \end{array} \\ \left[\begin{array}{cc} 0.1 & -0.1 \\ -0.1 & 0.1 \end{array}\right] & \begin{array}{c} 1 \\ 2 \end{array} \end{array}$$

$$[k^{(2)}] = \begin{array}{cc} & \begin{array}{cc} 2 & 3 \end{array} \\ \left[\begin{array}{cc} \dfrac{1}{R} & -\dfrac{1}{R} \\ -\dfrac{1}{R} & \dfrac{1}{R} \end{array}\right] & \begin{array}{c} 2 \\ 3 \end{array} \end{array}$$

$$[k^{(3)}] = \begin{array}{cc} & \begin{array}{cc} 2 & 3 \end{array} \\ \left[\begin{array}{cc} 0.1 & -0.1 \\ -0.1 & 0.1 \end{array}\right] & \begin{array}{c} 2 \\ 3 \end{array} \end{array}$$

$$[K] = \begin{array}{ccc} 1 & \quad 2 & \quad 3 \end{array}$$

$$[K] = \left[\begin{array}{ccc} 0.1 & -0.1 & 0 \\ -0.1 & 0.1+\dfrac{1}{R}+0.1 & \dfrac{-1}{R}-0.1 \\ 0 & \dfrac{-1}{R}-0.1 & \dfrac{1}{R}+0.1 \end{array}\right] \left\{\begin{array}{c} V_1 \\ V_2 \\ V_3 \end{array}\right\} = \left\{\begin{array}{c} I_1 \\ I_2 \\ I_3 \end{array}\right\}$$

Since it is given that $V_1 = 100$, we delete row 1 and modify others as shown below:

$$\left[\begin{array}{cc} 0.1+\dfrac{1}{R}+0.1 & \dfrac{-1}{R}-0.1 \\ \dfrac{-1}{R}-0.1 & \dfrac{1}{R}+0.1 \end{array}\right] \left\{\begin{array}{c} V_2 \\ V_3 \end{array}\right\} = \left\{\begin{array}{c} 10 \\ I_3 \end{array}\right\}$$

Since it is given that $V_3 = 0$, we delete row 3 and modify others as shown below:

$$\left[\begin{array}{c} 0.1+\dfrac{1}{R}+0.1 \end{array}\right] \left\{\begin{array}{c} V_2 \end{array}\right\} = \left\{\begin{array}{c} 10 \end{array}\right\}$$

Now we are left with one equation,

$$\left(0.2+\dfrac{1}{R}\right)(V_2) = 10.$$

We get,

$$0.2+\dfrac{2}{V_2} = \dfrac{10}{V_2}$$

or

$$0.2 = \dfrac{10}{V_2} - \dfrac{2}{V_2} = \dfrac{8}{V_2}$$

Thus, $V_2 = \dfrac{8}{0.2} = 40$

Substituting in the equation $\left(0.2 + \dfrac{1}{R}\right) V_2 = 10,$

$\left(0.2 + \dfrac{1}{R}\right)(40) = 10,$

or $\dfrac{1}{R} = \dfrac{10}{40} - 0.2 = 0.25 - 0.20 = 0.05$

or $R = \dfrac{1}{0.05} = 20 \ Ohms.$

Example 7.6 Solve the electrical circuit. shown in Fig. 7.4

Solution: We will use reciprocals of resistances. We begin by labeling the elements and the nodes. Then we write down the assembled stiffness matrix.

$$\left[k^{(1)}\right] = \begin{bmatrix} 0.1 & -0.1 \\ -0.1 & 0.1 \end{bmatrix} \begin{matrix} 1 \\ 2 \end{matrix} \quad \begin{matrix} 1 \quad\ 2 \end{matrix}$$

$$\left[k^{(2)}\right] = \begin{bmatrix} 0.1 & -0.1 \\ -0.1 & 0.1 \end{bmatrix} \begin{matrix} 2 \\ 3 \end{matrix} \quad \begin{matrix} 2 \quad\ 3 \end{matrix}$$

$$\left[k^{(3)}\right] = \begin{bmatrix} 0.1 & -0.1 \\ -0.1 & 0.1 \end{bmatrix} \begin{matrix} 3 \\ 4 \end{matrix} \quad \begin{matrix} 3 \quad\ 4 \end{matrix}$$

$$\left[k^{(4)}\right] = \begin{bmatrix} 0.1 & -0.1 \\ -0.1 & 0.1 \end{bmatrix} \begin{matrix} 2 \\ 4 \end{matrix} \quad \begin{matrix} 2 \quad\ 4 \end{matrix}$$

$$\left[k^{(5)}\right] = \begin{bmatrix} 0.1 & -0.1 \\ -0.1 & 0.1 \end{bmatrix} \begin{matrix} 1 \\ 5 \end{matrix} \quad \begin{matrix} 1 \quad\ 5 \end{matrix}$$

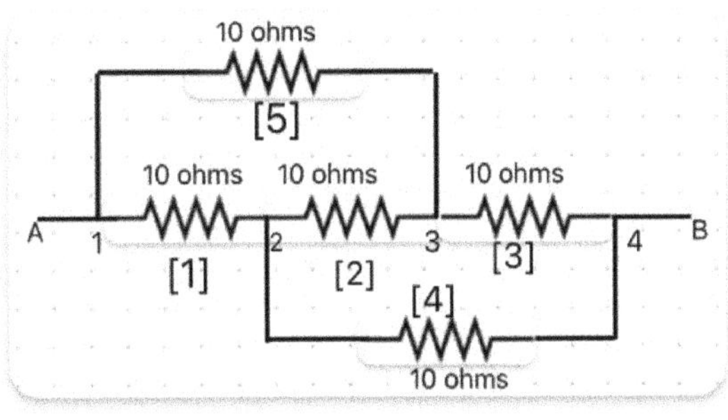

Fig. 7.6

$$[K] = \begin{array}{c} \quad\; 1 \qquad\qquad 2 \qquad\qquad\quad 3 \qquad\qquad 4 \\ \begin{bmatrix} 0.1+0.1 & -0.1 & -0.1 & \\ -0.1 & 0.1+0.1+0.1 & -0.1 & -0.1 \\ -0.1 & -0.1 & 0.1+0.1+0.1 & -0.1 \\ & & -0.1-0.1 & 0.1+0.1 \end{bmatrix} \begin{array}{c} 1 \\ 2 \\ 3 \\ 4 \end{array} \end{array}$$

$$[K] = \begin{array}{c} \; 1 \quad\;\; 2 \quad\;\; 3 \quad\;\; 4 \\ \begin{bmatrix} 0.2 & -0.1 & -0.1 & 0 \\ -0.1 & 0.3 & -0.1 & -0.1 \\ -0.1 & -0.1 & 0.3 & -0.1 \\ 0 & -0.1 & -0.1 & 0.2 \end{bmatrix} \begin{array}{c} 1 \\ 2 \\ 3 \\ 4 \end{array} \end{array}$$

Thus, *The global force equation*, $[K]\{V\} = \{I\}$ *gives,*

$$\begin{bmatrix} 0.2 & -0.1 & -0.1 & 0 \\ -0.1 & 0.3 & -0.1 & -0.1 \\ -0.1 & -0.1 & 0.3 & -0.1 \\ 0 & -0.1 & -0.1 & 0.2 \end{bmatrix} \begin{Bmatrix} V_1 \\ V_2 \\ V_3 \\ V_4 \end{Bmatrix} = \begin{Bmatrix} I_1 \\ I_2 \\ I_3 \\ I_4 \end{Bmatrix}$$

Since $V_1 = 100$ *and* $V_3 = 0$, we remove row 1 row and row 4 except for the diagonal terms. The product of v_1 with the diagonal term in the first row is used to replace I_1 in the right-most column. Similarly, the product of V4 with the diagonal term in the fourth row is used to replace I4 in the right-most column.

Since I2 and I3 are nodal current, these should be taken as zero each. Thus,

$$\begin{bmatrix} 0.2 & 0 & 0 & 0 \\ -0.1 & 0.3 & -0.1 & -0.1 \\ -0.1 & -0.1 & 0.3 & -0.1 \\ 0 & 0 & 0 & 0.2 \end{bmatrix} \begin{Bmatrix} 100 \\ V_2 \\ V_3 \\ 0 \end{Bmatrix} = \begin{Bmatrix} 20 \\ 0 \\ 0 \\ 0 \end{Bmatrix}$$

Shift the product of the remaining terms of column 1 with v_1 to the right-most column to replace I_1. Similarly, Shift the product of the remaining terms of column 4 with v_4 to the right-most column to replace I_4.

Similarly, shift the product of the remaining terms of column 4 with v_4 to the right-most column.

$$\begin{bmatrix} 0.2 & 0 & 0 & 0 \\ 0 & 0.3 & -0.1 & 0 \\ 0 & -0.1 & 0.3 & 0 \\ 0 & 0 & 0 & 0.2 \end{bmatrix} \begin{Bmatrix} 100 \\ V_2 \\ V_3 \\ 0 \end{Bmatrix} = \begin{Bmatrix} 20 \\ 10 \\ 10 \\ 0 \end{Bmatrix}$$

Now we solve the above set of equations. Here we have just two equations to solve,

$$0.3\,V_2 - 0.1\,V_3 = 10$$

$$-0.1\,V_2 + 0.3\,V_3 = 10$$

Thus, $V_2 = 50$ *and* $V_3 = 50$

Example 7.7 An electrical circuit is shown below. The node numbers and the resistances shown in the circuit elements. Find the voltages at all nodes.

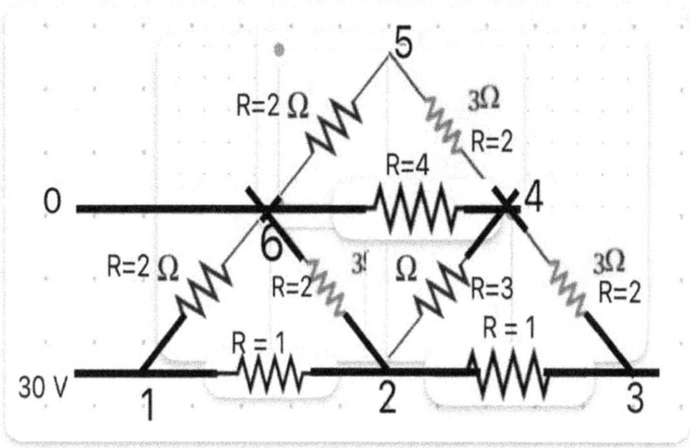

Fig. 7.7

Solution: We will use reciprocal of each given resistance.

$$[K] = \begin{bmatrix} 1+0.5 & -1 & 0 & 0 & 0 & -0.5 \\ -1 & 1+1+0.333+0.5 & -1 & -0.333 & 0 & -0.5 \\ 0 & -1 & 1+0.5 & -0.5 & 0 & 0 \\ 0 & -0.333 & -0.5 & 0.5++0.333+0.25+0.5 & -0.5 & -0.25 \\ 0 & 0 & 0 & -0.5 & 0.5+0.5 & -0.5 \\ -0.5 & -0.5 & 0 & -0.25 & -0.5 & 0.25+0.5+0.5+0.5 \end{bmatrix}$$

$$= \begin{bmatrix} 1.5 & -1 & 0 & 0 & 0 & -0.5 \\ -1 & 2.83 & -1 & -0.333 & 0 & -0.5 \\ 0 & -1 & 1.5 & -0.5 & 0 & 0 \\ 0 & -0.333 & -0.5 & 1.583 & -0.5 & -0.25 \\ 0 & 0 & 0 & -0.5 & 1 & -0.5 \\ -0.5 & -0.5 & 0 & -0.25 & -0.5 & 1.75 \end{bmatrix}$$

$$\{V\} = \begin{Bmatrix} V_1 \\ V_2 \\ V_3 \\ V_4 \\ V_5 \\ V_6 \end{Bmatrix}, \quad \{I\} = \begin{Bmatrix} I_1 \\ I_2 \\ I_3 \\ I_4 \\ I_5 \\ I_6 \end{Bmatrix}$$

Matrix [K] stands for inverse of circuit resistances. Its product with voltage vector will give current vector.

After substituting known values, the global equation to solve, that is, $[K]\{V\} = \{I\}$ *is,*

$$
\begin{bmatrix}
1.5 & -1 & 0 & 0 & 0 & -0.5 \\
-1 & 2.83 & -1 & -0.333 & 0 & -0.5 \\
0 & -1 & 1.5 & -0.5 & 0 & 0 \\
0 & -0.333 & -0.5 & 1.583 & -0.5 & -0.25 \\
0 & 0 & 0 & -0.5 & 1 & -0.5 \\
-0.5 & -0.5 & 0 & -0.25 & -0.5 & 1.75
\end{bmatrix}
\begin{Bmatrix}
V_1 \\ V_2 \\ V_3 \\ V_4 \\ V_5 \\ V_6
\end{Bmatrix}
=
\begin{Bmatrix}
I_1 \\ I_2 \\ I_3 \\ I_4 \\ I_5 \\ I_6
\end{Bmatrix}
$$

We can put nodal current as zero at each interior node. This is because of the reason that the Inflow current = outflow current at each interior node.

Note in the above table that $V_1 = 30$ as given

We thus delete row 1 and modify others as shown below:

$$
\begin{bmatrix}
2.83 & -1 & -0.333 & 0 & -0.5 \\
-1 & 1.5 & -0.5 & 0 & 0 \\
-0.333 & -0.5 & 1.583 & -0.5 & -0.25 \\
0 & 0 & -0.5 & 1 & -0.5 \\
-0.5 & 0 & -0.25 & -0.5 & 1.75
\end{bmatrix}
\begin{Bmatrix}
V_2 \\ V_3 \\ V_4 \\ V_5 \\ V_6
\end{Bmatrix}
=
\begin{Bmatrix}
30 \\ I_3 \\ I_4 \\ I_5 \\ 15
\end{Bmatrix}
$$

Note in the above table that $V_6 = 0$ as given

We thus delete row 6 and modify others as shown below:

$$
\begin{bmatrix}
2.83 & -1 & -0.333 & 0 & 0 \\
-1 & 1.5 & -0.5 & 0 & 0 \\
-0.333 & -0.5 & 1.583 & -0.5 & 0 \\
0 & 0 & -0.5 & 1 & 0
\end{bmatrix}
\begin{Bmatrix}
V_2 \\ V_3 \\ V_4 \\ V_5
\end{Bmatrix}
=
\begin{Bmatrix}
0 \\ 0 \\ 7.5 \\ 15
\end{Bmatrix}
$$

Or

$$2.83\, V_2 - V_3 - 0.333\, V_4 = 0$$

$$-1\, V_2 + 1.5\, V_3 - 0.5\, V_4 = 0$$

$$-0.333\, V_2 - 0.5\, V_3 + 1.583\, V_4 - 0.5\, V_5 = 7.5$$

$$-0.5\, V_4 + V_5 = 15$$

The solution of the above set of algebraic equations gives,

$$V_2 = 4.807;\ V_3 = 8.407\,;\ V_4 = 15.607;\ V_5 = 22.804$$

We already know that $V_1 = 0$ *and* $V_6 = 30$.

CHAPTER 8

THREE-DIMENSIONAL PROBLEMS APPROXIMATED AS TWO-DIMENSIONAL PROBLEMS

Some Important Relations

Gradient Matrix, [B]

Let us consider temperature T inside a linear line element (e) with two nodes i and j.

The nodal temperatures are T_i and T_j. Thus, $T = N_i T_i + N_j T_j$, where N_i and N_j are shape functions of the element (e).

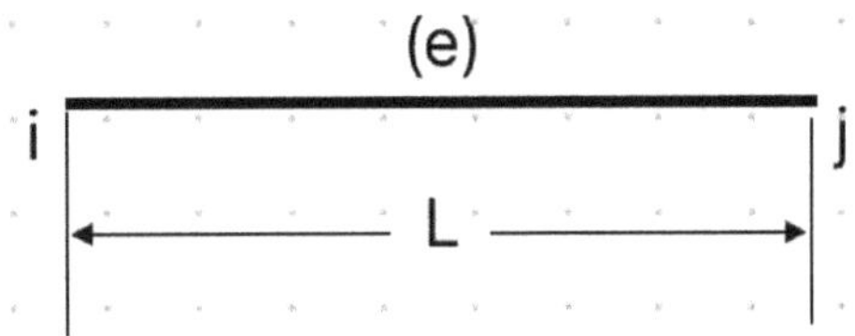

Rewriting T, we get, $T = \begin{bmatrix} N \end{bmatrix} \begin{Bmatrix} T_i \\ T_j \end{Bmatrix}$,

$$\frac{dT}{dx} = \begin{bmatrix} \dfrac{dN_i}{dx} & \dfrac{dN_j}{dx} \end{bmatrix} \begin{Bmatrix} T_i \\ T_j \end{Bmatrix}$$

$$= \begin{bmatrix} -\dfrac{1}{L} & \dfrac{1}{L} \end{bmatrix} \begin{Bmatrix} T_i \\ T_j \end{Bmatrix}$$

$$= \frac{1}{L} \begin{bmatrix} -1 & 1 \end{bmatrix} \begin{Bmatrix} T_i \\ T_j \end{Bmatrix}$$

Heat flux or heat conduction per unit area in the positive x direction $= -k\dfrac{dT}{dx}$

$$= -k\frac{1}{L}\begin{bmatrix} -1 & 1 \end{bmatrix}\begin{Bmatrix} T_i \\ T_j \end{Bmatrix} = -k\,[B]\begin{Bmatrix} T_i \\ T_j \end{Bmatrix}, \text{ where } [B] = \frac{1}{L}\begin{bmatrix} -1 & 1 \end{bmatrix} \text{ is called the gradient matrix.}$$

Stress-Strain Relationship [D] in 3 dimensions

$$\begin{Bmatrix} \sigma_x \\ \sigma_y \\ \sigma_z \\ \tau_{xy} \\ \tau_{yz} \\ \tau_{zx} \end{Bmatrix} = \frac{E}{(1+\mu)(1-2\mu)}\begin{bmatrix} 1-\mu & \mu & \mu & 0 & 0 & 0 \\ \mu & 1-\mu & \mu & 0 & 0 & 0 \\ \mu & \mu & 1-\mu & 0 & 0 & 0 \\ 0 & 0 & 0 & \frac{1}{2}-\mu & 0 & 0 \\ 0 & 0 & 0 & 0 & \frac{1}{2}-\mu & 0 \\ 0 & 0 & 0 & 0 & 0 & \frac{1}{2}-\mu \end{bmatrix}\begin{Bmatrix} e_x \\ e_y \\ e_z \\ \gamma_{xy} \\ \gamma_{yz} \\ \gamma_{zx} \end{Bmatrix}$$

A three-noded triangular element is shown below. This element may be a plane stress element or a plane strain element. Any point on this element has two displacements, u being the horizontal displacement and v the vertical displacement.

Thus,

$$u = N_i\,U_{2i-1} + 0\,U_{2i} + N_j\,U_{2j-1} + 0\,U_{2j} + N_k\,U_{2k-1} + 0\,N_{2k}$$

$$v = 0\,U_{2i-1} + N_i\,U_{2i} + 0\,U_{2j-1} + N_j\,U_{2j} + 0\,U_{2k-1} + N_k\,U_{2k}$$

We may write the above two equations as a single matrix equation,

$$\begin{Bmatrix} u(x,y) \\ v(x,y) \end{Bmatrix} = \begin{bmatrix} N_i & 0 & N_j & 0 & N_k & 0 \\ 0 & N_i & 0 & N_j & 0 & N_k \end{bmatrix}\begin{Bmatrix} U_{2i-1} \\ U_{2i} \\ U_{2j-1} \\ U_{2j} \\ U_{2k-1} \\ U_{2k} \end{Bmatrix}$$

The strain- displacement equation for the two-dimensional triangular element is,

$$\begin{Bmatrix} e_{xx} \\ e_{yy} \\ e_{xy} \end{Bmatrix} = \frac{1}{2A}\begin{bmatrix} b_i & 0 & b_j & 0 & b_k & 0 \\ 0 & c_i & 0 & c_j & 0 & c_k \\ c_i & b_i & c_j & b_j & c_k & b_k \end{bmatrix}\begin{Bmatrix} U_{2i-1} \\ U_{2i} \\ U_{2j-1} \\ U_{2j} \\ U_{2k-1} \\ U_{2k} \end{Bmatrix} = [B]\begin{Bmatrix} U_{2i-1} \\ U_{2i} \\ U_{2j-1} \\ U_{2j} \\ U_{2k-1} \\ U_{2k} \end{Bmatrix}$$

where, for a plane stress or a plane strain triangular element, the derivative matrix [B] is given by,

$$[B] = \frac{1}{2A} \begin{bmatrix} b_i & 0 & b_j & 0 & b_k & 0 \\ 0 & c_i & 0 & c_j & 0 & c_k \\ c_i & b_i & c_j & b_j & c_k & b_k \end{bmatrix}$$

For a plane stress or a plane strain triangular element, the stiffness matrix is,

$$[k^{(e)}] = [B]^T[D][B]\,A\,t$$

$$[B] = \begin{bmatrix} \dfrac{z_{22}}{det[J]} & 0 & \dfrac{z_{31}}{det[J]} & 0 & \dfrac{z_{12}}{det[J]} & 0 \\[2ex] 0 & \dfrac{r_{32}}{det\,[J]} & 0 & \dfrac{r_{13}}{det\,[J]} & 0 & \dfrac{r_{21}}{det\,[J]} \\[2ex] \dfrac{r_{32}}{det\,[J]} & \dfrac{z_{23}}{[J]} & \dfrac{r_{13}}{det\,[J]} & \dfrac{z_{31}}{det\,[J]} & \dfrac{r_{21}}{det\,[J]} & \dfrac{z_{12}}{det[J]} \\[2ex] \dfrac{N_1}{r} & 0 & \dfrac{N_2}{r} & 0 & \dfrac{N_3}{r} & 0 \end{bmatrix}$$

where, $[J] = \begin{bmatrix} r_{12} & z_{13} \\ r_{23} & z_{23} \end{bmatrix}$ and $det[J] = r_{12}z_{23} - r_{23}z_{13} = (r_1 - r_2)(z_2 - z_3) - (r_2 - r_3)(z_1 - z_3)$

[J] is called the Jacobian matrix.

$r_{12} = r_1 - r_2,\ z_{13} = z_1 - z_3$ and so on.

Stiffness matrix for an axisymmetric triangular element,

$$[k^{(e)}] = 2\pi\, r\, A\, [B]^T[D][B]$$

Stress Components

$$[\sigma] = [B]\{U^{(e)}\}$$

Thermal Strain Vector

$$\{\varepsilon_T\} = \begin{Bmatrix} \alpha\,\delta T \\ \alpha\,\delta T \\ 0 \end{Bmatrix}, \text{ where } \alpha \text{ is the coefficiet of thermal expansion.}$$

Note that we use the symbol e for total strain and the symbol ε for the elastic strain. Thus, Total strain = elastic strain + thermal strain.

Or $e = \varepsilon + \varepsilon_T$

Axisymmetric Problems

There are some types of three-dimensional problems which can be simplified and solved as two-dimensional problems. Axisymmetric problems, plane stress problems and plain strain problems in elasticity are examples of such problems.

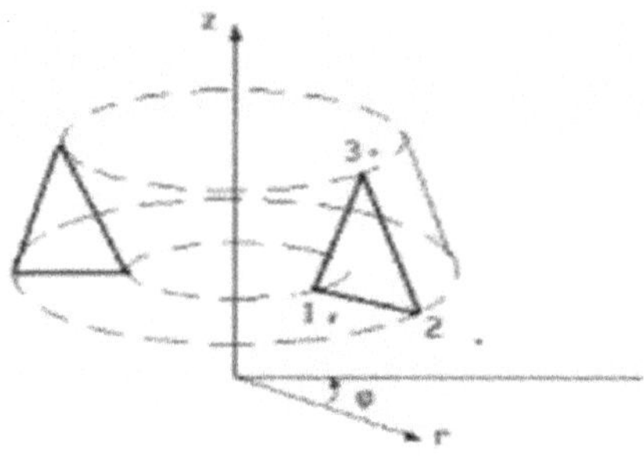

Fig. 8.1

Let us consider a triangle in a vertical plane This triangle has nodes 1,2 and 3 and is imagined as revolved about a vertical axis z. The revolved element so created may be called a revolved triangular axisymmetric element.

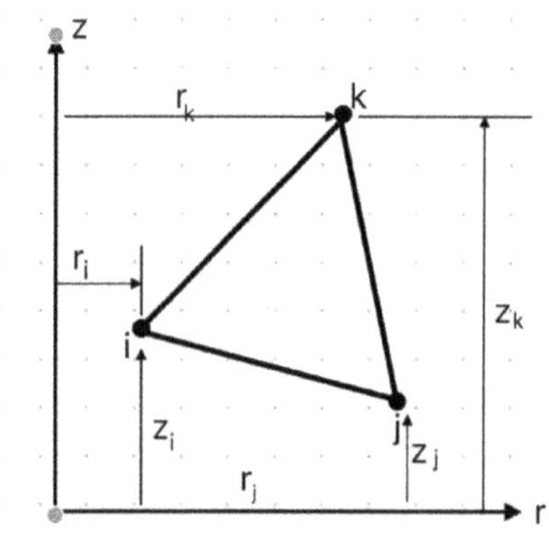

Fig. 8.2

Gradient Matrix, [B]

For a three noded triangle in plane stress problem in elasticity, the gradient matrix is,

$$[B] = \frac{1}{2A} \begin{bmatrix} b_i & 0 & b_j & 0 & b_k & 0 \\ 0 & c_i & 0 & c_j & 0 & c_k \\ c_i & b_i & c_j & b_j & c_k & b_k \end{bmatrix}$$

The strain – displacement relationship is,

$$\left\{ \begin{array}{c} \varepsilon_{xx} \\ \varepsilon_{yy} \\ \varepsilon_{xy} \end{array} \right\} = [B] \left\{ \begin{array}{c} u_{2i-1} \\ u_{2i} \\ u_{2j-1} \\ u_{2j} \\ u_{2k-1} \\ u_{2k} \end{array} \right\} = \left[B \right] \{U\}, \text{ where U is called the displacement vector.}$$

For a plane stress problem or the plain strain problem, the element stiffness matrix,

$$[k^{(e)}] = [B]^T [D] [B] A\, t$$

In an axisymmetric problem, the element stiffness matrix

$$[k]^{(e)} = \int_V [\mathrm{B}]^T[\mathrm{D}][\mathrm{B}]\, dV = 2\,\pi\, \mathrm{r}\, \mathrm{A}[\mathrm{B}]^T[\mathrm{D}][\mathrm{B}]$$

where,

$$r_m = r = \frac{r_1 + r_2 + r_3}{3} \quad \text{is the mean radius of the element.}$$

A is the area of the triangular element, [B] is the strain-displacement matrix and [D] is the stress-strain relation matrix. $[B]^T$ is the transpose of matrix [B].

Strain- Displacement Matrix

$$[B] = \begin{bmatrix} \dfrac{z_{22}}{det[J]} & 0 & \dfrac{z_{31}}{det[J]} & 0 & \dfrac{z_{12}}{det[J]} & 0 \\[2ex] 0 & \dfrac{r_{32}}{det\,[J]} & 0 & \dfrac{r_{13}}{det\,[J]} & 0 & \dfrac{r_{21}}{det\,[J]} \\[2ex] \dfrac{r_{32}}{det\,[J]} & \dfrac{z_{23}}{[J]} & \dfrac{r_{13}}{det\,[J]} & \dfrac{z_{31}}{det\,[J]} & \dfrac{r_{21}}{det\,[J]} & \dfrac{z_{12}}{det[J]} \\[2ex] \dfrac{N_1}{r} & 0 & \dfrac{N_2}{r} & 0 & \dfrac{N_3}{r} & 0 \end{bmatrix}$$

where, $[J]=\begin{bmatrix} r_{12} & z_{13} \\ r_{23} & z_{23} \end{bmatrix}$ and $det[J] = r_{12}\,z_{23} - r_{23}z_{13} = \left(r_1 - r_2\right)\left(z_2 - z_3\right) - \left(r_2 - r_3\right)\left(z_1 - z_3\right)$

[J] is called the Jacobian matrix.

$$r_{12} = r_1 - r_2,\ z_{13} = z_1 - z_3 \ \text{ and so on.}$$

$$det[J] = r_{12}\,z_{23} - r_{23}z_{13} = \left(r_1 - r_2\right)\left(z_2 - z_3\right) - \left(r_2 - r_3\right)\left(z_1 - z_3\right)$$

Area of a triangle

$$A = \frac{\det[J]}{2} = = \frac{1}{2}\left(r_{13}z_{23} - r_{23}z_{13}\right)$$

$$[D] = \frac{E(1-\mu)}{(1+\mu)(1-2\mu)} \begin{bmatrix} 1 & \dfrac{\mu}{(1-\mu)} & 0 & \dfrac{\mu}{1-\mu} \\[2mm] \dfrac{\mu}{1-\mu} & 1 & 0 & \dfrac{\mu}{1-\mu} \\[2mm] 0 & 0 & \dfrac{1-2\mu}{2(1-\mu)} & 0 \\[2mm] \dfrac{\mu}{1-\mu} & \dfrac{\mu}{1-\mu} & 0 & 1 \end{bmatrix}$$

Consider a pressurized cylinder analyzed using axisymmetric triangular elements.

1. Mesh the cylinder cross-section using triangular elements.
2. Compute the stiffness matrix for each element.
3. Apply boundary conditions (e.g., zero displacement at one end).
4. Solve for nodal displacements {d} using: [K]{d} = {F}
5. Compute stresses and strains using: {0} = [D][B]{d} ↓

Example 8.1 A long cylinder of inside diameter 80 mm and outside diameter of 120 mm snugly fits into a hole over its entire length. The cylinder is then subjected to an internal pressure of 2 MPa. Using two elements on the 10 mm length shown, find the displacement at the inner radius. *Take* $E = 2 \times 10^5 \dfrac{N}{mm^2}$ *and* $\mu = 0.3$. Nodes 3 and 4 are fixed. Nodes 1 and 2 are on horizontal rollers thus allowing displacement in the r direction.

Solution: Here we will use 2 axisymmetric triangular elements, with nodes 1, 2, 3 and 4 in the anti-clockwise direction. We see that element 1 has the nodes 1, 2, 4 and element 2 has the nodes 2, 3 and 4.

As before, we will use the global equation, $[K]\{U\}=\{F\}$ to find nodal displacements at each node: For displacements, we use the convention that at node i, u_{2i-1} is the horizontal displacement and u_{2i} is the vertical displacement.

Thus, $u_2 = u_4 = u_6 = u_8 = 0$. *Also,* $u_5 = u_7 = 0$.

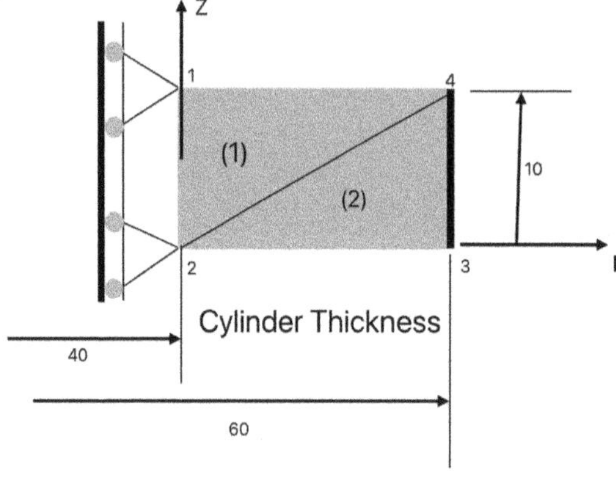

Fig. 8.3

$$[k]^{(e)} = \int_V [B]^T[D][B]\,dV = 2\pi r\, A[B]^T[D][B],$$

where A is the area of the triangular element, [B] is the strain- displacement matrix and [D] is the stress-strain relation matrix. $[B]^T$ is the transpose of matrix [B].

Strain- Displacement Matrix

$$[B] = \begin{bmatrix} \dfrac{z_{22}}{det[J]} & 0 & \dfrac{z_{31}}{det[J]} & 0 & \dfrac{z_{12}}{det[J]} & 0 \\[2ex] 0 & \dfrac{r_{32}}{det[J]} & 0 & \dfrac{r_{13}}{det[J]} & 0 & \dfrac{r_{21}}{det[J]} \\[2ex] \dfrac{r_{32}}{det[J]} & \dfrac{z_{23}}{[J]} & \dfrac{r_{13}}{det[J]} & \dfrac{z_{31}}{det[J]} & \dfrac{r_{21}}{det[J]} & \dfrac{z_{12}}{det[J]} \\[2ex] \dfrac{N_1}{r} & 0 & \dfrac{N_2}{r} & 0 & \dfrac{N_3}{r} & 0 \end{bmatrix}$$

where, $[J] = \begin{bmatrix} r_{12} & z_{13} \\ r_{23} & z_{23} \end{bmatrix}$ and $det[J] = r_{12}\,z_{23} - r_{23}z_{13} = \left(r_1 - r_2\right)\left(z_2 - z_3\right) - \left(r_2 - r_3\right)\left(z_1 - z_3\right)$

[J] is called the Jacobian matrix.

$r_{12} = r_1 - r_2,\ z_{13} = z_1 - z_3$ and so on.

$det[J] = r_{12}\,z_{23} - r_{23}z_{13} = \left(r_1 - r_2\right)\left(z_2 - z_3\right) - \left(r_2 - r_3\right)\left(z_1 - z_3\right)$

$= (40 - 60)(-10) = 200$

Strain- Displacement Matrix

$$[B] = \begin{bmatrix} \dfrac{z_{22}}{det[J]} & 0 & \dfrac{z_{31}}{det[J]} & 0 & \dfrac{z_{12}}{det[J]} & 0 \\[2ex] 0 & \dfrac{r_{32}}{det[J]} & 0 & \dfrac{r_{13}}{det[J]} & 0 & \dfrac{r_{21}}{det[J]} \\[2ex] \dfrac{r_{32}}{det[J]} & \dfrac{z_{23}}{[J]} & \dfrac{r_{13}}{det[J]} & \dfrac{z_{31}}{det[J]} & \dfrac{r_{21}}{det[J]} & \dfrac{z_{12}}{det[J]} \\[2ex] \dfrac{N_1}{r} & 0 & \dfrac{N_2}{r} & 0 & \dfrac{N_3}{r} & 0 \end{bmatrix}$$

where, $[J] = \begin{bmatrix} r_{12} & z_{13} \\ r_{23} & z_{23} \end{bmatrix}$ and $det[J] = r_{12}\,z_{23} - r_{23}z_{13} = \left(r_1 - r_2\right)\left(z_2 - z_3\right) - \left(r_2 - r_3\right)\left(z_1 - z_3\right)$

[J] is called the Jacobian matrix.

$r_{12} = r_1 - r_2,\ z_{13} = z_1 - z_3$ and so on.

$det[J] = r_{12}\,z_{23} - r_{23}z_{13} = \left(r_1 - r_2\right)\left(z_2 - z_3\right) - \left(r_2 - r_3\right)\left(z_1 - z_3\right)$

$= (40 - 60)(-10) = 200$

Area of a triangle

$$A = \frac{det\,[J]}{2} = \ = \frac{1}{2}\left(r_{13}\,z_{23} - r_{23}\,z_{13}\right) = \frac{200}{2} = 100.$$

For element 1, $r = \dfrac{r_1 + r_2 + r_3}{3} = \dfrac{40 + 40 + 60}{4} = 46.67$

For element 2, $r = \dfrac{r_2 + r_3 + r_4}{3} = \dfrac{40 + 60 + 60}{4} = 53.333$

Stress-Strain Relationship Matrix, [D]

$$[D] = \frac{E(1-\mu)}{(1+\mu)(1-2\mu)} \begin{bmatrix} 1 & \dfrac{\mu}{(1-\mu)} & 0 & \dfrac{\mu}{1-\mu} \\[2ex] \dfrac{\mu}{1-\mu} & 1 & 0 & \dfrac{\mu}{1-\mu} \\[2ex] 0 & 0 & \dfrac{1-2\mu}{2(1-\mu)} & 0 \\[2ex] \dfrac{\mu}{1-\mu} & \dfrac{\mu}{1-\mu} & 0 & 1 \end{bmatrix}$$

On substitution of the given values, we get

$$[D] = 2.692 \times 10^5 \begin{bmatrix} 1 & 0.4285 & 0 & 0.4285 \\ 0.4285 & 1 & 0 & 0.4285 \\ 0 & 0 & 0.2857 & 0 \\ 0.4285 & 0.4285 & 0 & 1 \end{bmatrix}$$

Strain-Displacement Matrix, [B] for Element 1

$$[B^{(1)}] = \begin{bmatrix} \dfrac{z_{23}}{det\,[J]} & 0 & \dfrac{z_{31}}{det\,[J]} & 0 & \dfrac{z_{12}}{det\,[J]} & 0 \\[2ex] 0 & \dfrac{r_{32}}{det\,[J]} & 0 & \dfrac{r_{13}}{det\,[J]} & 0 & \dfrac{r_{21}}{det\,[J]} \\[2ex] \dfrac{r_{32}}{det\,[J]} & \dfrac{z_{23}}{det\,[J]} & \dfrac{r_{13}}{detb\,[J]} & \dfrac{z_{31}}{det\,[J]} & \dfrac{r_{21}}{det\,[J]} & \dfrac{z_{12}}{det\,[J]} \\[2ex] \dfrac{N_1}{r} & 0 & \dfrac{N_2}{r} & 0 & \dfrac{N_3}{r} & 0 \end{bmatrix}$$

Substituting the given values, we get

$$[B^{(1)}] = \begin{bmatrix} 0 & 0 & -0.05 & 0 & 0.05 & 0 \\ 0 & 0.1 & 0 & 0.1 & 0 & 0 \\ 0.1 & 0 & -0.1 & 0.05 & 0 & 0.05 \\ 0.0071 & 0 & 0.0071 & 0 & 0.0071 & 0 \end{bmatrix}$$

Strain-Displacement Matrix, [B] for Element 2

$$[B^{(2)}] = \begin{bmatrix} \dfrac{z_{34}}{det\,[J]} & 0 & \dfrac{z_{42}}{det\,[J]} & 0 & \dfrac{z_{23}}{det\,[J]} & 0 \\[2ex] 0 & \dfrac{z_{43}}{det\,[J]} & 0 & \dfrac{z_{24}}{det\,[J]} & 0 & \dfrac{z_{32}}{det\,[J]} \\[2ex] \dfrac{r_{43}}{det\,[J]} & \dfrac{z_{34}}{det\,[J]} & \dfrac{r_{24}}{det\,[J]} & \dfrac{z_{42}}{det\,[J]} & \dfrac{r_{32}}{det\,[J]} & \dfrac{z_{23}}{det\,[J]} \\[2ex] \dfrac{N_1}{r} & 0 & \dfrac{N_2}{r} & 0 & \dfrac{N_3}{r} & 0 \end{bmatrix}$$

$$= \begin{bmatrix} -0.05 & 0 & 0.05 & 0 & 0 & 0 \\ 0 & 0 & 0 & 0.1 & 0 & 0.1 \\ 0 & -0.05 & 0.1 & 0.05 & 0.1 & 0 \\ 0.00625 & 0 & 0.00625 & 0 & 0.00625 & 0 \end{bmatrix}$$

For element 1, substituting values in $\left[k^{(1)}\right] = \displaystyle\int_V [\mathrm{B}]^{\mathrm{T}}[\mathrm{D}][\mathrm{B}]\, dV = 2\pi r\, \mathrm{A}\left[\mathrm{B}^{(1)}\right]^{\mathrm{T}}[\mathrm{D}]\left[\mathrm{B}^{(1)}\right]$,

we get,

$$
7.8939 \times 10^9
\begin{array}{cccccc}
1 & 2 & 3 & 4 & 7 & 8 \\
\end{array}
\begin{bmatrix}
0.0288 & 3.038\times10^{-4} & 2.67\times10^{-3} & 1.73\times10^{-3} & 2.024\times10^{-4} & 1.43\times10^{-3} \\
3.04\times10^{-4} & 0.01 & 0.002142 & 0.01 & 0.002446 & 0 \\
2.67\times10^{-3} & 2.44\times10^{-3} & 5.72\times10^{-3} & 0.0202 & 2.67\times10^{-3} & 7.15\times10^{-4} \\
1.133\times10^{-3} & -0.01 & -0.0137 & -9.285\times10^{-3} & -2.44\times10^{-4} & 7.16\times10^{-4} \\
2.02\times10^{-4} & 2.17\times10^{-3} & 2.85\times10^{-3} & 0.0217 & 2.854\times10^{-3} & 0 \\
1.43\times10^{-3} & 0 & 1.43\times10^{-3} & 7.15\times10^{-4} & 0 & 7.15\times10^{-4}
\end{bmatrix}
\begin{Bmatrix} u_1 \\ u_2 \\ u_3 \\ u_4 \\ u_7 \\ u_8 \end{Bmatrix}
=
\begin{Bmatrix} F_1 \\ F_2 \\ F_3 \\ F_4 \\ F_7 \\ F_8 \end{Bmatrix}
$$

$$
7.8939 \times 10^7
\begin{array}{cccccc}
1 & 2 & 3 & 4 & 7 & 8 \\
\end{array}
\begin{bmatrix}
0.0288 & 3.038\times10^{-4} & -2.67\times10^{-3} & 1.73\times10^{-3} & 2.024\times10^{-4} & 1.43\times10^{-3} \\
3.04\times10^{-4} & 0.01 & 0.002142 & 0.01 & 0.002446 & 0 \\
-2.67\times10^{-3} & 2.44\times10^{-3} & 5.72\times10^{-3} & 0.0202 & 2.67\times10^{-3} & 7.15\times10^{-4} \\
1.133\times10^{-3} & -0.01 & -0.0137 & -9.285\times10^{-3} & -2.44\times10^{-4} & 7.16\times10^{-4} \\
2.02\times10^{-4} & 2.17\times10^{-3} & 2.85\times10^{-3} & 0.0217 & 2.854\times10^{-3} & 0 \\
1.43\times10^{-3} & 0 & 1.43\times10^{-3} & 7.15\times10^{-4} & 0 & 7.15\times10^{-4}
\end{bmatrix}
\begin{Bmatrix} u_1 \\ 0 \\ u_3 \\ 0 \\ 0 \\ 0 \end{Bmatrix}
=
\begin{Bmatrix} F_1 \\ 0 \\ F_3 \\ 0 \\ 0 \\ 0 \end{Bmatrix}
$$

$$
F_1 = F_3 = \frac{2\pi r L p}{2} = 2513.27\ \mathrm{N}
$$

The following two equations result from the matrix equation:

$$
0.0288\, u_1 - 0.00267 \times u_3 = \frac{2513.27}{7.8939\times10^9} = 0.0003184
$$

$$
-2.67\times10^{-3}\, u_1 + 5.72\times10^{-3}\, u_3 = \frac{2513.27}{7.8939\times10^9} = 0.0003184
$$

Or

$$
0.00267 u_1 - 0.0002475 u_3 = 0.00002952
$$

$$
-00267 u_1 + 0.00572 u_3 = 0.0003184
$$

Or

$$
0.0054725\, u_3 = 0.00034792
$$

$$
u_3 = 0.06358\ mm\ 0.00868\ \mathrm{mm}
$$

$$
u_1 = 0.01695\ mm\ 0.1154\ \mathrm{mm}
$$

Plane stress and Plain Strain

Plain Stress

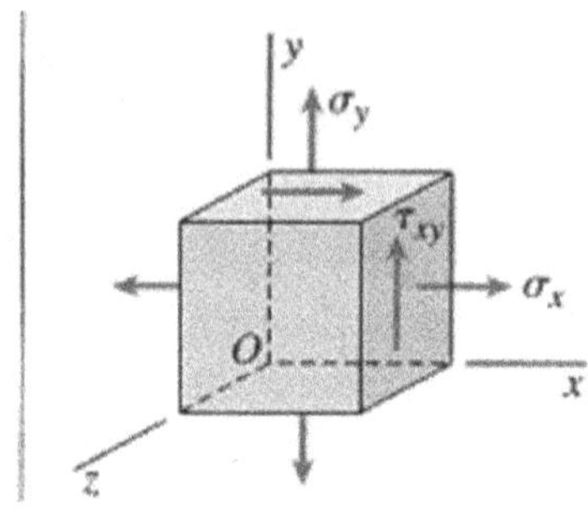

Fig. 8.4: A point on the plane stress plane x y

A plane stress problem is one in which stresses at any point on it occur in x and y directions but none in the z direction. This means that $\sigma_z = 0$, $\sigma_{xz} = 0$, $\sigma_{yz} = 0$. however, σ_x, σ_y, σ_z and τ_{xy} may not be zero. Plane stress occurs in the x, y plane (or a thin sheet of a body long which long in the z direction). Normal Shear strains, ε_x, ε_y, ε_z *and shear strain* γ_{xy} *may not be zero*.

Plain strain

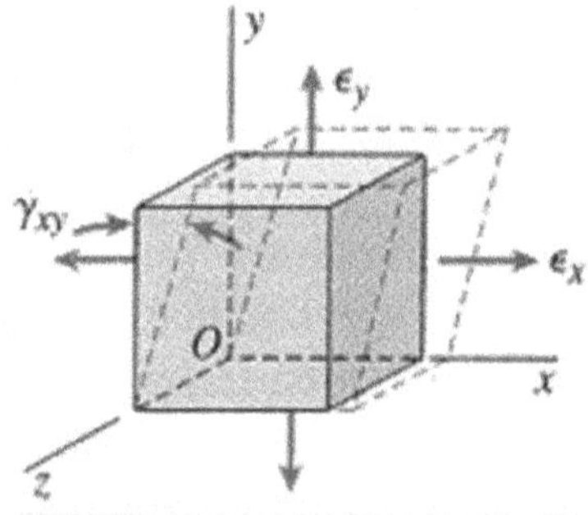

Fig. 8.5 A point on the plane strain plane x y

Plain stress and Plain Strain Problems

A plane strain problem is one in which strains at any point on it occur in x and y directions but none in the z direction. This means that $\tau_{xz} = 0$, $\tau_{yz} = 0$. However, σ_x, σ_y, σ_z and τ_{xy}

Plane strain occurs in the x, y plane (or a thin sheet). Shear strains, ε_x, ε_y, ε_z *and shear strain* γ_{xy} *may not be zero*.

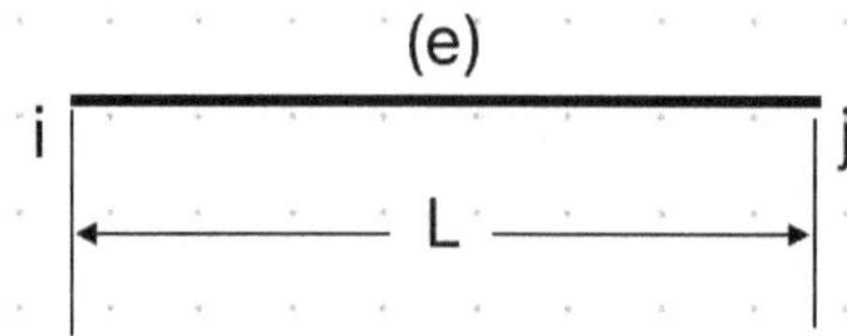

Fig. 8.6

Stress-Displacement Vector for the Plane Stress Element

$$\begin{Bmatrix} \sigma_{xx} \\ \sigma_{yy} \\ \sigma_{xy} \end{Bmatrix} = [B][D]\{U\}, \text{ where } [D] = \frac{E}{1-\mu^2} \begin{bmatrix} 1-\mu & \mu & 0 \\ \mu & 1-\mu & 0 \\ 0 & 0 & \frac{1}{2}(1-\mu) \end{bmatrix}$$

For the plane strain element,

$$[D] = \frac{E(1-\mu)}{(1-2\mu)(1+\mu)} \begin{bmatrix} 1-\mu & \mu & 0 \\ \mu & 1-\mu & 0 \\ 0 & 0 & \frac{1}{2}(1-2\mu) \end{bmatrix}$$

Example 8.2 In the plane stress triangular element shown in Fig. 7.4, at

Node 1 $u_1 = 2\ mm$; $u_2 = 1\ mm$

Node 2 $u_3 = 1\ mm$; $u_4 = 1.5\ mm$

Node 3 $u_5 = 2.5\ mm$; $u_6 = 0.5\ mm$

Element thickness = 10 mm

Young's modulus, $E = 2 \times 10^5\ N/mm^2$

Poisson's ratio $\mu = 0.3$

Find the stresses in this element.

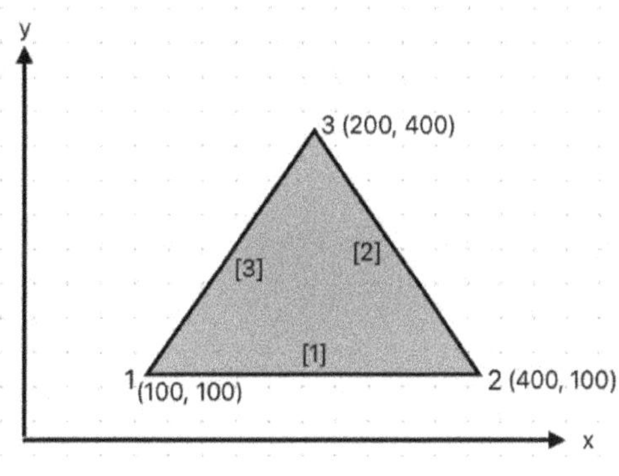

Fig. 8.7

Solution: The plane stress triangular element is shown in Fig. 7.2.

$$Area\ of\ the\ element = \frac{1}{2} \times base \times height = \frac{1}{2}(400-100)(400-100) = 45000\ mm^2$$

$$[D] = \frac{E}{(1-\mu^2)} \begin{bmatrix} 1 & \mu & 0 \\ \mu & 1 & 0 \\ 0 & 0 & \frac{1-\mu}{2} \end{bmatrix} = \frac{E}{(1-\mu^2)} \begin{bmatrix} 1 & \mu & 0 \\ \mu & 1 & 0 \\ 0 & 0 & \frac{1-\mu}{2} \end{bmatrix} = \frac{200000}{1-0.09} \begin{bmatrix} 1 & 0.3 & 0 \\ 0.3 & 1 & 0 \\ 0 & 0 & 0.35 \end{bmatrix} =$$

$$\begin{bmatrix} 219780.2 & 65934.1 & 0 \\ 65934.1 & 219780.2 & 0 \\ 0 & 0 & 76923.1 \end{bmatrix}$$

$$[B] = \frac{1}{2A} \begin{bmatrix} b_i & 0 & b_j & 0 & b_k & 0 \\ 0 & c_i & 0 & c_j & 0 & c_k \\ c_i & b_i & c_j & b_j & c_k & b_k \end{bmatrix}$$

where

$$b_i = y_j - y_k = 100 - 400 = -300$$

$$b_j = y_k - y_i = 400 - 100 = 300$$

$$b_k = y_i - y_j = 100 - 100 = 0$$

$$c_i = x_k - x_j = 200 - 400 = -200$$

$$c_j = x_i - x_k = 100 - 200 = -100$$

$$c_k = x_j - x_i = 400 - 100 = 300$$

Thus,

$$[B] = \frac{1}{2A} \begin{bmatrix} b_i & 0 & b_j & 0 & b_k & 0 \\ 0 & c_i & 0 & c_j & 0 & c_k \\ c_i & b_i & c_j & b_j & c_k & b_k \end{bmatrix}$$

$$= \frac{1}{90000} \begin{bmatrix} -300 & 0 & 300 & 0 & 0 & 0 \\ 0 & -200 & 0 & -100 & 0 & 300 \\ -200 & -300 & -100 & 300 & 300 & 0 \end{bmatrix}$$

$$= \begin{bmatrix} -\dfrac{1}{300} & 0 & \dfrac{1}{300} & 0 & 0 & 0 \\ 0 & -\dfrac{1}{450} & 0 & -\dfrac{1}{900} & 0 & \dfrac{1}{300} \\ -\dfrac{1}{450} & -\dfrac{1}{300} & -\dfrac{1}{900} & \dfrac{1}{300} & \dfrac{1}{300} & 0 \end{bmatrix}$$

$$\{U^{(e)}\} = \begin{Bmatrix} u_1 \\ u_2 \\ u_3 \\ u_4 \\ u_5 \\ u_6 \end{Bmatrix} = \begin{Bmatrix} 2 \\ 1 \\ 1 \\ 1.5 \\ 2.5 \\ 0.5 \end{Bmatrix}$$

$$\begin{Bmatrix} \sigma_1 \\ \sigma_2 \\ \sigma_3 \end{Bmatrix} = [D][B]\{U^{(e)}\}$$

$$= \frac{1}{90000}\begin{bmatrix} 219780.2 & 65934.1 & 0 \\ 65934.1 & 219780.2 & 0 \\ 0 & 0 & 76923.1 \end{bmatrix}\begin{bmatrix} -300 & 0 & 300 & 0 & 0 & 0 \\ 0 & -200 & 0 & -100 & 0 & 300 \\ -200 & -300 & -100 & 300 & 300 & 0 \end{bmatrix}\begin{Bmatrix} 2 \\ 1 \\ 1 \\ 1.5 \\ 2.5 \\ 0.5 \end{Bmatrix}$$

$$= \frac{1}{90000}\begin{bmatrix} 219780.2 & 65934.1 & 0 \\ 65934.1 & 219780.2 & 0 \\ 0 & 0 & 76923.1 \end{bmatrix}\begin{Bmatrix} -300 \\ -200 \\ 400 \end{Bmatrix}$$

$$= \begin{Bmatrix} -879.12 \\ -708.18 \\ 341.88 \end{Bmatrix} N/mm^2$$

Example 8.3 Find the element stiffness matrix for the three-noded triangular element of example 8.2.

Solution: Matrices $[B]$ and $[D]$ have already been calculated. All that we need to do now is to calculate the transpose $[B]^T$ of $[B]$ and substitute in the relation $[k^{(e)}] = [B]^T[D][B]\,A\,t$.

$$[B]^T = \frac{1}{2A}\begin{bmatrix} b_i & 0 & c_i \\ 0 & c_i & b_i \\ b_j & 0 & c_j \\ 0 & c_j & b_j \\ b_k & 0 & c_k \\ 0 & c_k & b_k \end{bmatrix} = \frac{1}{90000}\begin{bmatrix} -300 & 0 & -200 \\ 0 & -200 & -300 \\ 300 & 0 & -100 \\ 0 & -100 & 300 \\ 0 & 0 & 300 \\ 0 & 300 & 0 \end{bmatrix} = \begin{bmatrix} -\dfrac{1}{300} & 0 & -\dfrac{1}{450} \\[2mm] 0 & -\dfrac{1}{450} & -\dfrac{1}{300} \\[2mm] \dfrac{1}{300} & 0 & -\dfrac{1}{900} \\[2mm] 0 & -\dfrac{1}{900} & \dfrac{1}{300} \\[2mm] 0 & 0 & \dfrac{1}{300} \\[2mm] 0 & \dfrac{1}{300} & 0 \end{bmatrix}$$

$$[D][B] = \begin{bmatrix} 219780.2 & 65934.1 & 0 \\ 65934.1 & 219780.2 & 0 \\ 0 & 0 & 76923.1 \end{bmatrix}\begin{bmatrix} -\dfrac{1}{300} & 0 & \dfrac{1}{300} & 0 & 0 & 0 \\[2mm] 0 & -\dfrac{1}{450} & 0 & -\dfrac{1}{900} & 0 & \dfrac{1}{300} \\[2mm] -\dfrac{1}{450} & -\dfrac{1}{300} & -\dfrac{1}{900} & \dfrac{1}{300} & \dfrac{1}{300} & 0 \end{bmatrix}$$

Or

$$[D][B] = \begin{bmatrix} -732.60 & -146.52 & 732.60 & -73.26 & 0 & 219.78 \\ -219.78 & -488.4 & 219.78 & -244.20 & 0 & 732.60 \\ -170.94 & 256.41 & -85.47 & 256.41 & 256.41 & 0 \end{bmatrix}$$

$$[B]^T[D][B] = \begin{bmatrix} -\dfrac{1}{300} & 0 & -\dfrac{1}{450} \\[2mm] 0 & -\dfrac{1}{450} & -\dfrac{1}{300} \\[2mm] \dfrac{1}{300} & 0 & -\dfrac{1}{900} \\[2mm] 0 & -\dfrac{1}{900} & \dfrac{1}{300} \\[2mm] 0 & 0 & \dfrac{1}{300} \\[2mm] 0 & \dfrac{1}{300} & 0 \end{bmatrix} \begin{bmatrix} -732.60 & -146.52 & 732.60 & -73.26 & 0 & 219.78 \\ -219.78 & -488.4 & 219.78 & -244.20 & 0 & 732.60 \\ -170.94 & 256.41 & -85.47 & 256.41 & 256.41 & 0 \end{bmatrix}$$

Or

$$[B]^T[D][B] = \begin{bmatrix} 2.82 & -0.08 & -2.25 & -0.33 & -0.57 & -0.73 \\ -0.08 & 1.94 & -0.77 & 1.40 & 0.85 & -1.63 \\ -2.25 & -0.77 & 2.54 & -0.53 & -0.28 & 0.73 \\ -0.33 & 1.40 & -0.53 & 1.13 & 0.85 & -0.81 \\ -0.57 & 0.85 & -0.28 & 0.85 & 0.85 & 0 \\ -0.73 & -1.63 & 0.73 & -0.81 & 0 & 2.44 \end{bmatrix}$$

$$[k^{(e)}] = [B]^T[D][B]\,A\,t = (45000)(10) \begin{bmatrix} 2.82 & -0.08 & -2.25 & -0.33 & -0.57 & -0.73 \\ -0.08 & 1.94 & -0.77 & 1.40 & 0.85 & -1.63 \\ -2.25 & -0.77 & 2.54 & -0.53 & -0.28 & 0.73 \\ -0.33 & 1.40 & -0.53 & 1.13 & 0.85 & -0.81 \\ -0.57 & 0.85 & -0.28 & 0.85 & 0.85 & 0 \\ -0.73 & -1.63 & 0.73 & -0.81 & 0 & 2.44 \end{bmatrix}$$

$$= 10^6 \begin{bmatrix} 16 & 0 & 0 & 4 & -16 & -4 \\ 4 & 0 & 0 & 16 & -4 & -16 \\ 0 & 6 & 6 & 0 & -6 & -6 \end{bmatrix} \begin{Bmatrix} 0.003 \\ 0 \\ 0.001 \\ -0.0003 \\ 0.0015 \\ 0 \end{Bmatrix} = 10^6 \begin{Bmatrix} 0.0228 \\ 0.0012 \\ -0.003 \end{Bmatrix} = \begin{Bmatrix} 22800 \\ 1200 \\ -300 \end{Bmatrix}$$

$$= 10^6 \begin{bmatrix} 16 & 0 & 0 & 4 & -16 & -4 \\ 4 & 0 & 0 & 16 & -4 & -16 \\ 0 & 6 & 6 & 0 & -6 & -6 \end{bmatrix} \begin{Bmatrix} 0.003 \\ 0 \\ 0.001 \\ -0.0003 \\ 0.0015 \\ 0 \end{Bmatrix} = 10^6 \begin{Bmatrix} 0.0228 \\ 0.0012 \\ -0.003 \end{Bmatrix} = \begin{Bmatrix} 22800 \\ 1200 \\ -300 \end{Bmatrix}$$

Example 8.4 A triangular two-dimensional element is shown in Fig. 8. The nodal displacements of this element are given below. Find the stiffness matrix the element.

Horizontal displacement at node i = 0.003 cm

Horizontal displacement at node j = 0.001 cm

Horizontal displacement at node k = 0.0 cm

Vertical displacement at node I = 0.0 cm

Vertical displacement at node j = -0.0003 cm

Vertical displacement at node k = 0.0 cm

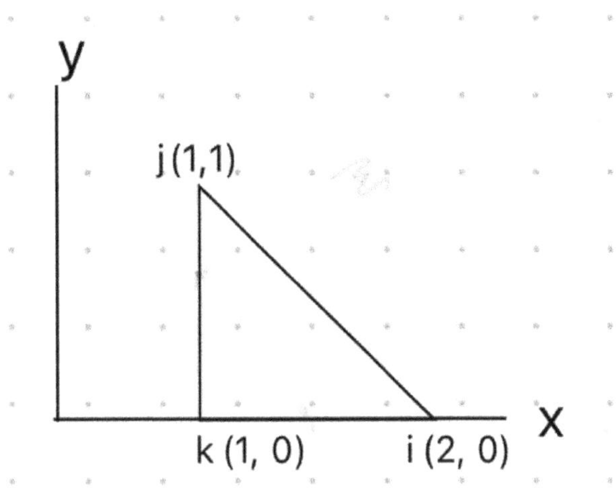

Fig. 8.8

Solution:

$$b_i = y_j - y_k = 1-0 = 1, \quad b_j = y_k - y_i = 0-0 = 0, \quad b_k = y_i - y_j = 0-1 = -1$$

$$c_i = x_k - x_j = 1-1 = 0, \quad c_j = x_i - x_k = 2-1 = 1, \quad c_k = x_j - x_i = 1-2 = -1$$

$$[B] = \frac{1}{2A}\begin{bmatrix} b_i & 0 & b_j & 0 & b_k & 0 \\ 0 & c_i & 0 & c_j & 0 & c_k \\ c_i & b_i & c_j & c_j & c_k & b_k \end{bmatrix} = \frac{1}{2\frac{1}{2}}\begin{bmatrix} 1 & 0 & 0 & 0 & -1 & 0 \\ 0 & 0 & 0 & 1 & 0 & -1 \\ 0 & 1 & 1 & 0 & -1 & -1 \end{bmatrix}$$

$$= \begin{bmatrix} 1 & 0 & 0 & 0 & -1 & 0 \\ 0 & 0 & 0 & 1 & 0 & -1 \\ 0 & 1 & 1 & 0 & -1 & -1 \end{bmatrix}$$

$$[B]^T = \begin{bmatrix} 1 & 0 & 0 \\ 0 & 0 & 1 \\ 0 & 0 & 1 \\ 0 & 1 & 0 \\ -1 & 0 & -1 \\ 0 & -1 & -1 \end{bmatrix}$$

$$[D] = 10^6 \begin{bmatrix} 16 & 4 & 0 \\ 4 & 16 & 0 \\ 0 & 0 & 6 \end{bmatrix}$$

$$[D] \times [B] = 10^6 \begin{bmatrix} 16 & 4 & 0 \\ 4 & 16 & 0 \\ 0 & 0 & 6 \end{bmatrix} \times \begin{bmatrix} 1 & 0 & 0 & 0 & -1 & 0 \\ 0 & 0 & 0 & 1 & 0 & -1 \\ 0 & 1 & 1 & 0 & -1 & -1 \end{bmatrix} = 10^6 \begin{bmatrix} 16 & 0 & 0 & 4 & -16 & -4 \\ 0 & 6 & 6 & 0 & -6 & -6 \\ 0 & 6 & 6 & 0 & -6 & -6 \end{bmatrix}$$

The triangular element is subject to the following forces which are constant in the element:

$$\begin{Bmatrix} \sigma_1 \\ \sigma_2 \\ \sigma_3 \end{Bmatrix} = [D][B]\{U\} = 10^6 \begin{bmatrix} 16 & 0 & 0 & 4 & -16 & -4 \\ 0 & 6 & 6 & 0 & -6 & -6 \\ 0 & 6 & 6 & 0 & -6 & -6 \end{bmatrix} \begin{Bmatrix} 0.003 \\ 0 \\ 0.001 \\ -0.0003 \\ 0 \\ 0 \end{Bmatrix} = 10^6 \begin{Bmatrix} 0.0468 \\ 0.0078 \\ 0 \end{Bmatrix}$$

$$[k^{(e)}] = [B]^T[D][B]\,A\,t = \begin{bmatrix} 1 & 0 & 0 \\ 0 & 0 & 1 \\ 0 & 0 & 1 \\ 0 & 1 & 0 \\ -1 & 0 & -1 \\ 0 & -1 & -1 \end{bmatrix} \times 10^6 \begin{bmatrix} 16 & 4 & 0 \\ 4 & 16 & 0 \\ 0 & 0 & 6 \end{bmatrix} \times \begin{bmatrix} 1 & 0 & 0 & 0 & -1 & 0 \\ 0 & 0 & 0 & 1 & 0 & -1 \\ 0 & 1 & 1 & 0 & -1 & -1 \end{bmatrix} \times \frac{1}{2} \times 2.$$

Thus,

$$[k^{(e)}] = \begin{bmatrix} 16000000 & 0 & 0 & 4000000 & -16000000 & -4000000 \\ 0 & 6000000 & 6000000 & 0 & -6000000 & -6000000 \\ 0 & 6000000 & 6000000 & 0 & -6000000 & -6000000 \\ 0 & 4000000 & 0 & 0 & 16000000 & -16000000 \\ -16000000 & -6000000 & -6000000 & -4000000 & 22000000 & 10000000 \\ -4000000 & -6000000 & -6000000 & -16000000 & 10000000 & 22000000 \end{bmatrix} \begin{Bmatrix} 0.004 \\ 0 \\ 0.001 \\ -0.00030. \\ 0.0015 \\ 0 \end{Bmatrix}$$

Example 8.5 A triangular element of a thin plate of thickness 10 mm is shown in Fig. 7.8. A traction force of 1000 $N/_{mm^2}$ is applied to the plate. Young's modulus, $E = 10^9/_{mm^2}$. Poisson's ratio, $\mu = 0.3$. Find element stiffness matrix, $[k^{(e)}]$ of this element.

$$[k^{(e)}] = [B]^T [D][B] A\, t$$

Solution:

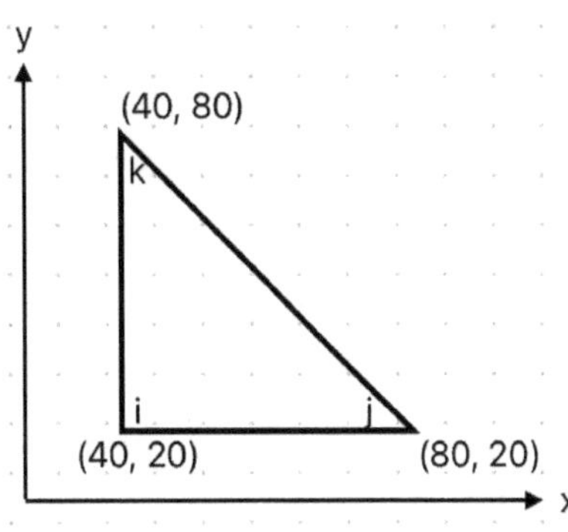

Fig. 8.9

$$[D] = \frac{E(1-\mu)}{(1-2\mu)(1+\mu)} \begin{bmatrix} 1-\mu & \mu & 0 \\ \mu & 1-\mu & 0 \\ 0 & 0 & \frac{1}{2}(1-2\mu) \end{bmatrix}$$

$$[D] = \frac{2\times 10^5(1-0.3)}{(1-0.6)(1+0.3)} \begin{bmatrix} 1-0.3 & 0.3 & 0 \\ 0.3 & 1-0.3 & 0 \\ 0 & 0 & \frac{1}{2}(1-0.6) \end{bmatrix} = \begin{bmatrix} 1.8844 & 0.8076 & 0 \\ 0.8076 & 1.8844 & 0 \\ 0 & 0 & 0.5384 \end{bmatrix}$$

From the given triangular element, we see that,

$$b_i = y_j - y_k = 20 - 80 = -60, \; b_j = y_k - y_i = 80 - 20 = 60, \; b_k = y_i - y_j = 20 - 20 = 0$$

$$c_i = x_k - x_j = 40 - 80 = -40, \; c_j = x_i - x_k = 40 - 40 = 0, \; c_k = x_j - x_i = 80 - 40 = 40$$

Area of the element, $A = 0.5\,(40)(60) = 1200$

$$[B] = \frac{1}{2A} \begin{bmatrix} b_i & 0 & b_j & 0 & b_k & 0 \\ 0 & c_i & 0 & c_j & 0 & c_k \\ c_i & b_i & c_j & b_j & c_k & b_k \end{bmatrix} = \frac{1}{2400} \begin{bmatrix} -60 & 0 & 60 & 0 & 0 & 0 \\ 0 & -40 & 0 & 0 & 0 & 40 \\ -40 & -60 & 0 & 60 & 40 & 0 \end{bmatrix}$$

$$= \begin{bmatrix} \dfrac{-1}{400} & 0 & \dfrac{1}{400} & 0 & 0 & 0 \\ 0 & \dfrac{-1}{600} & 0 & 0 & 0 & \dfrac{1}{600} \\ \dfrac{-1}{600} & \dfrac{-1}{400} & 0 & \dfrac{1}{400} & \dfrac{1}{600} & 0 \end{bmatrix}$$

$$
[B]^T =
\begin{bmatrix}
\dfrac{-1}{400} & 0 & \dfrac{-1}{600} \\[6pt]
0 & \dfrac{-1}{600} & \dfrac{-1}{400} \\[6pt]
\dfrac{1}{400} & 0 & 0 \\[6pt]
0 & 0 & \dfrac{1}{400} \\[6pt]
0 & 0 & \dfrac{1}{600} \\[6pt]
0 & \dfrac{1}{600} & 0
\end{bmatrix}
$$

$$
[B]^T [D] [B] = 10^5
\begin{bmatrix}
\dfrac{-1}{400} & 0 & \dfrac{-1}{600} \\[6pt]
0 & \dfrac{-1}{600} & \dfrac{-1}{400} \\[6pt]
\dfrac{1}{400} & 0 & 0 \\[6pt]
0 & 0 & \dfrac{1}{400} \\[6pt]
0 & 0 & \dfrac{1}{600} \\[6pt]
0 & \dfrac{1}{600} & 0
\end{bmatrix}
\begin{bmatrix}
1.8844 & 0.8076 & 0 \\
0.8076 & 1.8844 & 0 \\
0 & 0 & 0.5384
\end{bmatrix}
\begin{bmatrix}
\dfrac{-1}{400} & 0 & \dfrac{1}{400} & 0 & 0 & 0 \\[6pt]
0 & \dfrac{-1}{600} & 0 & 0 & 0 & \dfrac{1}{600} \\[6pt]
\dfrac{-1}{600} & \dfrac{-1}{400} & 0 & \dfrac{1}{400} & \dfrac{1}{600} & 0
\end{bmatrix}
$$

$$
[B]^T [D] [B] = 10^5
\begin{bmatrix}
\dfrac{-1}{400} & 0 & \dfrac{-1}{600} \\[6pt]
0 & \dfrac{-1}{600} & \dfrac{-1}{400} \\[6pt]
\dfrac{1}{400} & 0 & 0 \\[6pt]
0 & 0 & \dfrac{1}{400} \\[6pt]
0 & 0 & \dfrac{1}{600} \\[6pt]
0 & \dfrac{1}{600} & 0
\end{bmatrix}
\begin{bmatrix}
0.004711 & -0.001346 & 0.004711 & 0 & 0.001346 & 0 \\
-0.002019 & -0.001341 & 0.002019 & 0 & 0.001341 & 0 \\
-0.000897 & 0.001346 & 0 & 0.001346 & 0.000897 & 0
\end{bmatrix}
$$

$$= \begin{bmatrix} 1.3273 & 0.5608 & -1.1778 & -0.2243 & -0.4861 & 0 \\ 0.5608 & 0.8599 & -0.3365 & -0.3365 & -0.7478 & 0 \\ -1.1778 & -0.3365 & 1.1778 & 0 & 0.3365 & 0 \\ 0 & 0 & 0 & 0 & 0 & 0 \\ 0 & 0 & 0 & 0 & 0 & 0 \\ -0.3365 & -0.5234 & 0.3365 & 0 & 0.5234 & 0 \end{bmatrix}$$

$$[k^{(e)}] = [B]^T [D] [B] A \, T = (1200)\,(10) \begin{bmatrix} 1.3273 & 0.5608 & -1.1778 & -0.2243 & -0.4861 & 0 \\ 0.5608 & 0.8599 & -0.3365 & -0.3365 & -0.7478 & 0 \\ -1.1778 & -0.3365 & 1.1778 & 0 & 0.3365 & 0 \\ 0 & 0 & 0 & 0 & 0 & 0 \\ 0 & 0 & 0 & 0 & 0 & 0 \\ -0.3365 & -0.5234 & 0.3365 & 0 & 0.5234 & 0 \end{bmatrix}$$

$$= 10^3 \begin{bmatrix} 15.93 & 6.73 & -14.13 & -2.69 & -5.83 & 0 \\ 6.73 & 10.32 & -4.04 & -4.04 & -8.97 & 0 \\ -14.13 & -4.04 & 14.13 & 0 & 4.04 & 0 \\ 0 & 0 & 0 & 0 & 0 & 0 \\ 0 & 0 & 0 & 0 & 0 & 0 \\ -4.04 & -6.28 & 4.04 & 0 & 6.28 & 0 \end{bmatrix}$$

CHAPTER 9

UNSTEADY STATE HEAT CONDUCTION

Interpolation over an Element

Anything that varies over an element can be interpolated between the nodes of the element as

$$V = [N]\{V\} = \begin{bmatrix} N_i & N_j \end{bmatrix} \begin{Bmatrix} V_i \\ V_j \end{Bmatrix}$$

where V is something that varies linearly over the element with nodal values as

V_i and V_j.

Weighted Residual over the element is given by

$$R^{(e)} = \int_{X_i}^{X_j} [N]^T [N]\{V\} dx$$

These rules help us determine element matrices, force vectors and element capacitance matrices $[k^{(e)}]$, $\{f^{(e)}\}$ and $[c^{(e)}]$.

In unsteady, one-dimensional heat conduction, the applicable differential equation is,

$$D\frac{\partial^2 T}{\partial x^2} + Q = \lambda \frac{\partial T}{\partial t}, \ where \ \lambda = \frac{k}{\rho c}.$$

How to Solve One-dimensional Transient Heat Conduction

Problems

After dividing the given problem into a grid of elements and nodes,

1. Find $[k^{(e)}] = \dfrac{kA}{L}\begin{bmatrix} 1 & -1 \\ -1 & 1 \end{bmatrix}$ *for each element*

2. Find $\{\overline{f^{(e)}}\} = (1-\theta)\{f\}_a + \{f\}_b$ - for each element
3. Assemble [K] and $\{\overline{F}\}$ using the direct stiffness procedure
4. Decide the value of θ that you want to use depending on the scheme of your choice
5. Decide the formulation, say, lumped or consistent. Find $\left[c^{(e)}\right]$ for each element
6. Assemble [C].
7. Calculate matrix $[A] = [C] + \Delta t \times \theta \times [K]$
8. Calculate matrix $[P] = [C] - \Delta t \times \theta \times [K]$
9. Calculate $[A]\{T\}_{t+\Delta t} = [P]\{T\}_t + \{\overline{F}\} = \{\widehat{F}\}$

If the temperature value at some node is prescribed to remain constant, the row in [A] corresponding to the prescribed node is deleted except for the diagonal term which is made equal to 1 and corresponding value in $\{\widehat{F}\}$ is replaced by the prescribed value of the temperature. The coefficients in the corresponding column are shifted to add to (or subtract from) the force vector $\{\widehat{F}\}$.

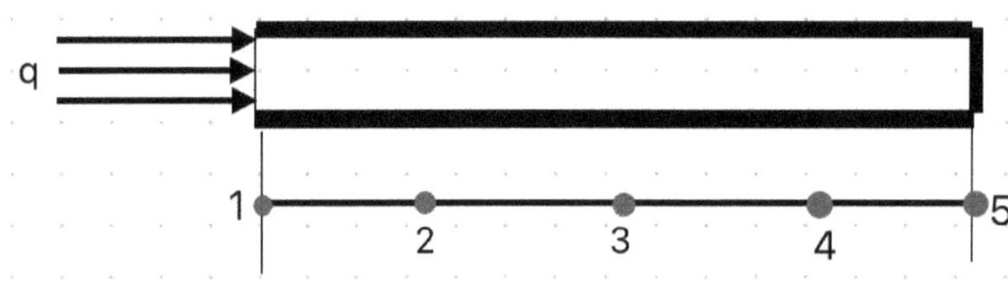

Fig. 9.1

Example 9.1 An insulated rod 12 cm in length is shown in Fig. 9.1. This rod is initially at $0°\,C$.

At time t = 0, the left end of the rod starts to receive heat flux at the rate 10 W/sq.cm and the right Pend is insulated.

Use the consistent formulation. Take $\theta = 0.5\ and\ \Delta t = 1\ second$. Take $D = 3\ \dfrac{W}{cm.\,°C}$, $\lambda = \dfrac{4\,J}{cm^3.\,°C}$, $q = 10\ W$, $A = 1\ cm^2$

Solution: The heat conduction equation that applies to a one-dimensional, time-dependent conduction is,

$$D\frac{\partial^2 T}{\partial x^2} + Q = \lambda\frac{\partial T}{\partial t}\text{, where}$$

$\lambda = \dfrac{k}{\rho\,c} = \dfrac{1}{\alpha}$, *where α is the thermal diffusivity of the material.*

$$[k^{(e)}] = \frac{kA}{L}\begin{bmatrix} 1 & -1 \\ -1 & 1 \end{bmatrix} = \frac{3\times1}{3}\begin{bmatrix} 1 & -1 \\ -1 & 1 \end{bmatrix} = \begin{bmatrix} 1 & -1 \\ -1 & 1 \end{bmatrix}$$

$$[c^{(e)}] = \frac{\lambda L}{6}\begin{bmatrix} 2 & 1 \\ 1 & 2 \end{bmatrix} = \begin{bmatrix} 4 & 2 \\ 2 & 4 \end{bmatrix}$$

There are 4 elements with 5 nodes in the given problem. As usual, the global stiffness [K] assembled from element stiffness matrices, given above.

$$[K] = \begin{bmatrix} 1 & -1 & 0 & 0 & 0 \\ -1 & 1+1 & -1 & 0 & 0 \\ 0 & -1 & 1+1 & -1 & 0 \\ 0 & 0 & -1 & 1+1 & -1 \\ 0 & 0 & 0 & -1 & 1 \end{bmatrix} = \begin{bmatrix} 1 & -1 & 0 & 0 & 0 \\ -1 & 2 & -1 & 0 & 0 \\ 0 & -1 & 2 & -1 & 0 \\ 0 & 0 & -1 & 2 & -1 \\ 0 & 0 & 0 & -1 & 1 \end{bmatrix}$$

The global capacitance matrix [C] is assembled from element capacitance matrices $[c^{(e)}]$. The element capacitance matrices are formed either by lumping or by using consistent formulation.

Consistent formulation has been used in the given problem to write down $[c^{(e)}]$ shown above. In the table given below, both methods are given.

Table 9.I: Element Capacitance Matrices

	Lumped Formulation	**Consistent Formulation**
One- dim line element	$[c^{(e)}] = \dfrac{\lambda L}{2}\begin{bmatrix} 1 & 0 \\ 0 & 1 \end{bmatrix}$	$[c^{(e)}] = \dfrac{\lambda L}{6}\begin{bmatrix} 2 & 1 \\ 1 & 2 \end{bmatrix}$
Two-dim, triangular element	$[c^{(e)}] = \dfrac{\lambda A}{3}\begin{bmatrix} 1 & 0 & 0 \\ 0 & 1 & 0 \\ 0 & 0 & 1 \end{bmatrix}$	$[c^{(e)}] = \dfrac{\lambda A}{12}\begin{bmatrix} 2 & 1 & 1 \\ 1 & 2 & 1 \\ 1 & 1 & 2 \end{bmatrix}$
Two-dim, rectangular element	$[c^{(e)}] = \dfrac{\lambda A}{4}\begin{bmatrix} 1 & 0 & 0 & 0 \\ 0 & 1 & 0 & 0 \\ 0 & 0 & 1 & 0 \\ 0 & 0 & 0 & 1 \end{bmatrix}$	$[c^{(e)}] = \dfrac{\lambda A}{36}\begin{bmatrix} 4 & 2 & 1 & 2 \\ 2 & 4 & 2 & 1 \\ 1 & 2 & 4 & 2 \\ 2 & 1 & 2 & 4 \end{bmatrix}$

The global capacitance matrix [C] is assembled from element capacitance matrices.

$$[C] = \begin{bmatrix} 4 & 2 & 0 & 0 & 0 \\ 2 & 4+4 & 2 & 0 & 0 \\ 0 & 2 & 4+4 & 2 & 0 \\ 0 & 0 & 2 & 4+4 & 2+2 \\ 0 & 0 & 0 & 2+2 & 4+4 \end{bmatrix} = \begin{bmatrix} 4 & 2 & 0 & 0 & 0 \\ 2 & 8 & 2 & 0 & 0 \\ 0 & 2 & 8 & 2 & 0 \\ 0 & 0 & 2 & 8 & 4 \\ 0 & 0 & 0 & 4 & 8 \end{bmatrix}$$

The main matrix equation to solve in a time-dependent problem is written down below:

$$([C] + \theta\,\Delta t\,[K])\,\{T\}_b = ([C] - (1-\theta)\,\Delta t\,[K])\,\{T\}_a + \Delta t((1-\theta)\,\{F\}_a + \theta\{F\}_b)$$

[C] is called the global capacitance matrix.

θ is a variable whose value is between 0 and 1 depending on the difference scheme

we need to use.

Δt *is the value of one time step used.*

We may write the main equation as

$$[A]\{T\}_b = [P]\{T\}_a + \{\overline{F}\}$$

where,

$$[A] = ([C] + \theta \, \Delta t \, [K]$$

$$[P] = ([C] - (1 - \theta) \, \Delta t \, [K])$$

$$\overline{F} = \Delta t \, (1 - \theta) \, \{F\}_a + \Delta t \, \theta \, \{F\}_b$$

Choice of θ

The derivatives of {T} with respect to time t may be replaced by one of the following choices. Each choice gives a different value of θ and each has some advantages and disadvantages.

Forward differences, $\theta = 0$.

Central differences, $\theta = 0.5$.

Glarkin's Method, $\theta = 0.667$

Backward differences, = 1.

The main equation to solve for different θ Values is shown below in a tabular form:

Table 9.2: Equations to Use

Type of formulation	Equation to use
Forward differences, $\theta = 0$	$[C]\{T\}_b = ([C] - \Delta t \, [K]) \, \{T\}_a + \Delta t \, \{F\}_a$
Central differences, $\theta = 0.5$	$\left([C] + \dfrac{1}{2}\Delta t \, [K]\right) \{T\}_b =$ $\left([C] - \dfrac{1}{2}\Delta t \, [K]\right) \{T\}_a + \dfrac{1}{2}\Delta t \left(\{F\}_a + \{F\}_b \right)$
Glarkin's Method, $\theta = 0.667$	$\left([C] + \dfrac{2}{3}\Delta t \, [K]\right) \{T\}_b = \left([C] - \dfrac{1}{3}\Delta t \, [K]\right) \{T\}_a + \dfrac{1}{3}\Delta t \left(\{F\}_a + 2\{F\}_b \right)$
Backward differences, $\theta = 1$	$([C] + \Delta t \, [K]) \, \{T\}_b = ([C]\{T\}_a + \Delta t \, \{F\}_b)$

We always need values of M and S to include the effect of convection at the boundary.

When <u>entering</u> flux per unit area is given, M = 0 and S = the given flux.

When <u>leaving</u> flux per unit area is given, M = 0 and S = - the given flux.

For example, in the problem given here, entering flux is 10 W. Thus, M = 0 and S = 10 W.

$$\{F\} = S \begin{Bmatrix} 1 \\ 0 \\ 0 \\ 0 \end{Bmatrix} = \begin{Bmatrix} 10 \\ 0 \\ 0 \\ 0 \end{Bmatrix}.$$

Note that subscript b refers to the values after the time step and subscript a refers to values before the time step. We now define two new matrices [A] and [P]:

$$[A] = \left([C] + \frac{1}{2}\Delta t\, [K]\right) = \begin{bmatrix} 4 & 2 & 0 & 0 & 0 \\ 2 & 8 & 2 & 0 & 0 \\ 0 & 2 & 8 & 2 & 0 \\ 0 & 0 & 2 & 8 & 2 \\ 0 & 0 & 0 & 2 & 4 \end{bmatrix} + \begin{bmatrix} 0.5 & -0.5 & 0 & 0 & 0 \\ -0.5 & 1 & -0.5 & 0 & 0 \\ 0 & -0.5 & 1 & -0.5 & 0 \\ 0 & 0 & -0.5 & 1 & -0.5 \\ 0 & 0 & 0 & -0.5 & 0.5 \end{bmatrix}$$

We get $[A] = \begin{bmatrix} 4.5 & 1.5 & 0 & 0 & 0 \\ 1.5 & 9 & 1.5 & 0 & 0 \\ 0 & 1.5 & 9 & 1.5 & 0 \\ 0 & 0 & 1.5 & 9 & 1.5 \\ 0 & 0 & 0 & 1.5 & 4.5 \end{bmatrix}$ and, $[P] = \begin{bmatrix} 3.5 & 2.5 & 0 & 0 & 0 \\ 2.5 & 7 & 2.5 & 0 & 0 \\ 0 & 2.5 & 7 & 2.5 & 0 \\ 0 & 0 & 2.5 & 7 & 2.5 \\ 0 & 0 & 0 & 2.5 & 3.5 \end{bmatrix}$.

Or

$$\begin{bmatrix} 4.5 & 1.5 & 0 & 0 & 0 \\ 1.5 & 9 & 1.5 & 0 & 0 \\ 0 & 1.5 & 9 & 1.5 & 0 \\ 0 & 0 & 1.5 & 9 & 1.5 \\ 0 & 0 & 0 & 1.5 & 4.5 \end{bmatrix} \begin{Bmatrix} T_1 \\ T_2 \\ T_3 \\ T_4 \\ T_5 \end{Bmatrix}_b = \begin{bmatrix} 3.5 & 2.5 & 0 & 0 & 0 \\ 2.5 & 7 & 2.5 & 0 & 0 \\ 0 & 2.5 & 7 & 2.5 & 0 \\ 0 & 0 & 2.5 & 7 & 2.5 \\ 0 & 0 & 0 & 2.5 & 3.5 \end{bmatrix} \begin{Bmatrix} 0 \\ 0 \\ 0 \\ 0 \\ 0 \end{Bmatrix} + \begin{Bmatrix} 10 \\ 0 \\ 0 \\ 0 \\ 0 \end{Bmatrix}$$

Thus, we get the following set of algebraic equations to solve:

$$4.5\,T_1 + 1.5\,T_2 = 10$$

$$1.5\,T_1 + 9\,T_2 + 1.5\,T_3 = 0$$

$$1.5\,T_2 + 9\,T_3 + 1.5\,T_4 = 0$$

$$1.5\,T_3 + 9\,T_4 + 1.5\,T_5 = 0$$

$$1.5\,T_4 + 4.5\,T_5 = 0$$

The solution of the above set of algebraic equations is,

$$T_1 = 2.357;\ T_2 = -0.404;\ T_3 = 0.069;\ T_4 = -0.012;\ T_5 = 0.004.$$

Note that the two temperature values shown above are below zero. This is violation of the

Second Law of Thermodynamics. The reason for this is that the step time of 1 second is large

The time step Δt needs to observe the limits,

$$\Delta t < \frac{\lambda L^2}{12 D\,(1-\theta)}\ for\ consistent\ formulation\ and\ \Delta t < \frac{\lambda L^2}{4 D\,(1-\theta)}\ for\ lumped\ formulation.$$

Example 9.2 A rod similar to that shown in Fig. 9.1 has a length of 4 cm. This rod is initially at $0°\,C$. At time t = 0, the left end of the rod starts to receive heat flux at the rate of 5 W/sq.cm and the right end is insulated.

Use the consistent formulation. Take $\theta = 0.5\ and\ \Delta t = 1\ second$. Take $D = 4\ \dfrac{W}{cm.\,°C}$. $\lambda = \dfrac{12\,J}{cm^3.\,°C}$,,

$A = 1\ cm^2$

Solution: The heat conduction equation that applies to a one-dimensional, time-dependent conduction is,

$$D\frac{\partial^2 T}{\partial x^2} + Q = \lambda\frac{\partial T}{\partial t}$$

$\lambda = \dfrac{k}{\rho\,c} = \dfrac{1}{\alpha}$, *where α is the thermal diffusivity of the material.*

$$[k^{(e)}] = \frac{kA}{L}\begin{bmatrix} 1 & -1 \\ -1 & 1 \end{bmatrix} = \frac{4\times 1}{2}\begin{bmatrix} 1 & -1 \\ -1 & 1 \end{bmatrix} = \begin{bmatrix} 2 & -2 \\ -2 & 3 \end{bmatrix}$$

$$[c^{(e)}] = \frac{\lambda L}{6}\begin{bmatrix} 2 & 1 \\ 1 & 2 \end{bmatrix} = \frac{12\times 2}{6}\begin{bmatrix} 2 & 1 \\ 1 & 2 \end{bmatrix} = \begin{bmatrix} 8 & 4 \\ 4 & 8 \end{bmatrix}$$

F

There are 2 elements with 3 nodes in the given problem. As usual, the global stiffness matrix [K] and the capacitance matrix [C] are,

$$[K] = \begin{bmatrix} 2 & -2 & 0 \\ -2 & 4 & -2 \\ 0 & -2 & 2 \end{bmatrix},\quad [C] = \begin{bmatrix} 8 & 4 & 0 \\ 4 & 16 & 4 \\ 0 & 4 & 8 \end{bmatrix}$$

Equation to solve is,

$$[A]\{T\}_b = [P]\{T\}_a + \{\overline{F}\}$$

Or

$$\left([C] + \frac{1}{2}\Delta t\,[K]\right)\{T\}_b = \left([C] - \frac{1}{2}\Delta t\,[K]\right)\{T\}_a + \frac{1}{2}\Delta t\left(\{F\}_a + \{F\}_b\right)$$

Or

$$\left([C] + \frac{1}{2}[K]\right)\{T\}_b = \left([C] - \frac{1}{2}[K]\right)\{T\}_a + \frac{1}{2}(5 + 5)$$

Or

$$\begin{bmatrix} 8 & 4 & 0 \\ 4 & 16 & 4 \\ 0 & 4 & 8 \end{bmatrix} + \frac{1}{2}\begin{bmatrix} 2 & -2 & 0 \\ -2 & 4 & -2 \\ 0 & -2 & 2 \end{bmatrix} = \begin{bmatrix} 8 & 4 & 0 \\ 4 & 16 & 4 \\ 0 & 4 & 8 \end{bmatrix} - \frac{1}{2}\begin{bmatrix} 2 & -2 & 0 \\ -2 & 4 & -2 \\ 0 & -2 & 2 \end{bmatrix} + \begin{Bmatrix} 5 \\ 0 \\ 0 \end{Bmatrix}$$

Or

Example 9.2 Solve example 9.1 if we fix the temperature at node 1 as $40°\,C$.

$$\begin{bmatrix} 4.5 & 1.5 & 0 & 0 & 0 \\ 1.5 & 9 & 1.5 & 0 & 0 \\ 0 & 1.5 & 9 & 1.5 & 0 \\ 0 & 0 & 1.5 & 9 & 1.5 \\ 0 & 0 & 0 & 1.5 & 4.5 \end{bmatrix} \begin{Bmatrix} T_1 \\ T_2 \\ T_3 \\ T_4 \\ T_5 \end{Bmatrix} = \begin{bmatrix} 3.5 & 2.5 & 0 & 0 & 0 \\ 2.5 & 7 & 2.5 & 0 & 0 \\ 0 & 2.5 & 7 & 2.5 & 0 \\ 0 & 0 & 2.5 & 7 & 2.5 \\ 0 & 0 & 0 & 2.5 & 3.5 \end{bmatrix} \begin{Bmatrix} 40 \\ 0 \\ 0 \\ 0 \\ 0 \end{Bmatrix} + \begin{Bmatrix} 0 \\ 0 \\ 0 \\ 0 \\ 0 \end{Bmatrix}$$

Substituting the given initial values of temperatures, we get

$$\begin{bmatrix} 4.5 & 1.5 & 0 & 0 & 0 \\ 1.5 & 9 & 1.5 & 0 & 0 \\ 0 & 1.5 & 9 & 1.5 & 0 \\ 0 & 0 & 1.5 & 9 & 1.5 \\ 0 & 0 & 0 & 1.5 & 4.5 \end{bmatrix} \begin{Bmatrix} T_1 \\ T_2 \\ T_3 \\ T_4 \\ T_5 \end{Bmatrix} = \begin{Bmatrix} 140 \\ 100 \\ 0 \\ 0 \\ 0 \end{Bmatrix}$$

We now clear row 1 except for 4.5. We multiply 40 and 4.5 and replace 140 by this product 180.

$$\begin{bmatrix} 4.5 & 0 & 0 & 0 & 0 \\ 1.5 & 9 & 1.5 & 0 & 0 \\ 0 & 1.5 & 9 & 1.5 & 0 \\ 0 & 0 & 1.5 & 9 & 1.5 \\ 0 & 0 & 0 & 1.5 & 4.5 \end{bmatrix} \begin{Bmatrix} 40 \\ T_2 \\ T_3 \\ T_4 \\ T_5 \end{Bmatrix} = \begin{Bmatrix} 180 \\ 100 \\ 0 \\ 0 \\ 0 \end{Bmatrix}$$

We now multiply 1.5 in column 1 with 40 and add it to (or subtract it from 100) in the right-most column.

$$\begin{bmatrix} 4.5 & 0 & 0 & 0 & 0 \\ 0 & 9 & 1.5 & 0 & 0 \\ 0 & 1.5 & 9 & 1.5 & 0 \\ 0 & 0 & 1.5 & 9 & 1.5 \\ 0 & 0 & 0 & 1.5 & 4.5 \end{bmatrix} \begin{Bmatrix} 40 \\ T_2 \\ T_3 \\ T_4 \\ T_5 \end{Bmatrix} = \begin{Bmatrix} 180 \\ 40 \\ 0 \\ 0 \\ 0 \end{Bmatrix}$$

Or

$4.5\,T_1 = 180$

$9\,T_2 + 1.5\,T_3 = 40$

$1.5\,T_2 + 9\,T_3 + 1.5\,T_4 = 0$

$1.5\,T_3 + 9\,T_4 + 1.5\,T_5 = 0$

$1.5\,T_4 + 4.5\,T_5 = 0$

The solution of the above set of algebraic equations is,

$$[T]^T = \begin{bmatrix} 40 & 4.4754 & -0.7857 & 0.1386 & -0.0462 \end{bmatrix}$$

Since the calculated temperatures at nodes 3 and 5 are unacceptable, we must use a much smaller value of time step.

For the second time step,

$$
\begin{bmatrix}
4.5 & 0 & 0 & 0 & 0 \\
1.5 & 9 & 1.5 & 0 & 0 \\
0 & 1.5 & 9 & 1.5 & 0 \\
0 & 0 & 1.5 & 9 & 1.5 \\
0 & 0 & 0 & 1.5 & 4.5
\end{bmatrix}
\begin{Bmatrix} T_1 \\ T_2 \\ T_3 \\ T_4 \\ T_5 \end{Bmatrix}
=
\begin{Bmatrix} 40 \\ 4.5754 \\ -0.7857 \\ 0.1386 \\ -0.0462 \end{Bmatrix}
+
\begin{Bmatrix} 0 \\ 0 \\ 0 \\ 0 \\ 0 \end{Bmatrix}
$$

Or

$$
\begin{bmatrix}
4.5 & 0 & 0 & 0 & 0 \\
1.5 & 9 & 1.5 & 0 & 0 \\
0 & 1.5 & 9 & 1.5 & 0 \\
0 & 0 & 1.5 & 9 & 1.5 \\
0 & 0 & 0 & 1.5 & 4.5
\end{bmatrix}
\begin{Bmatrix} T_1 \\ T_2 \\ T_3 \\ T_4 \\ T_5 \end{Bmatrix}
=
\begin{Bmatrix} 180 \\ 130.06 \\ 6.2851 \\ -1.1096 \\ 0.231 \end{Bmatrix}
$$

Or

$$
\begin{bmatrix}
4.5 & 0 & 0 & 0 & 0 \\
1.5 & 9 & 1.5 & 0 & 0 \\
0 & 1.5 & 9 & 1.5 & 0 \\
0 & 0 & 1.5 & 9 & 1.5 \\
0 & 0 & 0 & 1.5 & 4.5
\end{bmatrix}
\begin{Bmatrix} T_1 \\ T_2 \\ T_3 \\ T_4 \\ T_5 \end{Bmatrix}
=
\begin{Bmatrix} 180 \\ 130.06 \\ 6.2851 \\ -1.1096 \\ 0.231 \end{Bmatrix}
$$

We get following algebraic equations to solve:

$$4.5\,T_1 = 180$$

$$1.5\,T_1 + 9\,T_2 + 1.5\,T_3 = 130.06$$

$$1.5\,T_2 + 9\,T_3 + 1.5\,T_4 = 6.2851$$

$$1.5\,T_3 + 9\,T_4 + 1.5\,T_5 = -1.1096$$

$$1.5\,T_4 + 4.5\,T_5 = 0.231$$

The solution of the set of equation is as follows:

$$[T]^T = [40 \quad 7.89 \quad -0.61 \quad -0.03 \quad 0.06]$$

The temperatures at nodes 3 and 4 are still unacceptable, but improvement in temperatures is recognisable. This numerical oscillation will disappear in the next few time steps.

Example 9.3 Data on a bar is as follows:

$D = 2, \lambda = 6, \Delta t = 1, \theta = 0, L = 2.$

Use lumped formula with four elements of length L = 2 cm each.

Find the temperatures at the nodes where these are not known.

Solution:

$$[k^{(e)}] = \frac{kA}{L}\begin{bmatrix} 1 & -1 \\ -1 & 1 \end{bmatrix} = \frac{2 \times 1}{2}\begin{bmatrix} 1 & -1 \\ -1 & 1 \end{bmatrix} = \begin{bmatrix} 1 & -1 \\ -1 & 1 \end{bmatrix}$$

$$[K] = \begin{bmatrix} 1 & -1 & 0 & 0 & 0 \\ -1 & 2 & -1 & 0 & 0 \\ 0 & -1 & 2 & -1 & 0 \\ 0 & 0 & -1 & 2 & -1 \\ 0 & 0 & 0 & -1 & 1 \end{bmatrix}$$

$$[c^{(e)}] = \frac{\lambda L}{2}\begin{bmatrix} 1 & 0 \\ 0 & 1 \end{bmatrix} = \frac{6 \times 2}{2}\begin{bmatrix} 1 & 0 \\ 0 & 1 \end{bmatrix} = \begin{bmatrix} 6 & 0 \\ 0 & 6 \end{bmatrix}$$

$$[C] = \begin{bmatrix} 6 & 0 & 0 & 0 & 0 \\ 0 & 12 & 0 & 0 & 0 \\ 0 & 0 & 12 & 0 & 0 \\ 0 & 0 & 0 & 12 & 0 \\ 0 & 0 & 0 & 0 & 6 \end{bmatrix}$$

$$\{T\}_a = \begin{Bmatrix} 10 \\ 50 \\ 50 \\ 50 \\ 10 \end{Bmatrix}$$

$$\Delta t \{F\}_a = \begin{Bmatrix} 0 \\ 0 \\ 0 \\ 0 \\ 0 \end{Bmatrix}$$

$$[A] = = [C] + \Delta t\, \theta\, [K] = [C] + 1 \times 0 \times [K] = [C]$$

$$[P] = [C] - \Delta t\, (1-\theta)\, [K] = [C] - 1 \times 1 \times [K] = [C] - [K]$$

$$[C] = \begin{bmatrix} 6 & 0 & 0 & 0 & 0 \\ 0 & 12 & 0 & 0 & 0 \\ 0 & 0 & 12 & 0 & 0 \\ 0 & 0 & 0 & 12 & 0 \\ 0 & 0 & 0 & 0 & 6 \end{bmatrix} - \begin{bmatrix} 1 & -1 & 0 & 0 & 0 \\ -1 & 2 & -1 & 0 & 0 \\ 0 & -1 & 2 & -1 & 0 \\ 0 & 0 & -1 & 2 & -1 \\ 0 & 0 & 0 & -1 & 1 \end{bmatrix} = \begin{bmatrix} 5 & 1 & 0 & 0 & 0 \\ 1 & 10 & 1 & 0 & 0 \\ 0 & 2 & 10 & 1 & 0 \\ 0 & 0 & 1 & 10 & 1 \\ 0 & 0 & 0 & 1 & 5 \end{bmatrix}$$

The main equation to solve is,

$$[A]\{T\}_b = [P]\{T\}_a + \{\overline{F}\}$$

$$
\begin{bmatrix} 6 & 0 & 0 & 0 & 0 \\ 0 & 12 & 0 & 0 & 0 \\ 0 & 0 & 12 & 0 & 0 \\ 0 & 0 & 0 & 12 & 0 \\ 0 & 0 & 0 & 0 & 6 \end{bmatrix}
\begin{Bmatrix} T_1 \\ T_2 \\ T_3 \\ T_4 \\ T_5 \end{Bmatrix}
=
\begin{bmatrix} 5 & 1 & 0 & 0 & 0 \\ 1 & 10 & 1 & 0 & 0 \\ 0 & 1 & 10 & 1 & 0 \\ 0 & 0 & 1 & 10 & 1 \\ 0 & 0 & 0 & 1 & 5 \end{bmatrix}
\begin{Bmatrix} 10 \\ 50 \\ 50 \\ 50 \\ 10 \end{Bmatrix}
+
\begin{Bmatrix} 0 \\ 0 \\ 0 \\ 0 \\ 0 \end{Bmatrix}
=
\begin{Bmatrix} 100 \\ 560 \\ 600 \\ 560 \\ 100 \end{Bmatrix}
$$

$$
\begin{bmatrix} 6 & 0 & 0 & 0 & 0 \\ 0 & 12 & 0 & 0 & 0 \\ 0 & 0 & 12 & 0 & 0 \\ 0 & 0 & 0 & 12 & 0 \\ 0 & 0 & 0 & 0 & 6 \end{bmatrix}
\begin{Bmatrix} T_1 \\ T_2 \\ T_3 \\ T_4 \\ T_5 \end{Bmatrix}
=
\begin{Bmatrix} 60 \\ 560 \\ 600 \\ 560 \\ 60 \end{Bmatrix}
$$

$[T]^T = \begin{bmatrix} 10 & 46.667 & 50 & 46.667 & 10 \end{bmatrix}$, for the first time step.

$$
\begin{bmatrix} 6 & 0 & 0 & 0 & 0 \\ 0 & 12 & 0 & 0 & 0 \\ 0 & 0 & 12 & 0 & 0 \\ 0 & 0 & 0 & 12 & 0 \\ 0 & 0 & 0 & 0 & 6 \end{bmatrix}
\begin{Bmatrix} T_1 \\ T_2 \\ T_3 \\ T_4 \\ T_5 \end{Bmatrix}
= [T]^T = \begin{bmatrix} 10 & 43.89 & 49.44 & 43.89 & 10 \end{bmatrix},
$$

for the second time step.

$$
[C] =
\begin{bmatrix} 6 & 0 & 0 & 0 & 0 \\ 0 & 12 & 0 & 0 & 0 \\ 0 & 0 & 12 & 0 & 0 \\ 0 & 0 & 0 & 12 & 0 \\ 0 & 0 & 0 & 0 & 6 \end{bmatrix},
\quad
\{T\}_a =
\begin{Bmatrix} 10 \\ 50 \\ 50 \\ 50 \\ 10 \end{Bmatrix},
\quad
\Delta t\,\{F\}_a =
\begin{Bmatrix} 0 \\ 0 \\ 0 \\ 0 \\ 0 \end{Bmatrix}
$$

$$[A] == [C] + \Delta t\,\theta\,[K] = [C] + 1 \times 0 \times [K] = [C]$$

$$[P] = [C] - \Delta t\,(1-\theta)\,[K] = [C] - 1 \times 1 \times [K] = [C] - [K]$$

$$
[A] =
\begin{bmatrix} 6 & 0 & 0 & 0 & 0 \\ 0 & 12 & 0 & 0 & 0 \\ 0 & 0 & 12 & 0 & 0 \\ 0 & 0 & 0 & 12 & 0 \\ 0 & 0 & 0 & 0 & 6 \end{bmatrix}
$$

$$
[P] = [C] - [K] =
\begin{bmatrix} 6 & 0 & 0 & 0 & 0 \\ 0 & 12 & 0 & 0 & 0 \\ 0 & 0 & 12 & 0 & 0 \\ 0 & 0 & 0 & 12 & 0 \\ 0 & 0 & 0 & 0 & 6 \end{bmatrix}
-
\begin{bmatrix} 1 & -1 & 0 & 0 & 0 \\ -1 & 2 & -1 & 0 & 0 \\ 0 & -1 & 2 & -1 & 0 \\ 0 & 0 & -1 & 2 & -1 \\ 0 & 0 & 0 & -1 & 1 \end{bmatrix}
=
\begin{bmatrix} 5 & 1 & 0 & 0 & 0 \\ 1 & 10 & 1 & 0 & 0 \\ 0 & 2 & 10 & 1 & 0 \\ 0 & 0 & 1 & 10 & 1 \\ 0 & 0 & 0 & 1 & 5 \end{bmatrix}
$$

The main equation to solve is,

$$[A]\,\{T\}_b = [P]\,\{T\}_a + \{\overline{F}\}$$

$$
\begin{bmatrix} 6 & 0 & 0 & 0 & 0 \\ 0 & 12 & 0 & 0 & 0 \\ 0 & 0 & 12 & 0 & 0 \\ 0 & 0 & 0 & 12 & 0 \\ 0 & 0 & 0 & 0 & 6 \end{bmatrix}
\begin{Bmatrix} T_1 \\ T_2 \\ T_3 \\ T_4 \\ T_5 \end{Bmatrix}
=
\begin{bmatrix} 5 & 1 & 0 & 0 & 0 \\ 1 & 10 & 1 & 0 & 0 \\ 0 & 1 & 10 & 1 & 0 \\ 0 & 0 & 1 & 10 & 1 \\ 0 & 0 & 0 & 1 & 5 \end{bmatrix}
\begin{Bmatrix} 10 \\ 50 \\ 50 \\ 50 \\ 10 \end{Bmatrix}
+
\begin{Bmatrix} 0 \\ 0 \\ 0 \\ 0 \\ 0 \end{Bmatrix}
=
\begin{Bmatrix} 100 \\ 560 \\ 600 \\ 560 \\ 100 \end{Bmatrix}
$$

The right-hand side of the above matrix equation can be written as a single vector as shown below. Multiply this diagonal coefficient by T1 and replace 100 by this product 60.

Note that T5 is a fixed value 10, we make all coefficients (except the diagonal coefficient 6) in row 5 as zero. Multiply this diagonal coefficient by T5 and replace 100 by this product 60.

$$
\begin{bmatrix} 6 & 0 & 0 & 0 & 0 \\ 0 & 12 & 0 & 0 & 0 \\ 0 & 0 & 12 & 0 & 0 \\ 0 & 0 & 0 & 12 & 0 \\ 0 & 0 & 0 & 0 & 6 \end{bmatrix}
\begin{Bmatrix} T_1 \\ T_2 \\ T_3 \\ T_4 \\ T_5 \end{Bmatrix}
=
\begin{Bmatrix} 100 \\ 560 \\ 600 \\ 560 \\ 100 \end{Bmatrix}
$$

$$
\begin{bmatrix} 6 & 0 & 0 & 0 & 0 \\ 0 & 12 & 0 & 0 & 0 \\ 0 & 0 & 12 & 0 & 0 \\ 0 & 0 & 0 & 12 & 0 \\ 0 & 0 & 0 & 0 & 6 \end{bmatrix}
\begin{Bmatrix} T_1 \\ T_2 \\ T_3 \\ T_4 \\ T_5 \end{Bmatrix}
=
\begin{Bmatrix} 60 \\ 560 \\ 600 \\ 560 \\ 60 \end{Bmatrix}
$$

Thus, after the first-time step, the nodal temperatures are,

$$[T]^T = \begin{bmatrix} 10 & 46.667 & 50 & 46.667 & 10 \end{bmatrix}$$

For the second time step,

$$
\begin{bmatrix} 6 & 0 & 0 & 0 & 0 \\ 0 & 12 & 0 & 0 & 0 \\ 0 & 0 & 12 & 0 & 0 \\ 0 & 0 & 0 & 12 & 0 \\ 0 & 0 & 0 & 0 & 6 \end{bmatrix}
\begin{Bmatrix} T_1 \\ T_2 \\ T_3 \\ T_4 \\ T_5 \end{Bmatrix}
=
\begin{bmatrix} 5 & 1 & 0 & 0 & 0 \\ 1 & 10 & 1 & 0 & 0 \\ 0 & 1 & 10 & 1 & 0 \\ 0 & 0 & 1 & 10 & 1 \\ 0 & 0 & 0 & 1 & 5 \end{bmatrix}
\begin{Bmatrix} 10 \\ 46.67 \\ 50 \\ 46.67 \\ 10 \end{Bmatrix}
+
\begin{Bmatrix} 0 \\ 0 \\ 0 \\ 0 \\ 0 \end{Bmatrix}
=
\begin{Bmatrix} 96.67 \\ 526.67 \\ 593.33 \\ 526.68 \\ 96.67 \end{Bmatrix}
$$

Or

$$\begin{bmatrix} 6 & 0 & 0 & 0 & 0 \\ 0 & 12 & 0 & 0 & 0 \\ 0 & 0 & 12 & 0 & 0 \\ 0 & 0 & 0 & 12 & 0 \\ 0 & 0 & 0 & 0 & 6 \end{bmatrix} \begin{Bmatrix} T_1 \\ T_2 \\ T_3 \\ T_4 \\ T_5 \end{Bmatrix} = \begin{Bmatrix} 60 \\ 526.67 \\ 593.33 \\ 526.68 \\ 60 \end{Bmatrix}$$

$$[T]^T = \begin{bmatrix} 10 & 43.89 & 49.44 & 43.89 & 10 \end{bmatrix}$$

Example 9.4 A bar is initially at a temperature of 0 deg C. At time $t = 0$, its left end is raised to a temperature of 40 deg C. [A], [P] and {F} for this bar are given. Calculate the nodal temperatures after one time step.

$$[A] = \begin{bmatrix} 9 & 3 & 0 \\ 3 & 18 & 3 \\ 0 & 3 & 9 \end{bmatrix}, \ [P] = \begin{bmatrix} 7 & 5 & 0 \\ 5 & 14 & 5 \\ 0 & 5 & 7 \end{bmatrix}, \ [T]_a = \begin{Bmatrix} 40 \\ 0 \\ 0 \end{Bmatrix}, \ \{F\}_a = \begin{Bmatrix} 0 \\ 0 \\ 0 \end{Bmatrix}$$

Calculate the temperature at its other two nodes after one time step.

$$\begin{bmatrix} 9 & 3 & 0 \\ 3 & 18 & 3 \\ 0 & 3 & 9 \end{bmatrix} \begin{Bmatrix} T_1 \\ T_2 \\ T_3 \end{Bmatrix} = \begin{bmatrix} 7 & 5 & 0 \\ 5 & 14 & 5 \\ 0 & 5 & 7 \end{bmatrix} \begin{Bmatrix} 40 \\ 0 \\ 0 \end{Bmatrix} + \begin{Bmatrix} 0 \\ 0 \\ 0 \end{Bmatrix}$$

$$\begin{bmatrix} 9 & 3 & 0 \\ 3 & 18 & 3 \\ 0 & 3 & 9 \end{bmatrix} \begin{Bmatrix} T_1 \\ T_2 \\ T_3 \end{Bmatrix} = \begin{bmatrix} 7 & 5 & 0 \\ 5 & 14 & 5 \\ 0 & 5 & 7 \end{bmatrix} \begin{Bmatrix} 40 \\ 0 \\ 0 \end{Bmatrix} + \begin{Bmatrix} 0 \\ 0 \\ 0 \end{Bmatrix} = \begin{Bmatrix} 280 \\ 200 \\ 0 \end{Bmatrix}$$

$$\begin{bmatrix} 9 & 0 & 0 \\ 3 & 18 & 3 \\ 0 & 3 & 9 \end{bmatrix} \begin{Bmatrix} T_1 \\ T_2 \\ T_3 \end{Bmatrix} = \begin{Bmatrix} 360 \\ 200 \\ 0 \end{Bmatrix}$$

$$\begin{bmatrix} 9 & 0 & 0 \\ 0 & 18 & 3 \\ 0 & 3 & 9 \end{bmatrix} \begin{Bmatrix} T_1 \\ T_2 \\ T_3 \end{Bmatrix} = \begin{Bmatrix} 360 \\ 200 - 3 \times 40 = 80 \\ 0 \end{Bmatrix}$$

We now should solve two equations,

$$18T_2 + 3T_3 = 80$$

$$3T_2 + 9T_3 = 0$$

The solution is,

$$T_2 = 4.7058, \ T_3 = -1.5686$$

The temperature $T_3 = -1.5686$ is unacceptable because it violates the Second Law of Thermodynamics.

Example 9.5 A metal rod is initially at 30°C when, at time t = 0, the left end is reduced to 5°C and the right end is insulated. The rod has a length of 8 cm, thermal conductivity $= \dfrac{6\ W}{cm,°C}$, $\lambda = \dfrac{1}{\alpha} = \dfrac{\rho c}{k} = \dfrac{3\ W}{cm^2.°C}$ and the area of cross $-$ section $= 1\ cm^2$.

Use a grid of four elements, $\Delta t = 1s$, $\theta = 0$, and lumped formulation. Calculate the unknown temperatures at the nodes of the grid.

Solution: The differential equation that applies here is, $D\dfrac{\partial^2 T}{\partial x^2} = \lambda\dfrac{\partial T}{\partial t}$.

The element stiffness matrix is,

$$\left[k^{(1)}\right] = \left[k^{(2)}\right] = \left[k^{(3)}\right] = \left[k^{(4)}\right]$$

$$= \frac{kA}{L}\begin{bmatrix} 1 & -1 \\ -1 & 1 \end{bmatrix} = \frac{6 \times 1}{2}\begin{bmatrix} 1 & -1 \\ -1 & 1 \end{bmatrix} = \begin{bmatrix} 3 & -3 \\ -3 & 3 \end{bmatrix}$$

The global stiffness matrix is,

$$[K] = \begin{bmatrix} 3 & -3 & 0 & 0 & 0 \\ -3 & 6 & -3 & 0 & 0 \\ 0 & -3 & 6 & -3 & 0 \\ 0 & 0 & -3 & 6 & -3 \\ 0 & 0 & 0 & -3 & 3 \end{bmatrix}$$

The element capacitance matrix is,

$$\left[c^{(1)}\right] = \left[c^{(2)}\right] = \left[c^{(3)}\right] = \left[c^{(4)}\right] = \frac{\lambda L}{2}\begin{bmatrix} 1 & 0 \\ 0 & 1 \end{bmatrix} = \frac{3 \times 2}{2}\begin{bmatrix} 1 & 0 \\ 0 & 1 \end{bmatrix} = \begin{bmatrix} 3 & 0 \\ 0 & 3 \end{bmatrix}$$

The global capacitance matrix is,

$$[C] = \begin{bmatrix} 3 & 0 & 0 & 0 & 0 \\ 0 & 6 & 0 & 0 & 0 \\ 0 & 0 & 6 & 0 & 0 \\ 0 & 0 & 0 & 6 & 0 \\ 0 & 0 & 0 & 0 & 3 \end{bmatrix}$$

Thus, $[A] = [C] + \theta \times \Delta t \times [K] = [C]$

Or

$$[A] = [C] = \begin{bmatrix} 3 & 0 & 0 & 0 & 0 \\ 0 & 6 & 0 & 0 & 0 \\ 0 & 0 & 6 & 0 & 0 \\ 0 & 0 & 0 & 6 & 0 \\ 0 & 0 & 0 & 0 & 3 \end{bmatrix}$$

$[P] = ([C] - (1 - \theta)\Delta t [K]) = [C] - (1 - 0) \times 1 \times [K] = [C] - [K]$

Or

$$[P]=[C]-[K]=\begin{bmatrix} 3 & 0 & 0 & 0 & 0 \\ 0 & 6 & 0 & 0 & 0 \\ 0 & 0 & 6 & 0 & 0 \\ 0 & 0 & 0 & 6 & 0 \\ 0 & 0 & 0 & 0 & 3 \end{bmatrix}-\begin{bmatrix} 3 & -3 & 0 & 0 & 0 \\ -3 & 6 & -3 & 0 & 0 \\ 0 & -3 & 6 & -3 & 0 \\ 0 & 0 & -3 & 6 & -3 \\ 0 & 0 & 0 & -3 & 3 \end{bmatrix}$$

Or

$$[P]=\begin{bmatrix} 0 & 3 & 0 & 0 & 0 \\ 3 & 0 & 3 & 0 & 0 \\ 0 & 3 & 0 & 3 & 0 \\ 0 & 0 & 3 & 0 & 3 \\ 0 & 0 & 0 & 3 & 0 \end{bmatrix}$$

$$\{\overline{F}\} = (1-\theta)\,\Delta t\,\{F\}_a + \theta\,\Delta t\,\{F\}_b$$

$$=\{F\}_a=\begin{Bmatrix} 0 \\ 0 \\ 0 \\ 0 \\ 0 \end{Bmatrix}$$

The equation to solve here is,

$$[A]\{T\}_b = [P]\{T\}_a + \{F\}_a$$

Thus,

$$\begin{bmatrix} 3 & 0 & 0 & 0 & 0 \\ 0 & 6 & 0 & 0 & 0 \\ 0 & 0 & 6 & 0 & 0 \\ 0 & 0 & 0 & 6 & 0 \\ 0 & 0 & 0 & 0 & 3 \end{bmatrix}\begin{Bmatrix} T_1 \\ T_2 \\ T_3 \\ T_4 \\ T_5 \end{Bmatrix}_b = \begin{bmatrix} 0 & 3 & 0 & 0 & 0 \\ 3 & 0 & 3 & 0 & 0 \\ 0 & 3 & 0 & 3 & 0 \\ 0 & 0 & 3 & 0 & 3 \\ 0 & 0 & 0 & 3 & 0 \end{bmatrix}\begin{Bmatrix} 5 \\ 30 \\ 30 \\ 30 \\ 30 \end{Bmatrix} + \begin{Bmatrix} 0 \\ 0 \\ 0 \\ 0 \\ 0 \end{Bmatrix}$$

Or

$$\begin{bmatrix} 3 & 0 & 0 & 0 & 0 \\ 0 & 6 & 0 & 0 & 0 \\ 0 & 0 & 6 & 0 & 0 \\ 0 & 0 & 0 & 6 & 0 \\ 0 & 0 & 0 & 0 & 3 \end{bmatrix}\begin{Bmatrix} T_1 \\ T_2 \\ T_3 \\ T_4 \\ T_5 \end{Bmatrix}_b = \begin{Bmatrix} 15 \\ 105 \\ 180 \\ 180 \\ 90 \end{Bmatrix}$$

The algebraic equations corresponding to the above matrix equation are,

$$3\,T_1 = 15 \qquad T_1 = 5$$

$$6\,T_2 = 105 \qquad T_2 = 17.5$$

$$6\,T_3 = 180 \;\text{Or}\; T_3 = 30$$

$$6\,T_4 = 180 \qquad T_4 = 30$$

$$3\,T_5 = 90 \qquad T_5 = 30$$

Example 9.6: Consider a cylindrical rod of diameter 0.4 cm and length 0.02 m. This rod has its base at 85°C. Its other end is insulated. The ambient fluid is at 25°C. The thermal conductvity of the rod material is $400\ \dfrac{W}{m.K}$. *The convective heat transfer coefficient is* $150\ \dfrac{W}{m^2.K}$. Find the nodal temperatures by using 2 elements with 3 nodes. Solve this problem as a transient heat transfer problem with time step of 0.1 s using consisten formulation. Recall that this problem was solved as a steady state heat transfer problem as example 4.3. We saw in that example that [K] and {F}

$$[K] = \begin{bmatrix} 0.50893 & -0.49951 & 0 \\ -0.49951 & 1.01786 & -0.49951 \\ 0 & -0.49951 & 0.50893 \end{bmatrix}$$

$$\{\overline{F}\} = \begin{Bmatrix} 0.232561 \\ 0.47722 \\ 0.23561 \end{Bmatrix}$$

For transient heat conduction, we need to solve the equation,

$$([C] + \theta\,\Delta t\,[K])\,\{T\}_b = ([C] - (1-\theta)\,\Delta t\,[K])\,\{T\}_b + \Delta t\big((1-\theta)\,\{F\}_a + \theta\{F\}_b\big)$$

Or

$$[A]\,\{T\}_b = [P]\{T\}_a + \overline{F}$$

where, using consistent formulation,

$$\left[C^{(1)}\right] = \frac{\rho\,c\,A\,L}{6}\begin{bmatrix} 2 & 1 \\ 1 & 2 \end{bmatrix}$$

$$= \frac{8900 \times 375 \times \pi\,(0.02)^2 \times 0.01}{6}\begin{bmatrix} 2 & 1 \\ 1 & 2 \end{bmatrix}$$

$$= \begin{bmatrix} 0.13980 & 0.06990 \\ 0.06990 & 0.13980 \end{bmatrix}$$

$$\left[C^{(2)}\right] = \begin{bmatrix} 0.13980 & 0.06990 \\ 0.06990 & 0.13980 \end{bmatrix}$$

The assembled capacitance matrix is,

$$[K] = \begin{bmatrix} 0.50893 & -0.49951 & 0 \\ -0.49951 & 1.01786 & -0.49951 \\ 0 & -0.49951 & 0.50893 \end{bmatrix}$$

We will use $\theta = \dfrac{2}{3}$, *that is*, *Galekin's Scheme and* $\Delta t = 0.1 \ s$.

$$[A] = ([C] + \theta \, \Delta t \, [K])$$

$$[A] = \begin{bmatrix} 0.17374 & 0.036603 & 0 \\ 0.036603 & 0.34747 & 0.036603 \\ 0 & 0.036603 & 0.17374 \end{bmatrix}$$

$$[P] = ([C] - (1 - \theta) \, \Delta t \, [K])$$

$$[P] = \begin{bmatrix} 0.1228 & 0.08655 & 0 \\ 0.08655 & 0.2457 & 0.08655 \\ 0 & 0.08655 & 0.1228 \end{bmatrix}$$

$$\{\overline{F}\} = \Delta t \left((1 - \theta) \{F\}_a + \theta \{F\}_b \right)$$

$$\{\overline{F}\} = \begin{Bmatrix} 0.023561 \\ 0.047122 \\ 0.023561 \end{Bmatrix}$$

Initial temperature distribution is given as

$$\{T\}_a = \begin{Bmatrix} 25 \\ 25 \\ 25 \end{Bmatrix}_a$$

At time t = 0, the temperature at node 1 is fixed as 85.

Now we will solve this problem for one time step.

Solution: The main matrix equation to solve in a time-dependent problem is written down below:

$$([C] + \theta \, \Delta t \, [K]) \{T\}_b = ([C] - (1 - \theta) \, \Delta t \, [K]) \{T\}_a + \Delta t ((1 - \theta) \{F\}_a + \theta \{F\}_b$$

[C] is called the global capacitance matrix.

Or

$$[A]\{T\}_b = [P]\{T\}_a + \{\overline{F}\}, \text{ where } b \text{ and } a \text{ } refer \text{ } to \text{ } time \text{ } t \text{ } and \text{ } t + \Delta t.$$

$$[A] = \begin{bmatrix} 0.17374 & 0.036603 & 0 \\ 0.036603 & 0.34747 & 0.036603 \\ 0 & 0.036603 & 0.17374 \end{bmatrix} \begin{Bmatrix} T_1 \\ T_2 \\ T_3 \end{Bmatrix}_b = \begin{bmatrix} 0.1228 & 0.08655 & 0 \\ 0.08655 & 0.24567 & 0.08655 \\ 0 & 0.08655 & 0.1228 \end{bmatrix} \begin{Bmatrix} 25 \\ 25 \\ 25 \end{Bmatrix}_{a+} \quad \{F\} = \begin{Bmatrix} 0.023561 \\ 0.047122 \\ 0.023561 \end{Bmatrix}$$

Or

$$[A] = \begin{bmatrix} 0.17374 & 0.036603 & 0 \\ 0.036603 & 0.34747 & 0.036603 \\ 0 & 0.036603 & 0.17374 \end{bmatrix} \begin{Bmatrix} T_1 \\ T_2 \\ T_3 \end{Bmatrix}_b = \begin{bmatrix} 0.1228 & 0.08655 & 0 \\ 0.08655 & 0.24567 & 0.08655 \\ 0 & 0.08655 & 0.1228 \end{bmatrix} \begin{Bmatrix} 25 \\ 25 \\ 25 \end{Bmatrix}_a + \begin{Bmatrix} 0.023561 \\ 0.047122 \\ 0.023561 \end{Bmatrix}_a$$

Or

$$\begin{bmatrix} 0.17374 & 0.036603 & 0 \\ 0.036603 & 0.34747 & 0.036603 \\ 0 & 0.036603 & 0.17374 \end{bmatrix} \begin{Bmatrix} T_1 \\ T_2 \\ T_3 \end{Bmatrix} = \begin{bmatrix} 0.1228 & 0.08655 & 0 \\ 0.08655 & 0.24567 & 0.08655 \\ 0 & 0.08655 & 0.1228 \end{bmatrix} \begin{Bmatrix} 85 \\ 18.538 \\ 26.354 \end{Bmatrix} + \begin{Bmatrix} 0.023561 \\ 0.047122 \\ 0.023561 \end{Bmatrix}_a = \begin{Bmatrix} 12.066 \\ 14.239 \\ 4.864 \end{Bmatrix}$$

The resulting algebraic equations are,

$$T_1 = 85$$

$$0.34747 \, T_2 + 0.036603 \, T_3 = 7.405$$

$$0.036603 \, T_2 + 0.17374 \, T_3 = 5.2573$$

The solution of the above system of equations is:

$$T_1 = 85 \quad T_2 = 18.538 \quad T_3 = 26.354$$

Second time step of 0.1 seconds

$T_1 = 85$ as given fixed temperature, we modify row 1 and column 1

as shown below:

$$= \begin{bmatrix} 0.17374 & 0.036603 & 0 \\ 0.036603 & 0.34747 & 0.036603 \\ 0 & 0.036603 & 0.17374 \end{bmatrix} \begin{Bmatrix} T_1 \\ T_2 \\ T_3 \end{Bmatrix} = \begin{bmatrix} 0.1228 & 0.08655 & 0 \\ 0.08655 & 0.24567 & 0.08655 \\ 0 & 0.08655 & 0.1228 \end{bmatrix} \begin{Bmatrix} 85 \\ 18.538 \\ 26.354 \end{Bmatrix} + \begin{Bmatrix} 0.023561 \\ 0.047122 \\ 0.023561 \end{Bmatrix}_a$$

$$= \begin{Bmatrix} 85 \\ 14.239 \\ 4.864 \end{Bmatrix}$$

Modification

$$\begin{bmatrix} 1 & 0 & 0 \\ 0 & 0.34747 & 0.036603 \\ 0 & 0.036603 & 0.17374 \end{bmatrix} \begin{Bmatrix} T_1 \\ T_2 \\ T_3 \end{Bmatrix} = \begin{Bmatrix} 85 \\ 11.1277 \\ 4.864 \end{Bmatrix}$$

Or

$$0.34374 \, T_1 + 0.036603 \, T_2 = 11.1277$$

$$0.036603 \, T_1 + 0.34374 \, T_2 = 4.864$$

Solution of the 3 algebraic equations gives,

$$T_1 = 85, \, T_2 = 29.736, \quad T_3 = 21.731$$

References

1. **Segerlind, L. J.** (1984). *Applied Finite Element Analysis* (2nd ed.). Wiley.

2. **Stasa, F. L.** (1985). *Applied Finite Element Analysis for Engineers*. Prentice Hall.

3. **Incropera, F. P., & DeWitt, D. P.** (2002). *Fundamentals of Heat and Mass Transfer* (5th ed.). John Wiley & Sons.

4. **Bathe, K. J.** (1996). *Finite Element Procedures*. Prentice Hall.

5. **Lewis, R. W., Morgan, K., Thomas, H. R., & Seetharamu, K. N.** (1996). *The Finite Element Method in Heat Transfer Analysis*. John Wiley & Sons.

6. **Reddy, J. N.** (1993). *An Introduction to the Finite Element Method* (2nd ed.). McGraw-Hill

7. **Logan, D. L.** (2012). *A First Course in the Finite Element Method* (5th ed.). Cengage

CHAPTER 10

PROBLEMS FOR PRACTICE

1. A triangular element has nodes i (0, 0), j (4, 0.5) and k (2, 5). Find its shape functions.
    What are the interpolated values of temperature T at points (2.0, 1.5) and (2.67, 3.5) in this element?
    The nodal values of T are i (40), j (34) and k (46).
    Ans. (39.38, 41.97 °C)

2. A large wall is 4 cm thick and has a thermal conductivity of 0.5 W/m.°C. Its right-hand surface is kept
    at a temperature of 10°C and its left surface is convecting with a heat transfer coefficient of 1.5 W/m²·
    °C to a fluid at 5°C. Find the temperature at the left surface of the wall first using one element and then
    using two elements of equal length.
    Ans. (9.46 °C in either case)

3. A **cylindrical fin** has a base temperature of 100°C. Its other end is in contact with water at 4 °C with
    a transfer coefficient of 0.05 W/cm². °C. The exterior surface of the fin is in contact with air at 20 °C
    with a heat transfer coefficient of 0.025 W/cm². °C. The fin diameter = 1.25 cm and fin length = 9 cm.
    The thermal conductivity of the fin material is 1.0 W/cm °C. Use three equal-length finite elements
    to obtain nodal temperatures in the fin.
    Ans. (100, 55.1, 35.5, 27 °C)

4. Calculate the temperature distribution in a one-dimensional fin with length = 8 cm, area of cross-section
    4 x 1 and thermal conductivity $= 3 \dfrac{W}{cm.\,^{\circ}C}$ surrounded by air at 20°C via a heat transfer coefficient of 0.1
    $\dfrac{W}{cm^2.\,^{\circ}C}$. Take the fin base temperature as 80°C. Use 4 elements. (Ans. 80, 54.1, 40.2, 33.4, 31.4 °C)

5. Consider a square element of a two-dimensional fin. The fin is 0.25 cm thick and has a thermal
    conductivity of $\dfrac{4\,W}{cm.\,^{\circ}C}$ in each coordinate direction. The sides of the square element are 2.5 cm each.
    The heat transfer coefficient from the element surface is $\dfrac{10\,W}{cm^2.\,^{\circ}C}$. Take $T_f = 20\,^{\circ}C$. What differential
    equation will apply in this case? Calculate the matrices for the square element I, j, k, m including
    convection from the edges j k and k m. Find the rate of heat transfer from this single element.
    (Ans. 2.19 W)

6. In a problem Q varies linearly over the area of a triangular element. Evaluate $\{f_Q^{(e)}\}$

7. $= \int_A Q\,dA$ for the triangular element of problem 1.

8. A two-member truss is shown below. Determine the nodal displacements and the stresses in each member using the finite element method. Find also the reactions at the supports.
   Take E = 200 GPa and area of cross-section of each member as 200 sq mm.

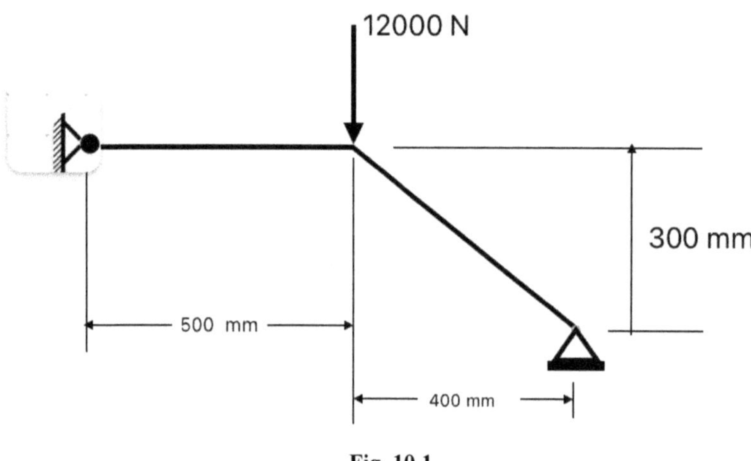

Fig. 10.1

9. A four-bar truss is shown below. Each member of this truss an area of cross-section of 6.25 cm^2 and Young's modulus of its material is E = $2\times 10^7/cm^2$. Calculate the supporting reactions for this truss

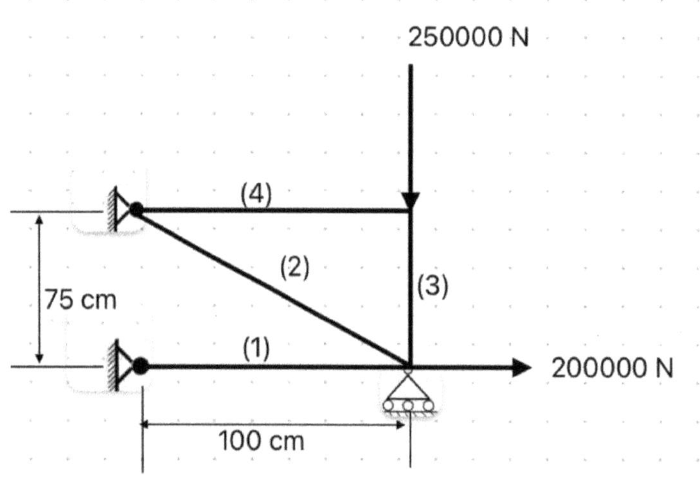

Fig. 10.2

10. Calculate the temperature distribution in a one-dimensional fin with length = 8 cm, area of cross-section 4 cm x 1 cm and thermal conductivity 3 W/cm.°C surrounded by air at 20°C via a heat transfer coefficient of 0.1.

11. The nodal coordinates of an interior rectangular element are i (0.31, 0.18), j (Xj = 0.38), k (Ym = 0.25). The nodal values of a variable ϕ of this element are 115, 85, 76, 105. Find the value of ϕ at the mid point of the rectangle. Ans. 95.25

12. Consider a circular fin whose base is held at $100\,°C$. The tip of the fin and its lateral surfaces undergo convection to a fluid at ambient temperature of 20°C. Assume $k = \dfrac{120\ W}{m\,.°\,C}$ and $h = \dfrac{40\ W}{m^2\,°\,C}$, fin length as 8 cm and fin diameter as 2 cm. Use a two-element finite element.

Ans. (100, 92.73, 90.35°C and heat flow rate = 6.86 W)

13. A five-member truss is shown in Fig. 10.3. All members of the truss are made of steel rods of 1.5 diameter rods. $20 \times 10^{10}\ N/_{m^2}$. Find the displacements of all members..

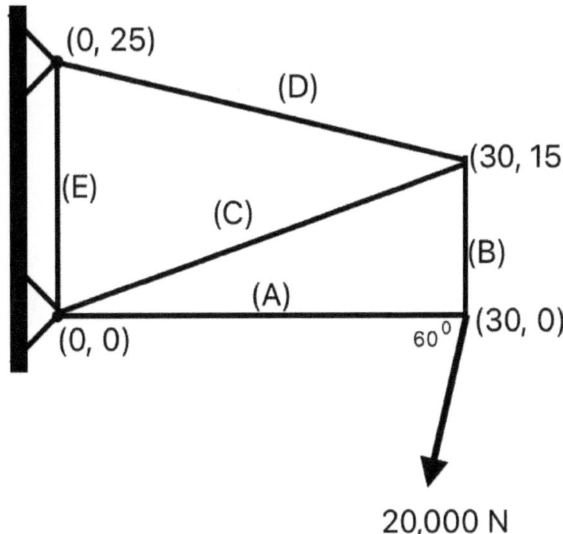

All coordinates are in centimeters

Fig 10.3

(Ans.	Member	Displacement, mm	Force, N)
	A	-1.67	-13676
	B	0.66	10735
	C	0.51	31777
	D	-1.27	-17320
	E	-2.07	-20343

14. A beam is rectangular in cross-section with a height of 4 cm and a width of 2 cm. An element of this beam is 1 cm in length. $E = 21 \times 10^{10}\ N/_{m^2}$. *Poisson's ratio is* 0.3. Find the stiffness matrix for this element.

$$(\text{Ans. } [k^{(e)}] = 10^8 \begin{bmatrix} 2688 & 13.44 & -2688 & 13.44 \\ 13.440 & 0.0896 & -13.44 & 0.0448 \\ -2688 & -13.44 & 2688 & -13.44 \\ 13.44 & 0.0448 & -13.44 & 0.0896 \end{bmatrix})\ N/m$$

15. Consider a beam loaded shown loaded in Fig. 10. Change the given FPS system of units into SI system of units and find the displacements, reactions, and the element loads.

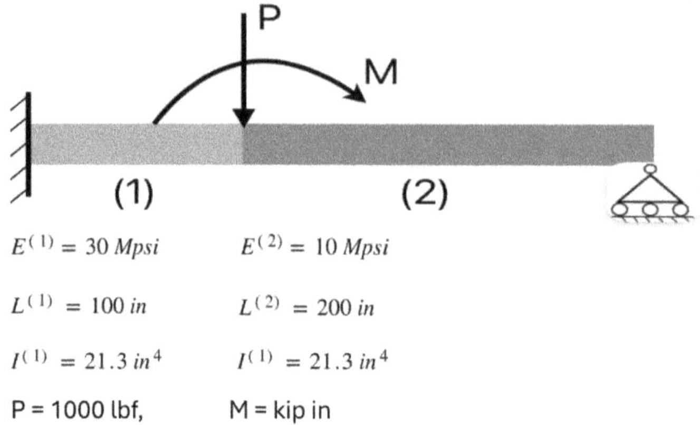

$E^{(1)} = 30\ Mpsi$ $E^{(2)} = 10\ Mpsi$

$L^{(1)} = 100\ in$ $L^{(2)} = 200\ in$

$I^{(1)} = 21.3\ in^4$ $I^{(1)} = 21.3\ in^4$

P = 1000 lbf,   M = kip in

Fig. 10.4

Use the following table for the conversion of units

$1\ inch = 2.54\ cm$

$1\ lbf = 0.4536\ kgf = 4.448\ N$

$1\ \dfrac{lbf}{in^2} = 0.6895\ \dfrac{N}{cm^2} = 6895\ \dfrac{N}{m^2} = 6895\ Pa$

$1\ kip = 1000\ lbf = 4448\ N$

$1\ lbf\ .in = 11.2985\ N.cm$

$1\ pascal = 1\ \dfrac{N}{m^2}$

$1\ bar = 10^5\ \dfrac{N}{m^2}$

$1\ GPa = 10^9\ \dfrac{N}{m^2}$

Ans. $\left(u_1 = 0,\ \theta_1 = 0 \right)$

$\left(u_2 = -0.01357\ m,\ \theta_2 = -0.00798\ rad \right)$

$\left(u_3 = -0.00856\ m,\ \theta_3 = 0.00828\ rad \right)$

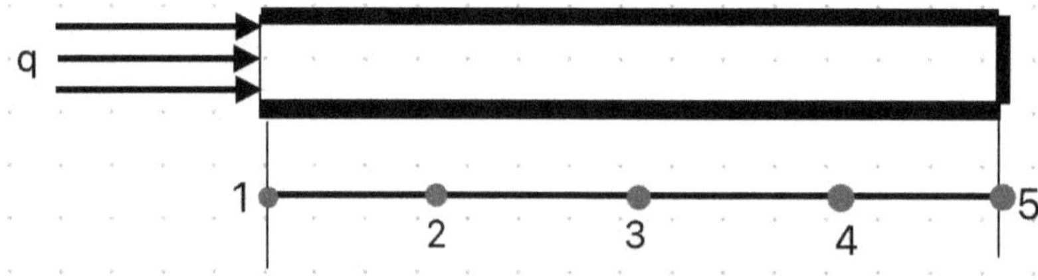

Fig. 10.5

16. An insulated rod 12 cm in length is shown in Fig. 9.1. This rod is initially at $0°\,C$.

    At time t = 0, the left end of the rod starts to receive heat flux at the rate 10 W/sq.cm and the right Pend is insulated.

    Use the **lumped formulation**. Take $\theta = 0.5\ and\ \Delta t = 0.1\ second$. Take

    $$D = 3\ \frac{W}{cm.\,°C}\,.\ \lambda = \frac{4\,J}{cm^3.\,°C},\ q = 10\,W,\ A = 1\ cm^2.$$

    Note: This is example 9.1 in the text. Now we want to solve it using lumped formulation and time step of 0.1 second.

17. Solve the following differential equation using the finite element method:

    $$\frac{d^2T}{dx^2} + 100 = 0 \qquad 0 \le x \le 10$$

    Subject to the boundary conditions: $T(0) = 0\ and\ T(10) = 0.$

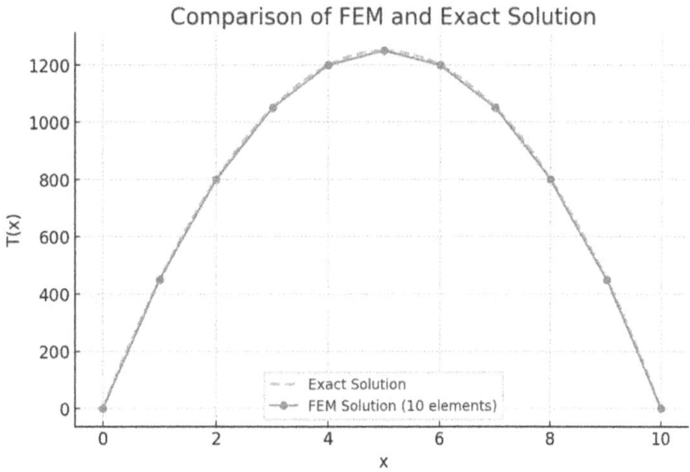

(Ans.with 10 elements)

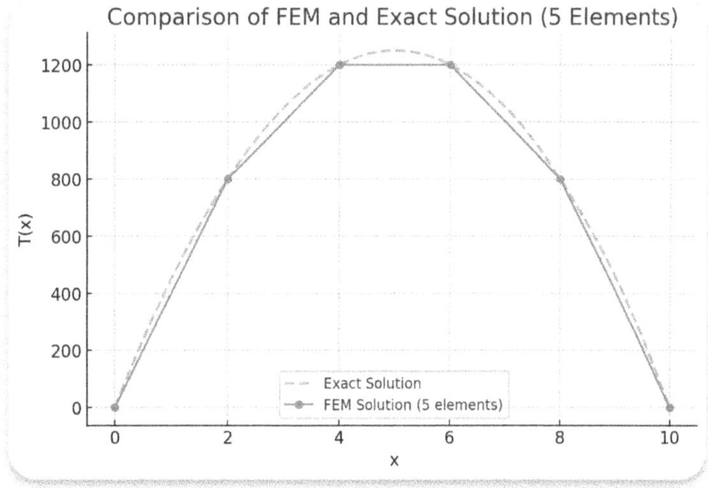

Fig. 10.6

(Ans with 5 elements)

APPENDIX I

SUMMARY OF ELEMENT MATRICES

For a linear, line element, displacement u at any point x on the element (e) is,

$$u = [N]\,\{U\} \ \ or \ \ u = \begin{bmatrix} N_i & N_j \end{bmatrix} \begin{Bmatrix} U_i \\ U_j \end{Bmatrix} \tag{A.1}$$

where i and j are the nodes of element (e).

Strain at any point on the element is given by,

$$\varepsilon = \frac{du}{dx} = \frac{1}{L}\begin{bmatrix} -1 & 1 \end{bmatrix}\begin{Bmatrix} U_i \\ U_j \end{Bmatrix} \tag{A.2}$$

where L is the length of the element and U_i and U_j are the nodal values of u.

Stress at any point on the element is given by,

$$\sigma = E\,\varepsilon = \frac{E}{L}\begin{bmatrix} -1 & 1 \end{bmatrix}\begin{Bmatrix} U_i \\ U_j \end{Bmatrix} \tag{A.3}$$

$$D\frac{d^2\phi}{dx^2} - G\phi + Q = 0 \tag{A.4}$$

This equation is a second order equation called one-dimensional field equation.

Element: Linear line element, e, with nodes i and j, length L and area of cross-section A.

Element stiffness matrix, $\left[k_D^{(e)} \right] = \dfrac{D}{L}\begin{bmatrix} 1 & -1 \\ -1 & 1 \end{bmatrix} + \dfrac{GL}{6}\begin{bmatrix} 2 & 1 \\ 1 & 2 \end{bmatrix}$ \hfill (A.5)

Element force vector, $\{ f_Q^{(e)} \} = \dfrac{QL}{2}\begin{Bmatrix} 1 \\ 1 \end{Bmatrix}$ \hfill (A.6)

Note that the first two terms in the differential equation (A.1) have the variable ϕ in them. Such terms contribute to the element stiffness matrix $\left[k_D^{(e)}\right]$. The third term Q in equation (A.1) which does not have variable ϕ in them are called constant terms and contribute to the element force vector.

<u>For derivative boundary conditions</u> (dbc),

Add $\left[k_M\right] = M\,A \begin{bmatrix} 1 & 0 \\ 0 & 0 \end{bmatrix}$ to $\left[k_D^{(e)}\right]$ if node i has the derivative boundary condition. Also add

Also add $\{f_S^{(e)}\} = S\,A \begin{Bmatrix} 1 \\ 0 \end{Bmatrix}$ to $\{f_Q^{(e)}\}$.

Add $\left[k_M\right] = M\,A \begin{bmatrix} 0 & 0 \\ 0 & 1 \end{bmatrix}$ to $\left[k_D^{(e)}\right]$ if node j has the derivative boundary condition.

Also add $\{f_S^{(e)}\} = S\,A \begin{Bmatrix} 0 \\ 1 \end{Bmatrix}$ to $\{f_Q^{(e)}\}$.

The differential equation applicable to steady state operation of a one-dimensional fin

$$k\,A\frac{d^2T}{dx^2} - h\,p\,T + h\,p\,T_f = 0 \tag{A.7}$$

This equation is the same as the one-dimensional field equation (1) with $kA = D$, $h\,p = G$ and $h\,p\,T_f = Q$. Note that p is the fin perimeter.

Two-dimensional Field Equation

$$D_x\frac{\partial^2\phi}{\partial x^2} + D_y\frac{\partial^2\phi}{\partial y^2} - G\phi + Q = 0 \tag{A.8}$$

is called two-dimensional field equation.

For heat transfer in long bodies in z-direction, equation (A.5) will reduce to $D_x\frac{\partial^2\phi}{\partial x^2} + D_y\frac{\partial^2\phi}{\partial y^2} + Q = 0$
In order to solve equation (A.5), two-dimensional elements are used. These elements may be either triangular or rectangular in shape.

Element: Triangular element, e, with nodes i, j, k and area A

Element stiffness matrix,

$$\left[k_D^{(e)}\right] = \frac{D_x}{4A}\begin{bmatrix} b_i^2 & b_i b_j & b_i b_k \\ b_j b_i & b_j^2 & b_k b_j \\ b_k b_i & b_k b_j & b_k^2 \end{bmatrix} + \frac{D_y}{4A}\begin{bmatrix} c_i^2 & c_i c_j & c_i c_k \\ c_j c_i & c_j^2 & c_k c_j \\ c_k c_i & c_k c_j & c_k^2 \end{bmatrix} + \frac{G\,A}{12}\begin{bmatrix} 2 & 1 & 1 \\ 1 & 2 & 1 \\ 1 & 1 & 2 \end{bmatrix} \tag{A.9}$$

Element Force Vector, $\{f\,_Q^{(e)}\} = \dfrac{QA}{3}\begin{Bmatrix} 1 \\ 1 \\ 1 \end{Bmatrix}$ (A.10)

For derivative boundary conditions or dbcs, add the matrix, $\left[k\,_M^{(e)}\right] = \dfrac{ML_{ij}}{6}\begin{bmatrix} 2 & 1 & 0 \\ 1 & 2 & 0 \\ 0 & 0 & 0 \end{bmatrix}$ to $\left[k_D^{(e)}\right]$

if line i j of element (e) has the dbc on it. Also, add $\{f\,_S^{(e)}\} = \dfrac{ML_{ij}T_f}{2}\begin{Bmatrix} 1 \\ 1 \\ 0 \end{Bmatrix}$ to $\{f\,_Q^{(e)}\}$.

if line i j of the element (e)

has the dbc on it. For derivative boundary conditions or dbcs, add the matrix,

$\left[k\,_M^{(e)}\right] = \dfrac{ML_{jk}}{6}\begin{bmatrix} 0 & 0 & 0 \\ 0 & 2 & 1 \\ 0 & 1 & 2 \end{bmatrix}$ to $\left[k_D^{(e)}\right]$ if line j k of element (e) has the dbc on it.

Also,

add $\{f\,_S^{(e)}\} = \dfrac{ML_{jk}T_f}{2}\begin{Bmatrix} 0 \\ 1 \\ 1 \end{Bmatrix}$ to $\{f\,_Q^{(e)}\}$. if line ij of the element (e) has the dbc on it. So on for line k i.

Two dimensional fins

For two dimensional fins the applicable steady state equation is:

$$k_x\,t\,\frac{\partial^2 T}{\partial x^2} + k_y\,t\,\frac{\partial^2 T}{\partial y^2} - 2\,h\,T + 2\,h\,T_f = 0$$ (A.11)

(t is the thickness of the fin)

We may rewrite the above equation as,

$$k_x\,\frac{\partial^2 T}{\partial x^2} + k_y\,\frac{\partial^2 T}{\partial y^2} - \frac{2\,h}{t}\,T + \frac{2\,h}{t}\,T_f = 0$$ (A.12)

This latter form, Equation (A.9), is more appropriate for the analysis of a two-dimensional fin, because M $= h$ and $S = hT_f$ can be used as previously defined for the derivative boundary condition.

Comparison with the field equation gives

$D_x = k_x,$

$D_y = k_y,$

$G = 2h/t,$

$Q = 2hT_f/t$

Element: Rectangular element, e, with nodes i, j, k and m and area A

Element stiffness matrix,

$$[k_D^{(e)}] = \frac{D_x a}{6b}\begin{bmatrix} 2 & -2 & -1 & 1 \\ -2 & 2 & 1 & -1 \\ -1 & 1 & 2 & -2 \\ 1 & -1 & -2 & 2 \end{bmatrix} + \frac{D_y b}{6a}\begin{bmatrix} 2 & 1 & -1 & -2 \\ 1 & 2 & -2 & -1 \\ -1 & -2 & 2 & 1 \\ -2 & -1 & 1 & 2 \end{bmatrix} + \frac{GA}{36}\begin{bmatrix} 4 & 2 & 1 & 2 \\ 2 & 4 & 2 & 1 \\ 1 & 2 & 4 & 2 \\ 2 & 1 & 2 & 4 \end{bmatrix} \tag{A.13}$$

Element force vector,

$$\{f_Q^{(e)}\} = \frac{QA}{4}\begin{Bmatrix} 1 \\ 1 \\ 1 \\ 1 \end{Bmatrix} \tag{A.14}$$

For derivative boundary conditions or dbcs, add the matrix

$$[k_M^{(e)}] = \frac{h L_{ij}}{6}\begin{bmatrix} 2 & 1 & 0 & 0 \\ 1 & 2 & 0 & 0 \\ 0 & 0 & 0 & 0 \\ 0 & 0 & 0 & 0 \end{bmatrix}$$

to $\left[k_D^{(e)}\right]$, if line i j of element (e) has the dbc. Also, then add

$$\{f_S^{(e)}\} = \frac{h T_f L_{ij}}{2}\begin{Bmatrix} 1 \\ 1 \\ 0 \\ 0 \end{Bmatrix} \text{ to } \{f_Q^{(e)}\}.$$

Similarly add

$$[k_M^{(e)}] = \frac{h L_{jk}}{6}\begin{bmatrix} 0 & 0 & 0 & 0 \\ 0 & 2 & 1 & 0 \\ 0 & 1 & 2 & 0 \\ 0 & 0 & 0 & 0 \end{bmatrix}$$

to $\left[k_D^{(e)}\right]$, if line j k of element (e) has the dbc. Also, then add

$$\{f_S^{(e)}\} = \frac{h T_f L_{jk}}{2}\begin{Bmatrix} 0 \\ 1 \\ 1 \\ 0 \end{Bmatrix} \text{ to } \{f_Q^{(e)}\}.$$

Structural Elements

Bar element:

$$[k^{(e)}] = \frac{A E}{L}\begin{bmatrix} 1 & -1 \\ -1 & 1 \end{bmatrix} \quad and \quad \{f^{(e)}\} = \begin{Bmatrix} -A E \alpha\, \delta T \\ A E \alpha\, \delta T \end{Bmatrix}, \quad Equation\ to\ solve,\ [K]\{U\} = \{P\} + \{F\}$$

Internal forces developed are calculated using

$$\begin{Bmatrix} R_i^{(e)} \\ R_j^{(e)} \end{Bmatrix} = \frac{A E}{L}\begin{bmatrix} 1 & -1 \\ -1 & 1 \end{bmatrix}\begin{Bmatrix} U_i \\ U_j \end{Bmatrix} - \begin{Bmatrix} -A E \alpha\, \delta T \\ A E \alpha\, \delta T \end{Bmatrix}$$

If $R_j^{(e)}$ is positive, the internal force in the member ij is tension.

Truss Element:

$$[k^{(e)}] = \frac{A E}{L}\begin{bmatrix} c^2 & cs & -c^2 & -cs \\ cs & s^2 & -cs & -s^2 \\ -c^2 & -cs & c^2 & cs \\ -cs & -s^2 & cs & s^2 \end{bmatrix} \quad and \quad \{f^{(e)}\} = A E \alpha\, \Delta T \begin{Bmatrix} -1\,c \\ -1\,s \\ c \\ s \end{Bmatrix}$$

with columns $2i-1$, $2i$, $2j-1$, $2j$.

where, $C = \cos\theta$

$S = \sin\theta$

Equation to solve: $[K]\{U\} = \{F\} + \{P\}$

Internal forces developed are calculated using

$$\begin{Bmatrix} R_i^{(e)} \\ R_j^{(e)} \end{Bmatrix} = \frac{A E}{L}\begin{bmatrix} 1 & -1 \\ -1 & 1 \end{bmatrix}\begin{Bmatrix} U_i \\ U_j \end{Bmatrix} - \begin{Bmatrix} -A E \alpha\, \delta T \\ A E \alpha\, \delta T \end{Bmatrix}$$

If $R_j^{(e)}$ is positive, the internal force in the member ij is tension.

Beam element:

$$[k^{(e)}] = \frac{E I}{L^3}\begin{bmatrix} 12 & 6L & -12 & 6L \\ 6L & 4L^2 & -6L & 2L^2 \\ -12 & -6L & 12 & -6L \\ 6L & 2L^2 & 6L & 4L^2 \end{bmatrix}$$

with columns $2i-1$, $2i$, $2j-1$, 2.

Equation to solve: $[K]\{U\} = \{P\}$

Internal forces developed are calculated using

$$\begin{Bmatrix} V_i^{(e)} \\ M_i^{(e)} \\ V_j^{(e)} \\ M_j^{(e)} \end{Bmatrix} = [k^{(e)}]\{U^{(e)}\}$$

If $V_j^{(e)}$ is positive, the internal force in the member ij is tension.

If $M_j^{(e)}$ is positive, the bending moment in the member ij at node j is counterclockwise.

COMPUTER PROGRAMS

Some Educational FEM programs

Here are some FEM programs available for those who want to learn more. There are also many commercial programs in the market for practical applications. Some programs are listed below:

Software	Structural Analysis	Heat Transfer	Fluid Mechanics	Ease of Use
SimScale	✓	✓	✓	★★★★★
Fusion 360	✓	✓	☐ Limited	★★★★
ANSYS Discovery	✓	✓	✓	★★★★
Elmer FEM	✓	✓	✓	★★★
COMSOL	✓	✓	✓	★★★★
SolidWorks Simulation	✓	✓	☐ Limited	★★★★

We have used the manual calculations method to solve problems in this book. The purpose of this book has been to demonstrate the basis of calculations. However, even in the solution of problems, small to large, use of computers is needed. Computer programs are written in many ways and run to obtain solutions. We have used Matlab to write and solve **Example 4.2** of this book.

This example is repeated here.

A cylindrical fin has a base temperature of 80 deg C. Its other end is in contact with water at 5 deg C with a transfer coefficient of $0.06 \dfrac{W}{cm^2 .^\circ C}$. The exterior surface of the fin is in contact with air at 5 deg C with a heat transfer coefficient of $0.03 \dfrac{W}{cm^2 .^\circ C}$. The fin diameter = 1.25 cm and fin length = 9 cm.

The thermal conductivity of the fin material is 1.0. Use three equal length finite elements to obtain solution for the temperature distribution in the fin.

The temperature values obtained by running this program are the same as those obtained previously by the manual calculations.

MATLAB Script for example 4.2

```matlab
% Parameters
k = 1.0;             % Thermal conductivity (W/cm°C)
h = 0.03;            % Heat transfer coefficient along the fin surface (W/cm²°C)
d = 1.25;            % Diameter of the fin (cm)
L = 9.0;             % Length of the fin (cm)
T_base = 80.0;       % Base temperature (°C)
T_inf = 5.0;         % Ambient temperature (°C)

% Discretization
num_elements = 3;
element_length = L / num_elements;

% Geometry
A = pi * (d^2) / 4;  % Cross-sectional area (cm²)
P = pi * d;          % Perimeter (cm)

% Element stiffness matrix and load vector
k_element = (k * A / element_length) * [1, -1; -1, 1];
h_correction = (h * P * element_length / 6) * [2, 1; 1, 2];
k_element_final = k_element + h_correction;
f_element = (h * P * element_length * T_inf / 2) * [1; 1];

% Global stiffness matrix and load vector
K_global = zeros(4, 4);
F_global = zeros(4, 1);

% Assembly
for i = 1:num_elements
    K_global(i:i+1, i:i+1) = K_global(i:i+1, i:i+1) + k_element_final;
    F_global(i:i+1) = F_global(i:i+1) + f_element;
end

% Apply boundary conditions
% T_0 = 80°C (Dirichlet condition at the base)
K_reduced = K_global(2:end, 2:end);
F_reduced = F_global(2:end) - K_global(2:end, 1) * T_base;

% Solve the reduced system
T_internal = K_reduced \ F_reduced;

% Full temperature distribution including the base temperature
T_distribution = [T_base; T_internal];

% Display results
disp('Temperature distribution along the fin (°C):');
disp(T_distribution);
```

APPENDIX III

COMPUTER PROGRAMS

Some Educational FEM programs

Here are some FEM programs available for those who want to learn more. There are also many commercial programs in the market for practical applications. Some programs are listed below:

Software	Structural Analysis	Heat Transfer	Fluid Mechanics	Ease of Use
SimScale	✓	✓	✓	★★★★★
Fusion 360	✓	✓	☐ Limited	★★★★
ANSYS Discovery	✓	✓	✓	★★★★
Elmer FEM	✓	✓	✓	★★★
COMSOL	✓	✓	✓	★★★★
SolidWorks Simulation	✓	✓	☐ Limited	★★★★

We have used the manual calculations method to solve problems in this book. The purpose of this book has been to demonstrate the basis of calculations. However, even in the solution of problems, small to large, use of computers is needed. Computer programs are written in many ways and run to obtain solutions. We have used Matlab to write and solve **Example 4.2** of this book.

This example is repeated below:

A cylindrical fin has a base temperature of 80 deg C. Its other end is in contact with water at 5 deg C with a transfer coefficient of $0.06 \frac{W}{cm^2 \cdot {}^\circ C}$. The exterior surface of the fin is in contact with air at 5 deg C with a heat transfer coefficient of $0.03 \frac{W}{cm^2 \cdot {}^\circ C}$. The fin diameter = 1.25 cm and fin length = 9 cm.

The thermal conductivity of the fin material is 1.0. Use three equal length finite elements to obtain solution for the temperature distribution in the fin.

The temperature values obtained by running this program are the same as those obtained previously by the manual calculations.

A Truss Problem Solved by Matlab Program

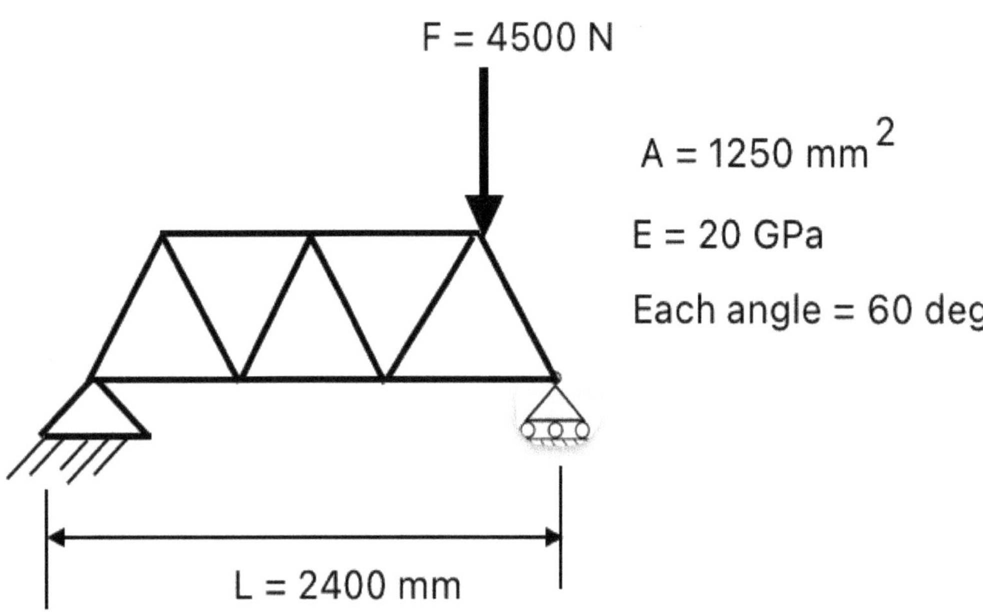

```matlab
clc; clear; close all;

% Define node coordinates (x, y)
nodes = [0, 0;     % Node 1
         4, 3;     % Node 2
         8, 0;     % Node 3
         12, 3;    % Node 4
         16, 0];   % Node 5

% Define element connectivity [node1, node2]
elements = [1, 2;
            2, 3;
            3, 4;
            4, 5;
            2, 4;
            1, 3;
            3, 5]; % Each row represents a truss mem

% Convert node numbers to zero-based indexing
elements = elements - 1;

% Material and geometric properties
E = 2e5;  % Young's modulus (MPa)
A = 200;  % Cross-sectional area (mm^2)

num_nodes = size(nodes, 1);
num_elements = size(elements, 1);
dof = num_nodes * 2;  % Degrees of freedom (2 per no

% Initialize global stiffness matrix
K = zeros(dof, dof);

% Assembly of global stiffness matrix
for i = 1:num_elements
    n1 = elements(i, 1);
    n2 = elements(i, 2);

    x1 = nodes(n1+1, 1);  % Node 1 x-coord
    y1 = nodes(n1+1, 2);  % Node 1 y-coord
    x2 = nodes(n2+1, 1);  % Node 2 x-coord
    y2 = nodes(n2+1, 2);  % Node 2 y-coord

    L = sqrt((x2 - x1)^2 + (y2 - y1)^2); % Element l
    c = (x2 - x1) / L; % Cosine of angle
    s = (y2 - y1) / L; % Sine of angle

    % Local stiffness matrix
    k_local = (E * A / L) * [c^2, c*s, -c^2, -c*s;
                             c*s, s^2, -c*s, -s^2;
                             -c^2, -c*s, c^2, c*s;
                             -c*s, -s^2, c*s, s^2];

    dof_indices = [2*n1, 2*n1+1, 2*n2, 2*n2+1];
```

```matlab
    % Assembly into global stiffness matrix
    K(dof, dof) = K(dof, dof) + k_local;
end

% Load Vector
F_ext = zeros(numDOF, 1);
F_ext(10) = -4500; % Applied downward force at Node

% Boundary Conditions
fixed_dofs = [1, 2, 13]; % Pinned support at Node 1
free_dofs = setdiff(1:numDOF, fixed_dofs);

% Solving for Displacements
U = zeros(numDOF, 1);
U(free_dofs) = K(free_dofs, free_dofs) \ F_ext(free_

% Reaction Forces
Reactions = K * U - F_ext;

% Compute Member Forces
element_forces = zeros(numElements,1);
for i = 1:numElements
    n1 = elements(i,1);
    n2 = elements(i,2);

    x1 = nodes(n1,1); y1 = nodes(n1,2);
    x2 = nodes(n2,1); y2 = nodes(n2,2);

    L_elem = sqrt((x2 - x1)^2 + (y2 - y1)^2);
    c = (x2 - x1) / L_elem;
    s = (y2 - y1) / L_elem;

    dof = [2*n1-1, 2*n1, 2*n2-1, 2*n2];

    Ue = U(dof);
    element_forces(i) = (E*A/L_elem) * [-c -s c s] *
end

% Display Results
disp('Nodal Displacements (m):');
disp(U);

disp('Reaction Forces (N):');
disp(Reactions);

disp('Member Forces (N):');
disp(element_forces);
```

INDEX